ALTERED STATES

CONTEMPORARY WORLDS explores the present and recent past.
Books in the series take a distinctive theme, geo-political entity
or cultural group and explore their developments over a period
ranging usually over the last fifty years. The impact of current
events and developments are accounted for by rapid but clear
interpretation in order to unveil the cultural, political, religious
and technological forces that are reshaping today's worlds.

SERIES EDITOR
Jeremy Black

In the same series

Britain since the Seventies
Jeremy Black

Sky Wars: A History of Military Aerospace Power
David Gates:

War since 1945
Jeremy Black

The Global Economic System since 1945
Larry Allen

A Region in Turmoil:
South Asian Conflicts since 1947
Rob Johnson

ALTERED STATES

America since the Sixties

JEREMY BLACK

REAKTION BOOKS

For Diane Atkinson, my favourite American aunt

Published by Reaktion Books Ltd
33 Great Sutton Street
London EC1V 0DX
www.reaktionbooks.co.uk

First published 2006

Printed and bound in Great Britain
by Cromwell Press, Trowbridge, Wiltshire

British Library Cataloguing in Publication Data
Black, Jeremy
    Altered states: America since the sixties. – (Contemporary worlds)
    1. United States – Social conditions – 1960–1980 2. United States – Social
    conditions – 1980– 3. United States – Civilization – 1945– 4. United States
    – Politics and government – 20th century 5. United States – Foreign relations
    – 20th century
    I. Title

ISBN-13: 978-1-86189-288-1
ISBN-10: 1 86189 288 8

Contents

Preface   7

1 Background   10
2 Changing Country   24
3 Changing People   57
4 Social Trends   81
5 Culture Wars   106
6 Politics   147
7 Imperial State   200
8 Conclusions   226

Selected Further Reading   241
Index   250

Preface

I grew up in Plano . . . The word conjures up drive-ins, tract homes,
waves of heat rising from the blacktop. My years there created for me
an expendable past, disposable as a plastic cup . . . On leaving home
I was able to fabricate a new and far more satisfying history, full of
striking, simplistic environmental influences; a colorful past, easily
accessible to strangers.

Donna Tartt, *The Secret History* (1992)

A continent pretending to be a country, the USA is not only the most
powerful state in the world, but also a culture and society that
commands attention around the globe. This impact is a crucial part of
the importance and history of the USA, and will be discussed in this
book, but putting the country in its context cannot distract from an
engagement with its character. This is to be found in the juxtaposition
of unitary and divisive pressures, which reflect and sustain the essential character of country, society and state. These themes are old ones,
but the resulting tensions remain both far-reaching and complex in
the American experience. Divisiveness can be seen as arising from a
pronounced variation in regional and local cultures and environments,
a variation that is sometimes expressed in antipathy.

This variation is frequently underrated or simplified. In the former
case, there is an essentialism seen in a tendency to treat America and
the Americans as the units for discussion and analysis, or to argue that,

although there are important differences in both categories, these are inherent to a federal system, and anyway should not be overly stressed. At the same time, differences that are acknowledged are frequently simplified to a misleading degree. In the 1960s there was a tendency to treat difference in terms of the South, with the implication that the rest of the USA was a homogenous society. More recently, there has been a dichotomous approach to difference within the USA, in terms of the overlapping, but far from coterminous, tendencies of Democratic, metropolitan and counter-culture versus Republican, suburban and conformist. This approach greatly underrates the variations that exist, their importance and their complexity. So also does an emphasis on geographical regions such as the South, the West or the North-East. Each is in practice very heterogeneous, and these variations are readily apparent to those who live in particular regions.

In contrast to the emphasis on divisiveness, there are powerful factors across the 3.5 million square miles of the country, aiding national integration, especially the nation-state, the constitution, consumerism, television culture and sport. These create a common currency of experiences and ideas that unite Americans of very different social, racial and geographical backgrounds. At the same time, they can also serve as spheres of contention, most obviously with the role of the Supreme Court as an arbitrator – and to critics a legislator by judicial interpretation – not only of differences over the criminal law but also over a range of social and political practices and events. More generally, no singular American mood at any given time has been apparent. Instead, there have been many, many moods, depending on class, race, place, personality and other factors both collective and individual. Both the bonds of citizenship and feelings of individualism have grown stronger among Americans during the last half-century.

The interplay of divisiveness and integration provides much of the history of recent decades. For example, the controversy over language, specifically the legal status of Spanish, owes much to the fear that dethroning English will encourage disintegrative tendencies. Conversely, affirmative action is pushed as a way to help incorporate those whose ethnic position is seen as disadvantageous, generally blacks.

The book will also draw attention to important central narratives that tend to be underrated, such as the changes stemming from suburbanization and the growing intensity of car culture. These are important not only to the history of American society, but also to its environmental impact and its changing politics. The pace of environmental change is particularly striking, and is an important aspect not only of America's impact on the world, but also of contention over its role as a power and over the nature of its society.

Ironically, the study of geography, the subject that focuses on spatial differentiation, is poorly developed in the modern USA, which is a pity because, as a result, some of the necessary empirical and analytical work on changing shifts is lacking. All history benefits from the geographical perspective, not least its focus on deeper transformations, and, in so far as space permits, this is offered in this book. At the same time, a geographical focus can lead to an emphasis on structural continuities, when it should rather see how spatial considerations help in the shaping of change. As Donna Tartt the novelist reminds us, this shaping also owes much to the human imagination, and one of the most conspicuous aspects of the aspirations that lead to individual reinventions is the imagination of change.

I would like to thank Larry Allen, Kristofer Allerfeldt, Paul Jeffery, Michael Leaman, Jeffrey Meriwether, Don Yerxa and two anonymous readers for their comments on an earlier draft, and Bill Marshall for those on a chapter, and Harvey Sicherman for his advice. It is a great pleasure to thank all those who have provided hospitality on repeated travels around the USA. This book was written in 2005-6, in which I visited Alabama, California, Connecticut, Georgia, Hawaii, Illinois, Kentucky, Maryland, Massachusetts, Mississippi, New Jersey, New York, North Carolina, Ohio, Pennsylvania, Rhode Island and Virginia. It is a particular pleasure to dedicate this book to Diane and to thank her for her hospitality in 1965, 1988, 2000 and 2005.

Chapter 1

Background

The flow of time, distant and recent, is felt in the moment. Recent history does not begin abruptly at any given date, and that of the USA, the country, its people and their government, cannot be abstracted from what came earlier. Patterns of causation and habits of thought provided, and provide, multiple links. Structures, institutions, narratives and memories are major parts of this situation of, at once, timelessness and the ever-present reality of time. Continuities are established by terrain and climate and are joined by the impact of past migration and consti-tutionalism. Yet the space available here does not permit an account of this deep history. Instead, we begin with an overview of some of the major developments and events earlier in the twentieth century.

At the start of the twentieth century America was already one of the world's leading states. It was also a prime beneficiary of the global economy, which was then characterized by free trade and international capital flows, and by large-scale migration. International investment from Western Europe helped to drive the American economy, and was a testimony to informed confidence in its profitability and growth. The 'huddled masses' that sailed to America were another testimony, one of even greater longer-term significance. Modern America owes much to their hopes, assumptions, efforts and experiences.

In 1914 American economic output was equivalent to that of the whole of Europe. By 1918 it had the capital to match. The American economy benefited from substantial natural resources, including coal, iron, copper, silver and timber, a large domestic market, extensive immigration, an openness to foreign investment, a legal code that protected property, a governmental system that supported economic growth and a political practice that avoided extremism. America's innovatory ethos derived in part from the shortages of skilled labour throughout the nineteenth century. Britain, in contrast, had invented and invested in heavy machinery in the early phases of the Industrial Revolution, making wholesale replacement expensive, while its plentiful supplies of cheap, skilled labour in any case militated against maximizing technological inputs.

America had demonstrated its power in war with Spain in 1898. The conquest of Cuba and Puerto Rico and the arrival of American troops in the Philippines followed rapid naval victories. The peace treaty with Spain left Puerto Rico, Guam and the Philippines to the USA, but, in the last, control was enforced only after nationalist opposition was suppressed in a bitter counter-insurgency war. By 1914 America was a major power in the Pacific, with Hawaii, Midway, Johnston, Palmyra, Tutula and Wake Islands, as well as Guam and the Philippines, and also increasingly assertive in Central America and in the Caribbean. American power was dramatized in the new geopolitics of the Panama Canal, which provided a link for warships and merchantmen between the eastern and western seaboards of the USA. A project originally – and unsuccessfully – begun with French capital ended as a triumph for American engineering and power: in 1903 Panama became an independent state carved out from Colombia under American protection, and the US gained control over the Canal Zone. America also demonstrated its power in 1907–9, when the sixteen battleships of the 'Great White Fleet' sailed round the world.

Already powerful, the USA was perhaps the prime beneficiary of World War One (1914–18), a conflict that was centred in Europe and hit its economies hard. The European powers, especially Britain, sold many of their foreign investments in order to finance the war effort, and this increased American control of the domestic economy. The disruption of European trade and the diversion of manufacturing to war production encouraged the growth of manufacturing elsewhere, and the USA, which did not enter the war until 1917, benefited most of all. The British war effort rapidly became heavily dependent on American financial and industrial resources. American forces on the Western Front played a role in the German defeat in 1918, and the prospect of many more American troops arriving was crucial in signalling a sense of shifting advantage towards the Allies.

After the war, the USA refused to join the League of Nations as President Wilson had planned, and therefore did not act as guarantor of the post-war international settlement, a fatal weakness for the settlement and the League. Furthermore, although the USA had purchased the Danish West Indian Isles (St Croix, St John and St Thomas) in 1917, it made no attempt to gain territories as a result of the war. In contrast, in a great colonial handout, Australia, Belgium, Britain, France, Japan, New Zealand and South Africa all gained control over parts of the German and/or Ottoman empires, as mandated territories under League of Nations' supervision. This gave Japan the Caroline, Mariana and Marshall Islands, which challenged the American position in the Western Pacific.

But the USA set the terms of the world economy. It became not only the world's largest industrial power, but also the principal trader and banker. New York replaced London as the world's financial centre. American industrial growth satisfied domestic demand, both in well-established sectors and in the growing consumer markets for cars and 'white goods', such as refrigerators and radios. Consumerism was encouraged by the availability of credit. The spreading use of electricity helped economic growth and the rise of plastic as a product affected several branches of manufacturing. New plant and scientific management techniques helped to raise American productivity, which increased profitability and consumer income, and, therefore, the domestic market.

THE 1920S

At the same time, World War One had put a brake on the liberal progressiveness seen in American society and political culture in the early years of the century. The war was followed by a conservative reaction that reflected hostility to socialism and concern about the example of the Russian Revolution. As a consequence, the 1920s saw an emphasis on a non-interventionist role by the state, although such a bland remark does not do justice to the depths and consequences of social tension in the years 1919–22, which included a very high level of labour conflict that had wider political and ethnic resonances. These included high levels of race violence between blacks and whites between 1917 and 1921, and widespread concern about anarchism and radicalism that focused on immigrants and led to repressive government action. Indeed, the US army devised War Plan Whites for action in the event of left-wing insurrection. Warren Harding, Calvin Coolidge and Herbert Hoover, the successive Republican Presidents between 1921 and 1933, benefited from the reaction against change, immigration and urban life that led to a stress on supposed white and Protestant values. This reaction contributed directly to Prohibition (1920–33), the banning of alcohol, which was a focus of the culture wars of the age, and which both criminalized what had hitherto been seen as normal and provided a major source of opportunity for organized crime. Prohibition, however, was also the last gasp of Progressivism and, in that light, was a reminder that the reformist-change impulse can overlap what is seen as reactionary. The reaction against change also led to a powerful revival of the anti-black Ku Klux Klan in the years 1921–6.

Although the connection was not a directly causal one, there was also a determination to control the 'informal' American empire in Central America and the West Indies. But this proved much harder than had been anticipated. In the 1920s popular guerrilla movements in Haiti and the Dominican Republic proved able to limit the degree of control enjoyed by the occupying American marine forces who found that ambushes restricted their freedom of movement. American bombing was no substitute, particularly in the face of guerrilla dominance of rural areas at night. Despite the fact that Americans were not defeated in battle, and in 1922 the guerrillas in the Dominican Republic conditionally surrendered, the marines sent to Nicaragua in the years 1928–33 failed to defeat a rebel peasant army, while the withdrawal from Haiti, which the USA had occupied from 1915 to 1934, owed much to a sense of the intractability of the conflict.

Although not equivalent to the economic growth of East Asia after World War Two, American economic expansion was not matched elsewhere. As a result, the USA became the major international lender in the 1920s. But American protectionism and economic strength reduced imports, so that other countries were unable to finance their borrowing from the USA – a major challenge to fiscal stability. Furthermore, the restrictions on immigration by the Emergency Quota Act of 1921 and the Immigration Act of 1924 helped to restrict the global benefit from American growth.

The overheating American economy collapsed in October 1929 (the Wall Street Crash), the result of a bursting speculative boom in share prices in New York. This bursting of an asset price bubble became far more serious when the inexperienced central bank cut the money supply, a mistake that was not repeated in 1987, or in 2000 with the dot.com crash. The tightening of the financial reins, which included calling in overseas loans, caused financial crisis elsewhere. At the same time, the Hawley-Smoot Act of 1930 put up American tariffs and depressed demand for imports. Other states followed suit, leading to a worldwide protectionism that dramatically cut world trade, and therefore the economic system that the USA dominated. As export industries were hit, unemployment rose substantially, to nearly 24 per cent in the USA in 1932, by which time manufacturing was at only 40 per cent of capacity. Depressed demand also hit commodity producers, such as mining and forestry, and agriculture.

THE NEW DEAL

The Slump and the subsequent Depression caused a notable fall of confidence in the old market economy. Despair led to higher levels of protest and violence. It also helped to put pay to the *laissez-faire* state and to end self-help in social welfare. Instead, there was greater federal economic intervention. The welfare and economic reforms known as the New Deal, which the Democrat Franklin Delano Roosevelt introduced after he became President in 1933, satisfied the powerful political need to be seen to be doing something. In gaining the initiative, this set a tempo for change that resisted deflation and kept non-governmental populist options at bay. Roosevelt backed public works and established work-creation schemes, such as the Works Project Administration, to fight unemployment. This led to the development of infrastructure, especially roads. Well-publicized work schemes helped to create a sense that a corner had been turned.

Partly as a result of such pump-priming measures, the federal debt rose from $22.5 billion in 1933 to $40.5 billion in 1939. Roosevelt favoured balanced budgets and put up taxes on the rich, rather than relying on deficit financing – a policy that contrasts greatly to that of recent years. He established social security, the Social Security Act being passed in 1935, but this was a very limited measure, not the state socialism decried by some alarmist critics. A combination of the conservative nature of American public opinion, hostility to interference with property rights, and growing political opposition from 1937, prevented him from doing more. Rather than during the New Deal, it was only in World War Two that the major moves towards a stronger and more expensive American state were made. Unemployment remained high in the 1930s, but GNP per capita recovered, rising from $615 in 1933 to $954 in 1940, and those in work became considerably better off, which increased domestic demand.

Roosevelt was rewarded with relatively easy re-elections in 1936 and, to a lesser extent, in 1940. He benefited from a coalition between Southern Democrats and their big-city Northern counterparts. If, in part, this was a yoking of contrasting traditions, it was typical of the coalitions that made up American politics, particularly when ideological conformity was of limited importance. Instead, politics owed much to coalitions between interests that were largely grounded in particular geographical areas and wielded power through dominance of state and local governments. This regionalism of politics has ebbed in recent decades, because ideological coherence has become more important, the Republicans becoming more clearly conservative. Phrased differently, politics has since become national rather than confederal, a process that created serious strains for many established party machines.

In the 1930s, in contrast, the Democrats were the party of the Solid South, resentful of defeat in the Civil War of 1861–5 at the hands of the

Republican North, and also brooding on the subsequent rule of the South during the Reconstruction era (1865–77) by Federal troops, outsiders and blacks. The Democrats thus stood in the 1930s for states' rights as the guardian of the (white) Southern way of life, at the same time as being the party of Northern outsiders – trade unionists and immigrants, particularly Catholics and Jews. The Republicans, in contrast, were the WASP (White Anglo-Saxon Protestant) party of the former Northern states, and were particularly the party of business and the affluent. They were very weak in the South: Louisiana's first Republican senator after Reconstruction was only elected in 2004.

WORLD WAR TWO

During World War Two, which the USA entered in 1941, American industry developed rapidly in one of the most dramatic economic leaps of the century. The Americans mobilized their resources far more speedily and extensively than they had done in World War One. The country's overall productive capacity increased by about 50 per cent between 1939 and 1944, a major shift that was of lasting importance to the American economy, and which indicated the close relationship between international and domestic circumstances. The dynamic of American resource build-up relied on lightly regulated capitalism, not coercion. Having had cool relations with much of business during the 1930s, Roosevelt now turned to them to create a war machine. The War Resources Board was established in 1939, in order to ready industry for a war footing, and the Office of Production Management under William Knudsen, head of the leading car manufacturer General Motors, followed in 1941. The attitudes and techniques of the production line were focused on war. $186 billion worth of munitions were produced, as well as an infrastructure to move them. By 1943–4 the US was making about 40 per cent of the world's total output of munitions. In 1944 it produced 89 million tons of steel, about half of the world's total production. Of the 42 million tons of shipping built by the Allies during the war, most were American-built. Many were Liberty Ships, often constructed in ten days using prefabricated components on production lines. The organizational ability to manage large-scale projects and to introduce new production processes was important: for example, all-welded ships replaced riveting, which speeded up production.

The flexibility of American society was a direct help: by 1944, 11.5 per cent of the workers in the shipbuilding industry were women. Major changes in the geography of America's people and economy flowed from the development of war production, particularly of aircraft and ships. The population of Washington, Oregon and, in particular, California, where many of the plants were located, rose greatly: by the end of the war, eight million people had moved permanently to different states. Some of the internal migrants were black: about 700,000 black civilians left the South, especially for California. The opportunities that war industrialization provided for black workers helped to loosen racial, as well as gender and social relations, although much segregation remained, and racial tension led to serious outbreaks of violence, particularly in Detroit in 1943. Nevertheless, there was nothing like the coercion or tension involved in the German or Soviet war economies. The USA benefited from its already sophisticated economic infrastructure. It surmounted the domestic divisions of the 1930s, in order to create a productivity-oriented political consensus that brought great international strength. The resources, commitments and role of the federal government all grew greatly, and taxes and government expenditure rose substantially. Government spending totalled $317 billion, and nearly 90 per cent of this was on the war.

The USA played a crucial role in the defeat of Germany and by far the leading part in the victory over Japan. When the war ended, American troops were on the River Elbe in central Germany and American bombers ruled the skies over Japan. The dropping of two atomic bombs on Japan in August 1945 was not only decisive in leading to its surrender, but also demonstrated America's unique technological capability and its ability to apply scientific advances. About $2 billion was spent in the rapid creation of a large nuclear industry. The electro-magnets needed for isotope separation were particularly expensive, and required 13,500 tons of silver. Roosevelt's successor, his former Vice President, Harry Truman, issued a statement shortly after the first atomic bomb was dropped on Hiroshima, in which he declared:

'Hardly less marvelous has been the capacity of industry to design, and of labour to operate, the machines and methods to do things never done before, so that the brain child of many minds came forth in physical shape and performed as it was supposed to do.'

At the time, there was very little controversy about the decision to drop the bombs, although it subsequently became an issue in the culture wars that divided liberals from conservatives (see chapter Five). When the National Air and Space Museum planned an exhibition for 1995 centred on the *Enola Gay*, the plane from which the bomb was dropped on Hiroshima, popular opinion berated the critical script as unpatriotic, and forced the substitution of a curtailed display. By contrast, in 2003, when the plane was displayed at Dulles Airport, there were protests that the effects of the bomb were not discussed. The plane was dented when someone threw a container of red paint at it, symbolizing blood.

THE POST-WAR INTERNATIONAL ORDER

At the end of World War Two in 1945 the American economy dominated the world even more than at its start. Of the other victors, the Soviet economy had been devastated and Britain had large debts. It was America that established the new economic order, and this reflected the global goals it was seeking. The international free trade and capital markets that had characterized the global economy of the 1900s were slowly re-established in the non-Communist world. The availability of American credit and investment was crucial to this process, since among the major powers only the USA enjoyed real liquidity in 1945. The dollar's role as the global reserve currency in a fixed exchange-rate system ensured that much of international trade, foreign-exchange liquidity and financial assets were denominated in US currency.

Under the Bretton Woods Agreement of 1944, American-supported monetary agencies, the World Bank and the International Monetary Fund (both of which had American headquarters), were established in order to play an active role in strengthening the global financial system. The Americans did not want a return to the beggar-my-neighbour devaluation of the 1930s. Free trade was also actively supported as part of a liberal economic order, and this was furthered as America backed decolonization by the European empires, and the creation of independent capitalist states, which were seen as likely to look to the USA for leadership. The General Agreement on Tariffs and Trade (GATT), signed in 1947, began a major cut in tariffs that slowly re-established free trade and helped it to boom.

The years 1945–73 marked a period of rapid economic development, later characterized as the Long Boom. The American model played a crucial role in the West. The economy produced consumer durables in large quantities, affordable to many, and the USA became a society of mass affluence, which helped to make it more generally attractive, not least as Hollywood and the television spread positive images of American life. These years were also later regarded as the formative ones for modern American society and culture, with contrasting accounts of what was best about, and for, the USA. This remains the case today, not least as culture wars are presented in terms of competing images derived from particular views of the 1950s and the 1960s. A society that is at once conservative and progressive lives in the past as much as in the future.

Furthermore, the period 1945–73 was a formative one in that there was no return to a peacetime of non-intervention and small government comparable to that which had followed World War One. Instead, the USA played the main role in the confrontation with Communism known as the Cold War. World War Two was followed by external commitment in the shape of membership of the United Nations and its Security Council, as well as the occupation of Japan and parts of Germany and Austria, and the placing of the former Japanese territories in the Western Pacific under American trusteeship. However, there was also demobilization in the late 1940s as the 'peace dividend' was taken. The number of amphibious ships fell from 610 in 1945 to 81 in 1950, and, in 1949, the army contained only one armoured division. Nevertheless, driven by concern about Soviet control of Eastern Europe, in 1949 the USA was a founder member of the North Atlantic Treaty Organization (NATO), creating a security framework for Western Europe – a clear contrast with its failure to support the League of Nations after World War One.

Furthermore, the military situation changed as a result of Communist North Korea's invasion of South Korea in 1950. In the resulting Korean War (1950–53), the USA played the leading role in the United Nations coalition that came to the help of South Korea, driving back the North Koreans and then resisting a large-scale intervention by (Communist) China. The Americans suffered 33,741 battle deaths and 2,827 non-battle deaths. The war also led to a major increase in military expenditure, as a percentage of total government expenditure, from 30.4 per cent in 1950 to 65.7 per cent in 1954. A military-industrial complex came to play a greater role in the economy and governmental structure. Conscription was revived, and the size of the armed forces expanded greatly, the army being increased to 3.5 million men. This helped to give the 1950s their particular character.

The Korean War greatly increased American sensitivity to developments and threats in East Asia. This led to an extension of its containment policy towards the Communist powers, the maintenance of American bases in Japan, a military presence in South Korea and a growing commitment to the Nationalist Chinese in Taiwan. From 1950 substantial American forces were also stationed in Western Europe, where they remained until the end of the Cold War. Behind the front line, the USA encouraged political, economic and cultural measures to limit support for Communism. It also pressed on with the development of advanced weaponry. The USA first tested a hydrogen bomb in 1952, destroying the Pacific island of Elugelab. Two years later, John Foster Dulles, the Secretary of State, outlined a willingness to launch massive nuclear retaliation against any Soviet attack. In response to NATO's vulnerability, President Eisenhower pushed the use of the atom bomb as a weapon of first resort, and in 1953 he even threatened to use it in order to bring the Korean War to an end. The deployment of B-52 heavy bombers in 1955 upgraded American delivery capability, but the Soviet launch in 1957 of Sputnik I, the first satellite, led to a fear of Soviet rocket attack. This led the USA to step up its long-range ballistic missile programme, and in 1958 the first one was fired. From the outset, the space race was linked to military dominance. The prospect of nuclear war cast a shadow over the widespread prosperity of 1950s America, particularly after the Soviets acquired a rocket capacity.

Another result of the Cold War was the National Security State. The CIA was created under the National Security Act of 1947. Anti-Communism reached its spectacular apogee in the claims about Communist influence in Hollywood and government made by Senator Joseph McCarthy, but in practice it was far more wide-ranging and contributed to the conservative ethos of the 1950s, which was reflected in the Republican Eisenhower presidency of 1953–61. The Democrats were portrayed as soft on Communism, and Eisenhower's re-election in 1956 with a margin of nine million votes displayed widespread satisfaction with the economic boom and social conservatism of these years. There was an upsurge in religiosity as church membership and attendance rose, and Eisenhower encouraged the addition of 'under God' to the Pledge of Allegiance and 'In God We Trust' on the currency. At the same time, the legacy of the Depression was such that Eisenhower left the New Deal intact. The Eisenhower years were to be the background to modern America. In many respects, the new social and political currents of the 1960s were to be a reaction to this conservatism, yet many of the shifts of the 1950s had a lasting impact, not least the growing suburbanization and car culture.

In the 1950s there was a major geographical shift in the pattern of American life. In the late nineteenth century the country had been dominated economically by a portion of the eastern seaboard – essentially from Baltimore to Boston, and the abutting area west to Chicago, Milwaukee and St Louis. Apart from financial and corporate dominance, this was also the region of manufacturing activity and of much of the population. Given the modest range of federal government activities, the remainder of the USA was essentially self-governing, through largely autonomous states, but, nevertheless, there was a feeling in the South and the West that the East dominated them economically, financially and politically. This lay behind much of the populism of the period and was the background to the anti-big business, trust-busting of the early twentieth century. However, the dominance of national life by the powerful zone remained a factor, and it was there that much of the industrial growth of the first four decades of the twentieth century occurred, not least in the car industry.

Wartime industrial activity shifted the balance of economic activity to the West Coast. This was part of a greater focus on the Pacific littoral that included the movement of many troops through West Coast ports to fight Japan. The shift might have occurred anyway, but the war accelerated it. Large-scale internal migration followed. In part, this was local, with suburban expansion reflecting the spreading use of cars, as well as decentralization in employment, and, increasingly, leisure, education and other service activities. Suburbanization was further encouraged because it was the product not only of movement from the inner cities but also from the rural heartlands. The shift from the land was a major theme in mid-twentieth-century American history.

There were also important changes in the relationship between regions. The South and West became far more important in economic and demographic terms during the 'baby boom', a period of rapid population growth. If California's growth attracted most attention, there were also spectacular developments in the 'New South', for example, the growing centres of Atlanta, Dallas and Houston, as well as in other parts of the West, such as Seattle. Nevertheless, although the population centre of the country moved westward in the 1950s, in 1960, as in 1950, it was still in southern Illinois. In part this reflected the continued demographic weight of the North-East. In 1960 the national population density was 50.5 people per square mile, but Massachusetts, Rhode Island, Connecticut and New Jersey had more than 500 people per square mile. When Alaska and Hawaii became states in 1958 and 1959 respectively – which, in part, reflected their Cold War strategic role and the movement there of veterans – the geographical centre of the country moved north and west, from northern Kansas in 1958 to western South Dakota in 1960, but, with 0.4 people per square mile, Alaska had little impact on national population trends. Idaho, Montana, Nevada, New Mexico, Wyoming and the Dakotas all also had fewer than ten people per square mile in 1960. In demographic terms, Florida's growing importance lessened the westward impact of the rise of California. Florida, Nevada and Alaska were the states with a population increase of more than 75 per cent in 1950–60, followed by Arizona with 50–75 per cent, and California, Colorado, Connecticut, Maryland, New Jersey, New Mexico and Utah with 25–50 per cent.

Culturally, a shift to the South and, far more, to the West challenged the influence of the East and, particularly, of New York. Indeed, there was a growing assertion on the part of regional centres. The most dramatic in the 1950s was the Beat movement, which focused on San Francisco. Popular music frequently still retains a regional flavour, as with crunk, a form of hip-hop in Atlanta. Alongside regional assertion, there was a move in the national focus of cultural activity, with a diminished emphasis on New York. This move had already happened with cinema, but television remained more New York-oriented. In 1972, however, the highly popular NBC Tonight Show, presented by Johnny Carson, moved from there to Burbank in the Los Angeles conurbation.

Space is defined by human activity. In the 1950s this involved the overcoming of the constraints of distance, most significantly with the extensive Interstate Highway System pushed forward by the Eisenhower administration, in part in order to help speed military response to any major war, and also with the development of civil aviation. The new transport system also helped to spread national brands. This was obvious to travellers, since chains selling homogenous products replaced local restaurants and hotels, but it was also important to companies seeking to create national markets for their products. The process was aided by television advertising. Television, cinema, popular music and sports' teams playing for national audiences all contributed to, if not homogenization, at least a growing awareness of what became national trends. This, ironically, was to provide a stronger adversarial basis for politics. In part, this was because some felt challenged by the more insistent emphasis on the national rather than the local and the regional, while others were able to accept this trend. A shifting emphasis towards national issues – and politicians – was encouraged by the growth of the federal government, which also emphasized a focus on the pursuit of views and policies at the national level. This was to link political contention to culture wars.

Chapter 2

Changing Country

The American environment has never been constant. There was no primitive state of perfection, rudely shattered by human action, or a holistic balance subsequently destroyed by the arrival of European settlers, however large a role such beliefs have played in discussion of environmental history. But the human impact on the American environment over the last 50 years has been especially striking. Not only has the context within which humans live and operate changed greatly, but all the other species living in America have also been affected. Furthermore, the environmental movement has testified to the extent to which a new and troubling sense of where human history will lead, or indeed end, has developed. This movement was not new – the influential Sierra Club was founded in 1892 – but it became much stronger. The period since the 1960s does have a unity in the sense of widespread concern about environmental pressure, if not calamity, and has helped to provide a narrative of issues for debate and contention. In his futuristic novel *Hello America* (1983), J. G. Ballard predicted a radical change: 'As they looked back over the stern-rails of the convoy ships . . . the departing Americans could already see the desert moving in to take over their towns and suburbs . . . The old dreams were dead, Manson and Mickey Mouse and Marilyn Monroe belonged to a past America.'

In part, the human impact on the environment is a result of the tremendous growth in knowledge about it, for this increase in human capability enabled exploitation and impact, linking scientific advance and economic drives to environmental pressures. The most dramatic example was provided by the mapping of resources by satellite-based systems. This was an aspect of the American dominance of the Space Age, a dominance that, in the face of Soviet competition in the 1950s and '60s, had seemed in embarrassing doubt. The Soviets launched an unmanned satellite in 1957 and, in 1961, put the first man into orbit. The Americans, however, were clearly seen as winning the Space Race when they landed men on the Moon in 1969, a success that was broadcast around the world in another triumph of American technology, which provided a novel sense of immediacy. The Apollo space missions also left photographs of the Earth as a legacy. If this was a potent image of one world, it was one very much derived from America. Similarly, in 1981, as another instance of American technology, the first orbital flight by the space shuttle took place, although some commentators saw the subsequent troubles of the programme, including the loss of shuttles, as indicators of over-reach or, at least, a failure of due diligence on the part of the National Aeronautics and Space Administration (NASA).

From the 1970s NASA also used remote sensing by Landsat imagery in order to generate satellite images of the Earth's surface from electromagnetic radiations outside the normal visual range – an enhancement of human capability that was a common theme of the technology of the age. The use of different wavelengths enabled viewers to see, and therefore 'know', different aspects of the world. Infrared, for example, is especially valuable for vegetation surfaces and for water resources.

The Americans used satellite technology for both public and private purposes. As so often in American history, consumerism and security were crucial and related themes. Global Positioning System navigation devices, particularly for cars, boats and private planes, massively enhanced the ability to plan an individual course across the environment, while media and telecommunications usage of space became crucial to the business and leisure worlds. Meanwhile, concern about national security led, from 1983, to the 'Star Wars' initiative, a commitment to space-based systems for detecting and intercepting missile attacks that has been maintained, despite only limited success.

While outer space was used to alter paradigms on Earth, unmanned space missions were sent to explore the solar system. Major advances in recording and communications technology enabled these missions to provide information on what humans could not reach. For example, two *Viking* probes, launched in 1975, landed on Mars in order to search for life. They were unsuccessful, as were the two robot rovers that landed on the planet in 2004. The *Voyager* mission, launched in 1977 to visit the outer planets, sent back pictures that also failed to record signs of life, as did the cometary probe *Deep Impact*. In 2003 President George W. Bush announced a major new initiative designed to send people to the Moon, as a centrepiece of a revival in human space flight, but this may fall victim to budgetary cuts.

The absence of an encounter with extra-terrestrial life forms ensured that there was no fundamental shift in American debates about the relative nature of human values and the role of religious and secular narratives and analyses. This was also in marked contrast to the predictive power of the imagination, since aliens frequently appeared in literature and on the screen, and profitably so, as in *Alien* (1979) and *War of the Worlds* (2005), a film that testified to a powerful sense of menace, with only limited confidence in human ability to defeat aliens. The biggest film hit of 1980 had been *The Empire Strikes Back*, followed by *E. T., the Extra-Terrestrial* in 1982, *Return of the Jedi* in 1983 and *Star Wars III: Revenge of the Sith* in 2005. Crop circles appeared to herald an alien invasion in *Signs* (2002). Far from the imaginative role of aliens becoming less common with human exploration, it became more pronounced. This role was used not only to offer adventure stories but also alternative narratives of meanings and origins. Universes without a deity offered a powerful challenge to the conventional belief in the divine ordering of life. As a result, religious groups criticized the *Harry Potter* stories and also the *Lord of the Rings* trilogy.

Greater knowledge of the environment served two different but related ends: utilization and protection of the environment, both of which were pushed with great energy in the USA. A greater understanding of the issues present in the protection of the environment indeed helped to clarify the damaging extent of utilization. Some of the latter was short-term in scope, and reversible, but much of it was long-term and cumulative, which made it difficult subsequently to effect radical improvement.

The 'development' of the western USA provides a good example of this process. The transformation of the 'waterscape' through irrigation played a central role in the new engineered landscape of dams and irrigation canals. This was designed to improve power generation and economic benefit, similar to those resulting elsewhere from deforestation, but, apparently, both superior and more scientific. But the predicted results of this development proved more difficult to ensure than had been anticipated. Furthermore, serious problems also arose. Long-term environmental consequences included raising soil salinity. In some areas, decades of flood irrigation led to this salinity, and thus to the need for more water to flush the land. High salinity poisoned plant roots. The irrigation run-off led to the build-up of alkalis in sink areas, and these affected wildlife. In particular, selenium, a toxic soil compound brought to the surface by agricultural practices, contributed to serious deformities in wildlife. There was a particularly serious crisis in the Sacramento-San Joaquin Delta ecosystem. Problems, in turn, brought renewed attempts at control. Throughout California, natural waterways (and native grasses) have been replaced or subordinated. The central role of human activity was partly displayed by dramatic dams, but by the end of the century the control of river flows by computer was a more insistent and symbolically appropriate symbol. The USA was not alone in this development. Water control was a major issue across much of the world, and the difficulties experienced in the USA can be matched, for example, in Australia.

The commodification and usage of natural resources was challenged in the USA, from the 1950s, by the proposition that the world was a biosphere operating in an organic fashion and using natural feedback mechanisms to sustain life. The workings of this system were increasingly clarified by the spread of environmental concern and knowledge. Thus, it became possible to track, dramatize and debate the movement of air- or water-borne pollutants, for example air-borne sulphur dioxide from the Mid-West to eastern Canada and Appalachia. Books such as *Silent Spring* (1962) by the ecologist Rachel Carson highlighted the environmental threat posed by pesticides, especially DDT. The Sierra Club, a significant forum for environmental awareness, saw a major rise in membership, from 15,000 in 1960 to nearly 60,000 in 1967, 114,000 in 1970, 250,000 in 1981, nearly 500,000 in 1991 and 750,000 in 2005.

This was linked to a major shift in consciousness, as an environmental counter-culture critical of existing usage developed. For long, the human imprint had been seen as clear progress, and as fundamental to the development of the USA. Thus *The March of Civilization in Maps and Pictures* (1950) declared of the USA: 'its freedom-loving people have devoted their energies to developing the riches that Nature has so lavishly supplied'. A teleology of development was combined with a sense of a God-given right to transform the environment for human benefit.

From the 1960s this interpretation was seriously challenged. Environmental concern began as part of the counter-culture, and, to a certain extent, remained there, as with the annual Earth Days held from 1970. Discussion of the environment, however, played a far more prominent role in public awareness than had been the case in the 1950s, and the mainstream political process responded. Much greater sensitivity was shown to environmental issues than in the Soviet Union or China. Legislation included the Wilderness Act of 1964, the National Environmental Policy Act of 1969, the Clean Air Act of 1970, the Clean Water Act of 1972, and Endangered Species Protection Acts in 1966 and 1973.

There was also, as a central theme of environmentalism, an attack on aspects of big business. Indeed, environmentalism permitted a revival of aspects of the Progressivist movement of the early twentieth century. There were attacks on particular companies, not least Ralph Nader's sustained critique of General Motors, the leading car maker, and also an assault in the arts on business, although business was one of the biggest sponsors of the arts. In David Mamet's play *The Water Engine: An American Fable* (1977), big business is presented as corrupt and dangerous as it seeks to suppress an engine that runs on water. The engine itself is destroyed. At the cinema, *The China Syndrome* (1979) was a thriller about safety cover-ups at a fictional nuclear plant, which was made apparently prescient when the Three Mile Island reactor went into a meltdown a week after the film was released, while *Silkwood* (1983) focused on the disappearance in 1974 of a union organizer who exposed serious safety breaches at the nuclear power plant where she worked.

It proved difficult, however, to make environmentalism a large-scale populist aspect of mainstream politics, in part because such concern was generally presented as opposed to growth, a crucial goal in public discussion, as well as a restriction on individual freedom. Green political activism remained very weak in comparison, for example, with Germany. There were also pronounced regional and local variations within the USA, with environmental concerns proving strongest in areas that were politically liberal and whose economy was focused on the service sector, although the 'What would Jesus drive?' campaign added an interesting strain of religious environmentalism, which testified to the strength of religion in American culture. Regional political cultures also played a role, environmentalism being seen as a goal in the North-East and as a distraction, if not effete self-indulgence, by many in the South and the West, and in Mid-Western states, such as Indiana, that shared much of their ethos.

It is very easy to attribute the pressure on the environment to the marked rise in America's population, and certainly that was of great importance. A clear implication is that this is all the fault of 'ordinary people', having lots of children, driving cars and consuming goods, and that the inevitable consequence of the rise in population is environmental degradation. But it is also necessary to look at how resources are used. Here, the pattern remained very skewed. The more affluent used their affluence in order to consume a greatly disproportionate share of American (and global) resources, and their affluence was, in part, measured by this consumption.

Pressure on the environment was far greater than ever before, particularly in Alaska and the West. This was not simply due to larger human numbers and directly related pressure on resources, such as water. Technology also helped in the exploitation of the environment. The flexibility of motor transport and roads, over railways, increased the tempo of human action. Furthermore, thanks to greater technological capability, the range and impact of extractive processes, such as mining, increased, as with oil extraction in Alaska. It is possible that global warming will accentuate this process, as minerals and oil currently under the Arctic ice become easier to exploit. Politics also play a role. In November 2005 the Republican-dominated Senate voted to open the Arctic National Wildlife Refuge to oil drilling.

HUMANS AND ANIMALS

The changes in habitats stemming from human development also affected other species. It has been easier to chart the process for larger animals, especially big mammals, than, say, for amphibians, let alone insects, and it is likely that the impact on smaller animals has been considerably underrated. The challenge also engaged imaginative attention. In the science fiction TV series *Tremors* (2003), El Blanco, a large underground worm-like creature in Nevada, is dangerously irritated by a genetically modified creature produced in an underground government biotechnology laboratory. The theme of malign human intervention also plays a major role in the *Jurassic Park* film trilogy (1993–2001).

The great expansion in population, and in man-made environments and products, ensured that animals that benefited from contact with humans increased in numbers. In part, this was a matter of animals that Americans wished to have around, such as farm animals and pets. Meat-eating was an important aspect of American affluence and popular culture, celebrated in the cult of the barbecue and the popularity of the beefburger. Some meat was imported, but most came from American animals. In turn, however, the meat industry produced serious pollution when animals were concentrated in large numbers, as in the Arkansas poultry industry. Chicken rubbish contains high levels of phosphorus, which cause problems in water supplies.

In agriculture, the emphasis on costs and profits, not least the yield of meat per acre, led to a relative move away from beef cattle (of which the USA, nevertheless, remained the world's largest producer), which were generally fed on pasture and which were part of the American image. Instead, there was a greater emphasis on animals that could be fed more intensively from feedlots throughout the year, especially pigs and chickens. In the resulting 'factory farming', land ceased to be the main factor of production in agriculture, since animals were kept, in high-density, in buildings throughout the year. This qualified ruralist conception, about the relationship between agriculture and land, led to concern about food safety, which was linked to that over the impact on humans of the consumption of 'fast food', and greatly increased the problems posed by animal waste. The dumping of waste products contaminated local rivers and groundwater. Americans, however, largely sought to ignore the conditions in which farm animals were kept, and very few challenged ruralist conceptions. The condition of the food industry, nevertheless, remains a matter of concern. Although the feeding of bone meal to cattle was banned in 1997, blood and gelatine were still part of their diet. In 1996 a survey indicated that one in five dairy herds had MAP, a bacterium that causes a wasting disease in cattle, Johne's Disease , that may itself be a cause of Crohn's Disease in humans, a disease that has become more common. Farmers themselves were under great pressure from meat-packers, such as Tyson Foods, which, in 2004, was found guilty of manipulating cattle prices.

In contrast to ignorance of the condition of farm animals, the demand for pets spawned a major industry that recorded many of the processes more generally characteristic of American society, including consumerism and the impact of fashion and social changes. The pet industry, for example, reflected the growing importance of developing and satisfying the sensibilities of children, a crucial element in changing consumerism. The trend from dogs to cats reflected the growing percentage of Americans living in small dwellings, as well as the decreased ability or willingness to take dogs for walks, which, in part, was a consequence of other leisure options, such as the cult of the gym, as well as pressure on leisure time. The greater independent role of women as consumers also played a part in pet choices. Pets also played a major role on film, both in family comedies and cartoons. They were an amusing 'underclass', essentially well treated, positive and offering no implicit criticism of human hierarchies and priorities. Pets proved a more conducive topic than poverty for a film industry that was far from strong on (social) realism.

The treatment of animals reflected the myriad tensions of American society. For example, in 1999 Macaw Native Americans decided that they would hunt the grey whale in the Pacific in order to train the younger members to appreciate traditional hunting methods. This caused enormous outcry, so the Coast Guard and the Washington National Guard had to protect the Macaw while they were out practising and then hunting. Critics pointed out that the Macaw hunted the whales with the far from traditional .50 calibre rifle. Macaw culture was attacked with calls for the acceptance of American norms. Pilgrim Congregational, a very liberal United Church of Christ church in Seattle, that was usually quite supportive of indigenous culture, argued that the whales' rights took precedence over those of the Macaw.

The human impact on the environment also had unintended consequences for animals. Global warming affected their habitats and breeding patterns, greatly in some cases, and may have been beneficial for some species. Birds and fish appeared in more northerly latitudes, the robin, for example, in Alaska. The warmer climate was believed responsible for an increase in the inroads of spruce bark beetles in Alaska, while grey whales, walruses and eider ducks moved into the northern Bering Sea as it warmed up. Other animals, however, suffered. The diminution of the ice in the Arctic made it harder for polar bears to hunt and led to them swimming further in search of food, some drowning. At a more local level, wastewater emissions from power stations and factories raised water temperatures, and led to greater animal and plant activity nearby.

Animals were also affected by human activity that removed predators. For example, the decline in the number of mountain lions helped the wild horse or mustang to multiply, and they became a serious problem in the fragile environment of the West, particularly in Nevada, as well as competing with cattle for the limited food available. In the Everglades in Florida, the disruption of the hydrological system by drainage led to the invasion of species, such as pythons and tropical fish, as well as a benefit for fish able to live off rotting vegetation. In the very different urban and suburban environment, rats, cockroaches and other wildlife benefited greatly from the growth in the volume of rubbish. In New York in 2005 a marked rise in complaints about rats and mice (to nearly 32,000 for the year March 2004–March 2005) became an issue in the mayoral election. Also in New York that year there was a marked rise in bedbug infestation. The growth in rubbish owed much to the greater unwillingness to reuse material, and was a product of rising affluence and of the transformation of material culture, including major changes in packaging. Animals such as squirrels, foxes, deer and bears altered their activity patterns in order to exploit sites of rubbish accumulation and disposal, for example, near fast-food restaurants.

Indeed, all these animals became increasingly urban. This was partly caused by the abandonment by farmers of economically marginal farmland, which lessened the buffer between towns and woodland. This was particularly seen in the North-East, where farms were smaller and, therefore, less economic than those in the Mid-West and West. The advance of suburban areas into woodland was also an important factor. In suburban Boston there is now a problem with coyotes, while raccoons and skunks are also very common. The spread of suburbia, moreover, was blamed for the widespread fires that broke out in California in 1993, 2003 and 2005, since houses were built too close to brush that was prone to fires. This tendency was also blamed on the drier climate, because the brush was very dry, although, as a reminder of the complexity of causation, such dryness was particularly serious if it followed heavy rainfall that encouraged vegetation growth. There were also serious fires in Colorado in 2001. Expanding settlement and low-density living meant that humans and animals shared habitats. In Louisiana and Florida some people moved into areas where the waterways were inhabited by alligators, Miami, for example, spreading into the Everglades. In a different sphere, the widespread increase in sewage levels ensured that bacteria found in human waste, such as *faecal coliform*, thrived.

The period certainly witnessed an accelerating race between humans and animals for profit from what Americans saw as their habitat, but which was also, of course, that of animals. Notions of God's creation and God-given rights were not generally extended to the latter. The successful film *Jaws* (1975) was the most vivid display of competition, and spawned sequels.

In part, Americans used animals of their own in the contest, and their animals were also victims. I can recall staying in Baton Rouge in an area in which alligators were eating domestic pets. More generally, hunting dogs helped shooters, while cats were still employed against rats and mice. On the whole, however, the remedy to animal competition was chemical, in both houses and fields. This increased dramatically the volume of chemicals in the USA, especially those not 'contained' in manufacturing plant. The rhetoric of exterminating natural enemies, such as cockroaches, became insistent, and was supported by the filmic depiction of sinister parasites and insects, as in *The Shivers* (1975) and the remake of *The Fly* (1986). The resulting 'war' on insects and other enemies, however, had unwanted side effects. In some cases, as in the battle against rats, there were signs of increasingly limited success, since the animals began to develop immunity to chemicals. There were other problems with chemical warfare. DDT was used, with good results, against mosquitoes in the long battle with malaria, for example in Florida, but it also affected the animal and human population. Malaria itself became more resistant to drugs.

AGRICULTURE

The chemical offensive was also employed in agriculture. The mono-culture that came from an emphasis on a few high-yield crop strains lessened bio-diversity and also provided a food source for particular pests. More generally, as a result of agricultural practices, the organic matter in soil was widely degraded, while cultivated land left without a protective cover of vegetation suffered from the large-scale erosion of soil by wind and water. This, in turn, encouraged the application of unprecedented levels of fertilizer. Fertilizers, herbicides and pesticides, however, increasingly affected the crops that were consumed. There was also a major impact on water resources as fertilizers ran off into rivers with groundwater, or were transferred into the water system through leaching into the soil (affecting well water), or evaporation and then distilling out in colder air. Decreases in the water supply accentuated concentrations of pollutants. The widespread application of nitrogenous fertilizers also had an effect on global warming as nitrogen evaporated from soils.

Pesticides had a more direct impact on the health of the agricultural workforce. This was one that was accentuated by technology in the shape of the aerial 'top-dressing' of fertilizers from crop-dusting aircraft. This system also spread fertilizers widely in areas where they were less welcome. Methyl bromide, a gas employed against parasites across the USA, in particular in the cultivation of peppers, strawberries, tomatoes and Christmas trees, causes neuromuscular and cognitive problems, and, although the government agreed to phase out its use by 2005 in order to help protect the ozone layer, it proved willing to obtain treaty exemptions in order to permit continued use.

The application of fertilizers helped to drive the increase in yields. Corn yields in the Corn Belt rose from 50 bushels an acre in 1950 to 125 bushels in 1980. Higher production, however, meant downward pressure on prices, leading to dependence on exports, and a financial crisis for many farmers in the 1980s, as falling revenues exacerbated the burdens of meeting heavy costs, including the debt arising from more expensive inputs such as machinery and fertilizers. This led to heavy drinking and a high rate of suicides among farmers. By 1987 Iowa suicides had reached the highest total since the 1930s. The crisis spread to hit the economies of local towns, and to lead to tension between lenders and borrowers. In 1985 there were attempts to prevent foreclosure farm sales in Minnesota.

Throughout the world a focus on particular crop strains lessened bio-diversity and therefore, however convenient the parallel might seem, cannot serve as an indicator of American social trends. This development does, nevertheless, serve to emphasize the role of standardization and scale in mass-consumer-driven economies, such as the USA. Like the standardization in manufactured goods, supermarket chains insisted on certain types of produce and emphasized certain physical characteristics as supposedly betokening wholesome produce.

What they advertised and displayed shaped as well as reflected public assumptions. This was seen in fruit and vegetables, as well as in meat, fish and wine (the USA became the world's fourth biggest wine producer). Technological advances interacted with the drive for standardization. Tomatoes, for example, became more ovoid in shape as a consequence of the emphasis on harvesting by machines rather than human pickers, because they were easier to pick. The rise in the sale of pre-cut and packaged vegetables and fruits reached $12.5 billion in 2004, nearly four times the figure of a decade earlier.

Politics also played a crucial role in American agriculture. The lobbying power of agriculture protected it from some of the environmental constraints that were increasingly affecting industry. Politics also helped to ensure subsidies, for example for growing alfalfa, cotton (a subsidy ruled illegal by the World Trade Organization in 2004) and rice, as well as discriminatory moves against imports, for example of Canadian lumber from 2002, moves that were a breach of the North American Free-Trade Agreement. In 2005 the Senate extended agricultural subsidies. The overall impact of politics was to provide a level of protectionism that accentuated environmental pressure (by keeping uneconomic crops in cultivation) and distorted free trade. This hit poorer countries, such as cotton producers in West Africa, for example Mali, and also affected the prices paid by American consumers.

FISHING

Consumer pressure and technological enhancement also affected fishing, but politics had less influence, reflecting the greater political clout of farmers. Waters off the American coast were fished intensively by large 'factory ships', which consumed substantial quantities of energy and were equipped with sophisticated finding devices. These industrial fleets hit fish stocks. American fishermen were by no means alone in the process of depletion, but over-fishing affected both the North Atlantic and the Pacific. North Atlantic squid was fished out in the 1980s, and, in the Pacific, over-fishing hit the major catches, such as the anchoveta in the 1970s and the chub mackerel in the 1980s. Red snapper stocks in the Gulf of Mexico were also hit. Legislative action sought to redress the situation, and reflected the extent to which capitalism could be regulated. The Magnuson-Stevens Fishery Conservation and Management Act (1976) required fishery managers to specify a time frame that was as short as possible in which to end over-fishing and to rebuild over-fished stocks. Pressure on stocks, however, ensured that the situation could not be defined simply in terms of benign management. Instead, there was tension, indeed conflict, between communities of fishermen. As was frequently the case in American society, such conflicts could be accentuated by ethnic differences, particularly on the Gulf of Mexico, where Vietnamese immigrants became important, especially in the shrimp industry.

An effort was also made to develop fish farming, which became more important in the last quarter of the century, especially for catfish. Although fish farming fitted the tendency to make the most intensive use possible of all land and water that could be utilized, it consumed resources, not least fishmeal, and led to a serious accumulation of waste and toxins.

CLIMATE CHANGE

American agriculture and fishing were affected by climate change, which was possibly the most significant development of the period. The trend in temperatures was upward, with important rises from 1980. When periodic falls in temperature occurred after 1980, for example in 1999, in every case they were to a higher level than the temperature in 1980. Furthermore, global warming was also an accelerating process. From 1975 until the end of the century, the USA's surface temperature rose by about half a degree Celsius, reaching a figure apparently higher than in any period of human habitation.

Environmental change became a major international issue from the 1990s. It was also revived as an important topic in American public discussion, but this fed into America's 'culture wars'. Conservatives and some business interests questioned the evidence for temperature change. James Inhofe, Chairman of the Senate Environment Committee, and

Senator for Oklahoma, a state with a large oil industry, described global warming as a 'hoax'. Supporters of George W. Bush queried the extent of warming and the degree of human responsibility, and therefore the value of trying to control human actions by, for example, limiting emissions of 'greenhouse gases', a course urged by environmentalists. Bush rejected this linkage, and the Republicans in the Senate blocked the Climate Stewardship Bill, which would have led to federal caps on emissions. As in the past, environmental policy was shaped by political partisanship.

In 2005, however, the National Academy of Sciences not only declared that there was strong evidence of such global warming, but also that 'it is likely that most of the warming in recent decades can be attributed to human activities'. Indeed, American scientists have provided crucial evidence both of global warming, a trend charted by the Institution of Oceanography in San Diego, and also of the impact of the burning of fossil fuels. Although their research has led to pressure on their funding from the Bush administration, there is more freedom to debate the issue than there would be in China. An analysis in 2005 by NASA's Goddard Institute for Space Studies of readings from 7,200 weather stations indicates that global temperatures have risen by 1.36° Fahrenheit (0.75 °Celsius) above the average between 1950 and 1980.

The devastating Hurricane Katrina in 2005 accentuated the issue, because some commentators linked the severity of the storm to the high temperature of the water in the Gulf of Mexico, at 80 °F. This was a controversial point, but an important issue nevertheless. Politicians and journalists, however, preferred to focus on the issue of governmental failures in preparation and response. The most acute failing, but one again that is far more uncomfortable than the issue of crisis management, is in the general issue of energy use, and official forecasts are grim, both for carbon emissions and for electricity consumption.

The extent to which rising emissions will lead to further warming, possibly an increase by another 1°F by 2030 and a total of 2–4 °F by 2100, as suggested in 2005 by David Rind of the Goddard Institute, is controversial. It is also unclear how far the process has become self-sustaining. For example, the shrinkage of the Arctic ice as a consequence of global warming will ensure that the Arctic will warm up more quickly, because open water absorbs more solar heat than ice, which, instead, reflects it. In 2005 NASA scientists, in a joint project with the University of Colorado, estimated that the Arctic ice cap now covers 500,000 fewer square miles than the average cover between 1979 and 2000. This might not mean much if you sit in the warmth of the Florida sun, but the consequence of such melting will be higher sea levels that threaten to drown parts of coastal Florida. By the early 2000s world sea levels were rising at a rate of 2 mm (0.08 inches) a year. To those reading this in Wyoming, it means higher taxes to pay for federal disaster relief.

As a result of warming, climate zones within the USA moved both geographically and in terms of the terrain: more northerly and higher regions both became warmer. This was significant for desertification in the West, while, across the US, greater heat had important consequences for the availability of freshwater on land. This increased pressure for irrigation, which contributed to the growing water crisis in the West, although water availability was not only an issue there. Rising water consumption was a product of high per capita usage (232 gallons per day in California in 2000) and greater numbers. Increased extraction of water from rivers ensured that river levels, for example of the Colorado and the Rio Grande, dropped, and the volume of water reaching the sea declined. Extraction from rivers also led to disputes with neighbouring countries, as well as between states. That over the Colorado, from which California took water through the Colorado River Aqueduct and the All-American Canal, led, after much bitterness, to an agreement between seven states and the Department of the Interior in 2003. Rising consumption also led to the depletion of natural aquifers and to the movement of salt to the surface, which greatly affected soil quality. Water levels were also hit by drought, particularly in the early 2000s. This ensured on the Mississippi that, in order to avoid scraping the bottom, barges had to be lighter, which affected the efficiency of barge traffic. Further down the river, the impact of Hurricane Katrina on New Orleans in 2005 owed much to the funnelling effect of the Mississippi River Gulf Outlet, which had been constructed to give ships a shorter route to the Gulf of Mexico.

The water crisis has been largely addressed by supply side solutions, particularly dam construction and related water transfer schemes. Los

Angeles, a megalopolis with 3.8 million residents in 2004, built in the middle of a desert, symbolized the determination to locate human activities as desired and to move resources accordingly. The role of water in local political culture and the struggles to control its supply had an echo in the arts, most powerfully with Roman Polanski's film *Chinatown* (1974).

Dams were the symbols of this determination to control, but they posed problems, not least cost, disruption to settlements in the areas flooded and serious changes to fluvial systems, particularly the trapping of silt, which, indeed, lessened their effectiveness. By the end of the twentieth century there was far more of an emphasis than hitherto on demand-side policies, in the shape of more effective water use, for example low-flush toilets, and on more appropriate costing. This led, in the early 2000s, to incentives in parts of the West to abandon garden plants requiring irrigation. Particular tension focused on golf courses, which required large quantities of water, and its lavish use was a response to assumptions that it would always be readily available, even in desert environments. Golf courses also reflected the extent to which environmental ownership and pressure were products of social structures.

Despite a degree of micro-management, the demands on the environment and, in particular, on water resources, from serious and sustained population growth were not firmly controlled, being left to local guidelines, rather than national planning. The fastest-growing states, Nevada, Arizona, Florida, Texas and Utah, were in water-shortage areas. This was part of a major move to the South and West that saw a major reordering in the urban hierarchy, with the metropolitan areas focused on Los Angeles, Dallas, Houston, Atlanta, San Diego, San Antonio, Phoenix and Las Vegas all becoming more important. In contrast, areas where water availability was less of a problem, for example most of the North-East, showed only modest population growth. In 2003 Phoenix displaced Philadelphia as the fifth most populous city in the country. Agriculture, an important sector of water demand, benefited greatly from subsidized pricing. This was particularly so in California, where close to 80 per cent of the water was used for farming, and this pricing was an aspect of the totemic character of agriculture in American public life, as well as of its strong grip on the politics of 'pork' (special interests).

As yet, the impact of a rising sea level has not been felt greatly in the USA, but, as the warming oceans expand when polar ice melts, it will become more of a feature. Shrinking glaciers, for example in Kenai Fjords National Park in Alaska, offer a clear warning. The melting of the snows in the Rockies also poses a serious problem, as water availability from snow is more consistent than if it falls as rain. Much of the latter becomes run-off that cannot be used so readily in the water system.

POLLUTION

Other changes that can be measured include carbon-dioxide emissions and acid deposition, the former the result of burning forests or fossil fuels, the latter a consequence of sulphur and nitrogen production from industrial processes. In 2005 the International Energy Agency warned that, unless energy consumption was limited, emissions of carbon dioxide would be 52 per cent higher by 2030. Carbon dioxide is the greenhouse gas, while acid rain damages woodland and hits both rivers and lakes. Pollution spread widely. When caused by 'high-stack emissions', it had the capacity to affect distant environments. It is very striking to stand on the Blue Ridge Parkway near Asheville and see air polluted by Mid-Western manufacturing plants being blown east. Exporting jobs, to Mexico under the North American Free-Trade Agreement (1994), or to China via the trade deficit, simply moved the pollution elsewhere.

The assault from pollution was also very varied and insistent. Lead emissions from traffic seriously affected air quality. This was particularly so in the cities, accentuating the appeal of suburban life, but suburban commuters then further damaged urban air quality, both in the suburbs and downtowns. The consumer society also produced greater and greater quantities of rubbish, much of it non-biodegradable, and some of it toxic. The nuclear industry, which contained 103 plants in 2005, posed particular problems.

Environmental damage as a consequence of accidents was also important. This was prominent at sea with the shipwreck of oil tankers, such as the *Exxon Valdez* off Alaska in 1989, but was more common on land, not least with leaks from oil pipelines. This damage led to particular sensitivity about the development of the Alaskan oil industry. In March 2006 a ruptured pipeline from which 950,000 litres of oil had spilt was discovered on Alaska's northern coast. The environmental problems caused by oil were also readily apparent in the toxic waters left in Hurricane Katrina's aftermath in 2005. The Three Mile Island accident in 1979 hit the development of the nuclear power industry, and no new nuclear power plants were commissioned after that. Indeed, more than 100 reactor orders were cancelled.

Noise and light pollution have also become more serious and widespread. The latter ensured that the view of the sky at night was increasingly affected, particularly as American society had the affluence to use large amounts of lighting, and the freedom to do so with scant regulation. Light pollution might seem an affectation of recent decades, but it was readily apparent from the sky, and brought home by nighttime photographs of the USA over a long period of time. More direct visual impact arose from industrial and mining activity. This was true both of economic activity and of its consequences. A particularly brutal example was provided by the West Virginia coal industry, which stripped mountains not only of their natural cover but also of their tops, helping to cause major problems with erosion, run-off and clogged waterways.

ENERGY SUPPLIES

There was particular pressure on energy supplies. Rising energy needs reflected the enormous growth in both per capita and aggregate energy consumption, in response to shifts in economic activity, social processes and living arrangements, but also the extent to which taxes on oil (petrol, gasoline) were low compared to those in Europe. The range of energy uses also increased. Oil-based additives became important in agriculture, while the spread of agricultural machinery increased demand for oil. In the 1990s the greater use of computers and the Internet pushed up demands for electricity. Despite a major rise in Chinese oil consumption from 2000, the USA consumed a quarter of world oil output in 2004, and its consumption per capita was considerably higher than in more densely populated Europe, let alone China. This was not only a matter of American prosperity, but also a product of the lack of investment in fuel economy, including public transport. In turn, this was a product of consumer preferences, corporate responses and a lack of serious government backing. The impact on the environment was grave. The highest per capita emissions of greenhouse gases were in the USA, in large part caused by the strength of the car culture there. Carbon dioxide was the most important greenhouse gas, but other emissions were also damaging. A combination of cars and the petrochemical industry led to the Houston conurbation sending skywards 200,000 tons of nitrogen oxide annually by the late 1990s. Petrochemical plants also bathed communities, such as Beaumont in Texas, the site of an Exxon Mobile refinery, in a perpetual smell. It is very unpleasant, even if it is the smell of jobs. A second visit did not improve the smell.

Energy use was linked to issues of finance and national security. Extensive coal reserves eased the need for imports – and coal fuels more than half of America's electricity needs. However, oil imports – close to 2 per cent of GDP in 2005 – were seen to put pressure on the balance of payments, and also to lead to a dangerous dependence on the politics of the Middle East and the stability of particular regimes, such as those of the Shah in Iran in the 1970s and the Saud dynasty in Saudi Arabia. In 2003 Saudi Arabia held 25 per cent of the world's oil reserves, and Iraq another 10 per cent, with the Middle Eastern OPEC states having two-thirds of the world's reserves. Whatever the future development of American supplies, particularly in Alaska, the Middle East will dominate future supply. Although the role of oil in the American decision to attack Iraq in 2003 was exaggerated, oil certainly played a major role in the geopolitics of American strategy. Indeed, this was an aspect of the cost that oil dependence forced on the USA, and thus the burden placed on its economy and consumers.

Oil imports rose sharply in the 1970s and then, having fallen in the early 1980s, again thereafter. These imports are projected to go on rising. In 2004 the US imported 58 per cent of the oil it consumed, compared to 34 per cent in 1973. The Energy Information Administration predicts this rising to 68 per cent by 2025, rising imports essentially meeting rising demand, although the shift from manufacturing to information and service industries has helped to limit the rise by reducing the economy's need for oil. Indeed, the consumption of energy per dollar of GDP fell by nearly a half from 1973 to 2002. Pressure on energy supplies, nevertheless, led to a major rise in oil and natural gas prices from November 2001. This hit American consumers particularly hard because of the relatively low rate of petrol taxation. In 1993 the federal tax was set at 18.4 cents per gallon. It has not been adjusted for inflation since. As a result of concern about oil costs, demand rose greatly for the new hybrid technology of petrol-electric cars, although that remained only a small percentage of the market.

Energy problems also led to a revival in interest in nuclear power on the part of the administration of George W. Bush, himself a supporter of subsidies for new plants. Concern about fossil fuels and carbon emissions led some environmentalists to support this goal. Given the very limited prospect of any reduction in energy use, environmentalists had to confront the problems posed by the various options for increased provision. For example, in Massachusetts in 2005 there was a debate over whether to place 130 large windmill turbines off Nantucket Island. It was claimed that there was enough potential energy in the winds off the east coast to replace much of the region's power-plant capacity. Environmentalists, however, joined by those who want to preserve the scenic beauty of Nantucket Sound, mounted a major counter-offensive.

The availability of passive safety features, rather than those dependent on operators, suggests that any new nuclear reactors will be safer than hitherto. Vulnerability to terrorist attack, however, is an issue. Energy had already precipitated a domestic political crisis in California in 2003, when it helped to cause the overthrow of Gray Davis, the Governor of California, whose popularity had suffered as a result of repeated electricity supply blackouts in 2001, and his subsequent attempts to deal with the crisis. Although the allocation and pricing of the available power were crucial to the crisis in 2001, the underlying problem was caused by a lack of capacity, because of the unwillingness to build unpopular power plants. In 2001 Vice President Cheney, who had major interests in the construction industry, had warned about the danger of a lack of energy threatening the economy, standard of living and national security, and argued the need for between 1,300 and 1,900 power plants. Government devoted far less attention to limiting demand or financing alternative technologies, despite the strategic value to be gained by lessening the need for oil imports. Bioethanol, indeed, can be produced in the USA, as could hydrogen, the basis of fuel-cell technology. At present, the use of corn-based ethanol as a fuel is costly, and only possible thanks to subsidies, but that may change if biotechnology makes it easier to produce. In his State of the Union address in 2006, George W. Bush proposed to finance research in this field, at the same time that he declared that 'America is addicted to oil', something he had singularly failed to tackle, not least in the Energy Act of 2005.

HOUSING

The car moulded the urban environment, facilitating the spread of suburbs over great distances. This ensured that the suburbs pressed on the natural environment, and also provided many problems for the provision of public services. In greatly expanding urban areas, such as Los Angeles, Houston and Atlanta, far-flung water and sewage services had to be established as the suburbs spread, creating new edge-cities. The combination of inexpensive new-build construction methods and the ready availability of mortgage support helped to make suburban expansion profitable and possible, and, throughout the period, most population growth in metropolitan areas has been suburban. Although the skyscrapers of downtowns reflected urban land values for offices, frequent talk of an urban renaissance as downtowns, or really parts of downtowns, became more fashionable as residential districts, ignored the extent to which population growth was faster in metropolitan peripheries than in their cores. This had political consequences. Whereas, in 1952, New York City had almost half the state's voters, by 2005 it had less than a third. The cultural consequences of suburban expansion included an important measure of homogenization, seen, for example, in the use of national patterns of urban layouts and housing types, as well as in shopping and leisure facilities, most of which were provided by national chains. This homogenization was an important aspect of the standardization that was seen throughout the economy and the consumer culture it fostered. Across the country, for example, light switches were the same, which was a tremendous boom to the economies of scale, as well as encouraging uniformity in design.

Private demand was the crucial element in housing, not public provision, and this demand responded to the major growth of GDP from the 1940s, and to the extent to which the lifestyle of the rich became that of the middle class. The kitchens and bathrooms of standard houses reflected this shift. The average house-purchaser came closer to realizing the standard dream of a detached house in a low-density area. This was crucial to the suburbanization of society, a classic case of 'pull', in the shape of aspirations for a particular lifestyle, and 'push', in the shape of fear of the city. This was a fear brilliantly captured in Tom Wolfe's novel *The Bonfire of the Vanities* (1987), and in *Batman*, the most successful film of 1989, which offered a very dark depiction of the city. The city was also seen as sinister and brutal in a tranche of films including *Sin City* (2005), a violent film based on Frank Miller's writing.

By August 2005 the annual rate of home sales was 7.29 million units (in October it fell to 7.1 million), while the median home price was $220,000, an annual increase of 15.8 per cent, the biggest rise on record in real terms (by October the annual increase was 16.6 per cent). In October the median price of new homes was $231,300, although it subsequently fell. Throughout 2000 the figure had been below $150,000, while it had been $22,600 in September 1970 and $68,300 in September 1980. Furthermore, the average size of houses continued to grow. By 2004 it was 2,349 square feet, an increase of 12 per cent in a decade. Tax cuts thus fed through into larger houses, while financial devices such as option adjustable-rate mortgages eased borrowing. Rising house prices encourage activity, and thus employment, in construction, increase net worth and make it easier to borrow. Borrowing against home equity as a share of disposable personal income indeed rose from 1 per cent in 1994 to 3 per cent in 2000 and 6.9 per cent in 2004; and in 2004 this added $600 billion to consumers' spending power. This was more than double the value of President Bush's tax cuts and put the latter in perspective. Rising home prices also make housing more expensive, enforce saving for, and in, property, and thus challenge expenditure in other spheres, such as leisure. In 2005 residential investment rose to 6 per cent of GDP, and property loans accounted for just over half of banks' total lending. An unwillingness to accept lower expenditure in other spheres led to a greater determination to borrow in order to fund house purchases. In 2005 households' mortgage debt rose to $1.8 trillion, an increase of close to a third in two years.

The major rise in house prices at a time of low inflation helped to take the combined revenue of the top ten house builders to about $73 billion in 2004, underlined social differentiation and also helped to make house purchase even more desirable. It was easiest for the upwardly mobile and youngish, and their ethos became particularly important in suburban areas, while the ability of the young to establish themselves helped to ensure the rise of the birth rate. The situation in Italy was the exact opposite: unable to establish themselves, children stayed in the parental home and the birth rate fell. An important aspect of social differentiation in the USA also arose from the increased percentage of properties that were second (or more) homes, whether for vacations or for investment. This was a very concrete manifestation of differences in wealth and opportunity. Whereas second homes were responsible for 7 per cent of new mortgages in 2000, the percentage for 2004 was 14, an unprecedented level.

TRANSPORT

The car was increasingly the dynamic hub at the intersection of a number of pressures and trends. Car use rose greatly and the car had a major impact on lifestyles, design, architecture and the economy. The car was very important in the demand for oil. By 2000 there were 486 cars per 1,000 people; by July 2005 there was a total number of about 225 million vehicles, which will possibly increase by about a half by 2025; and in February 2006 the seasonally adjusted annual rate of sales was 16.6 million. The state of car manufacturers such as General Motors and Ford was seen as crucial to the economy and to the trade balance, but a major part of the market was met by imports or by manufacturing within the USA by foreign companies. Japanese competition proved particularly effective. The spatial dimension of production was linked to socio-political considerations. Japanese and European plants in the South were mostly non-union and easier to manage than American-owned unionized plants in the North, particularly those of General Motors.

Alongside housing, the imprint of the car on social life was insistent, affecting a wide range of activities, including family relationships, courtship rituals and shopping. Greater personal mobility for most Americans, but by no means all, enabled, and was a necessary consequence of, lower-density housing and a declining role for public transport. This was linked to changes in employment patterns and urban structures, not least the shift from manufacturing to the service sector. Furthermore, in place of factories, or mines, that had large labour forces, most modern American industrial concerns are capital-intensive and employ less labour. They are located away from the central areas of cities, on flat and relatively open sites with good road links. There was a comparable shift in docks, away from city anchorages, for example in New York and San Francisco, to large, new, 'greenfield' container ports that employed far less labour – and were far from the trade-union problems of established docks. In 2000 approximately seven million trucks (lorries) in the country served docks, factories and the network of wholesale and retail distribution. Greenfield construction was also true of business, science and shopping parks, and, by 2004 suburbia accounted for about 90 per cent of new office building. It was far easier to deploy new technology, particularly the multiple electric networks required by computers, in new buildings. Related changes in location were also of great importance in such areas as education, health and leisure. Mega-churches were built in the suburbs, the prominent Southern Baptist Adrian Rogers moving Bellevue Baptist Church to a 6.5-acre site in the suburbs of Memphis in 1989. Roads provided not only access, but also the flexibility lacking in rapid-transit systems, and this made low-density development possible and profitable. Cars organized time as well as space, the journey-time by car becoming a prime unit of time and a way to organize people's lives.

Yet, as roads led to greater car use, so there was a need for more roads. In turn, they defined links and created physical barriers, producing a clear shaping of local environments that was linked to ethnic and social divisions, both real and psychological. This was the background to daily life, as experienced by many urban Americans, and also to the fictional world, as in the film *Crash* (2005).

As a result of the focus on the car, access for pedestrians declined markedly, and cycling was not generally an option, which further encouraged car use. An ironic aspect of this was that shopping malls themselves became important sites of exercise as well as challenges to the unfit. For some, getting to the mall from the parked car was a problem, as was moving within the mall, while others saw malls as a good place for indoor exercise, safely policed by the mall's security staff. Indeed, the Woodfield Mall in the Chicago suburb of Schaumburg advertised itself as a suitable location for walking exercise.

Cars also consumed an enormous amount of space. By the 2000s 'McMansions' had triple garages, while town centres and large parking garages and shopping malls were surrounded by acres of parking spaces. Parking attracted entrepreneurial activity (as well as corruption), and also played a major role in planning and in development battles. The scale of cars meanwhile was increased by the popularity of suvs (Sports Utility Vehicles), which are allowed by federal regulations to be less fuel efficient than other cars (as well as being far more dangerous to pedestrians). Their growing popularity in the 1990s ensured that average fuel economy for cars did not show the improvement it had displayed in the 1970s and '80s, when, in part as a result of the Corporate Average Fuel Economy legislation, it rose from 14 miles per gallon in 1974 to 22 miles per gallon in 1986, leading to a fall in oil use, a marked decline in oil imports and the weakness of OPEC. Polls in 2005, however, indicated that most Americans would prefer not to trade-down to a smaller, but more fuel-efficient, car, despite the attempt to add religious appeal to conservationism with the 'What would Jesus drive?' campaign of the early 2000s. The family that in November 2005 won $340 million in the Powerball Lottery celebrated by buying their dream car, a Humvee. An amendment to the Senate energy bill in 2005 that would have tightened vehicle fuel standards was rejected. This refusal to strengthen demand-side action testified to the responsiveness of legislators to widespread popular reluctance about fuel efficiency, which, like downward social mobility or public transport, is generally seen as for others.

In addition, large amounts of money were spent on the road system, in response to both rising demand in saturated areas and, far more generally, to a sense of entitlement to easy road use. In the early 2000s billions were spent on the costliest single public-works project in American history, the 'Big Dig' in Boston, to reorganize the central road artery and add tunnels to Logan airport – all based on road transport. The same amount of money would have greatly improved the railroads in the North-East: the sheer size of the country argues against developed rail travel, but in the Boston–Washington corridor much could be done. Rail travel is important in commuting into many major cities, for example New York, Chicago and Washington, DC, where the Metro system was begun in 1976. It also helped to turn towns into dormitory suburbs: Fredericksburg, for example, became one for Washington. However, rail was of minor importance in commuting into Southern cities or, indeed, for travel to them: Phoenix's passenger train service ended in 1996. Rail also remained very significant for long-distance freight, not least thanks to the use of containers. These were an American innovation, introduced on shipping in 1956, and then spreading to rail and road. This increased the speed, and cut the cost, of freight movements. Containerization was linked to the needs for labour productivity and product predictability that played a major role in the American economy, and helped it to sustain a powerful competitive edge. Nevertheless, the crisis of rail at the national level was shown with the bankruptcy of major companies, such as the Penn Central Railroad in 1970.

Whereas public funding for road building was very great, and major projects were completed, there was no comparable support for the rail system. Instead, there were frequent attempts by Republicans to cut the funding of Amtrak. Public transport lacked instinctive support among conservatives. It was disliked as a 'socialized' system, of prime benefit to metropolitan areas, particularly in the North-East. Subliminally, there was also a dislike of the social and racial mixing it represented, one comparable to the response to public hospitals. This mixing is very evident if local train services such as those of the New Jersey Transit Authority are taken. The limited provision for public transport helped to give the USA a distinctive character among developed societies. In *Who Framed Roger Rabbit?* (1988), corrupt government and the destruction of neighbourhoods, both in the interest of the car and against public transport, extended to the cartoon world. In practice, in 2005, 12 per cent of the voting-age population still did not have a driver's licence, but they lacked political influence. The emphasis on car culture was also shown with the average American only taking 28.4 bus trips in 2002 and with the six-year transport bill passed in 2005, which allocated $286.4 billion for roads and bridges; 35 per cent more than the previous bill. Because of this expenditure, the federal Highway Trust Fund is due to move into a 'negative cash balance' in 2008. Legislators were judged a success if they could deliver benefits, such as roads and bridges, to their constituencies, a process known as 'pork', and seen in the 6,371 earmarks in the 2005 transport bill. This expenditure contributed to the crisis in public finances in the mid-2000s, as well as to anger about the unwillingness of legislators to trim 'pork'. There was also activity on roads at the state level. The ten-year plan for California unveiled by the Governor in January 2006 promised 1,200 miles of new highway lanes.

Bridges symbolized human control over the environment, rather as dams had done for a previous generation. Furthermore, whereas major dams were largely confined to areas remote from centres of population, and particularly to the West, bridges were frequently close to or, indeed, part of these centres. Their impact was both local and regional, the latter reflecting their role in changing transport patterns. The engineering feats were frequently impressive, as with the Hampton Roads bridge-tunnel between Hampton and Norfolk, Virginia, completed in 1978, and the cost similarly high. The eight-lane Arthur J. Ravenel Jr Bridge, opened at Charleston in 2005, was, at 3.5 miles, the longest cable-stayed span bridge in North America, and cost $632 million. Its towers can be seen for more than 20 miles, and it is emblematic of the dominant role of bridges in low-country regions of the US. This bridge also reflects other tendencies of modern American bridge building. Although in response to pressure from environmental and cycling groups it includes a bicycle and pedestrian walkway, the bridge is for road, not rail, travel. Secondly, it replaces existing facilities in a far more dramatic fashion, in this case the Grace Bridge of 1929 and the Pearman Bridge of 1964. Elsewhere, for example in the Virginia Necks, bridges have replaced ferries, this contributing to the spread of the car in poor coastal communities that were hitherto partially self-sufficient, if not cut off. This is linked to the decline of local dialects in some areas, such as near Gloucester, Virginia.

If private transport transformed local geographies, electricity consumption in the shape of air conditioning did the same for regions, by making year-round living in the hot, wet South-East and the desert-dry South-West comfortable throughout the year. In an instructive example of the altered states referred to in the title of this book, this made these areas attractive to those who did not have to live there year-round, both attracting internal migrants and encouraging those who already lived there not to leave for part of the year. Air conditioning reflected the extent to which the constraints of physical geography could be altered and, more generally, this is true of recent American history. Nevertheless, air conditioning represented a major energy demand.

ENVIRONMENTALISM AND POLITICS

Anxiety about environmental pressures led to demands, in both the USA and globally, for what was termed sustainable development. This, however, proved a nebulous concept. It was difficult to define and enforce, and was also contested by local communities anxious for jobs, companies keen to maximize revenues, and state and federal governments determined on development. The George W. Bush administrations proved particularly reluctant to heed domestic and international pressure about energy conservation. In 1997 concern about global warming had led to the Kyoto Protocol, under which the major industrialized states agreed to reduce, by the years 2008–12, their emissions of the greenhouse gases held responsible for global warming to an average of about 5 per cent below their level in 1990. However, it proved difficult to reach agreement on how to enforce the agreement, and in 2001 the

USA, whose emissions had risen greatly in the 1990s, rejected the Kyoto agreement. As such, it found itself opposed to Canada, the European Union and Japan. By 2003 US emissions were 13 per cent above those in 1990, although many other countries, including Canada (up more than 25 per cent), were even more off course.

There are prudential reasons for doubting aspects of the Kyoto process. In the discussions held at Gleneagles in 2005 by the leaders of the Group of Eight nations, President Bush argued that there were uncertainties about Kyoto's science and economics. More specifically, he claimed that the agreement entailed substantial costs, but only limited benefits, for the USA; that proposals to deal with greenhouse-gas emissions excluding developing countries, especially China and India, were flawed, and put the USA at a competitive disadvantage; and that expenditure on new technologies, such as trapping CO_2 in deep salt-water-laden rock formations, should take precedence over emission reductions. Bush appears to be driven most by concern about the possible economic consequences. Indeed, in March 2001 he had declared: 'In terms of the CO_2 issue, I will explain as clearly as I can today and every other chance I get that I will not do anything that harms our economy. Because first things first are the people who live in America. That is my priority.'

The entire debate was also an aspect of America's bitter culture wars. To most conservatives, environmental concern was an aspect of the counter-culture, while, to the religious right, there was a sense of a God-given right to make use of the Earth. Sectional interests and cultural factors ensured that American policy-making was not greatly informed by scientific knowledge or characterized by secular processes of cause and debate. Given America's role as the world's leading economy and consumer, this was very unfortunate, and represented a major qualification of the argument that collective progress represents a way to deal with problems that cannot be handled at the individual level.

The issue also greatly contributed to anti-Americanism. Hurricane Katrina led Jürgen Trittin, the German Environment Minister, to describe the USA in 2005 as 'climate-polluter headquarters'. It is important, however, not to use the issue simply as one for America- or Bush-bashing. Many other states have displayed a far worse care for the environment as they industrialized in recent decades, most obviously China and India, while high unemployment levels across much of the European Union are, in part, a comment on the consequences of the over-regulation of business there. Furthermore, George W. Bush's faults were an accentuation of those of much of American society, which, indeed, is a reason why he appeared to move some of his critics to despair.

Within the USA the debate over environmental pressures was not simply a matter of Kyoto, an approach that could be readily subsumed by conservatives into their ideas of national sovereignty and, in particular, the rejection of international constraints that they trumpeted. There was also the question of the impact of climate change within the USA. This was dramatized in 2005 as a result of the consequences for the ultimate American wilderness, Alaska. A bi-partisan senatorial tour provided public confirmation of this impact, which had received attention from the late 1990s. Then, the thinning of the sea ice attracted comment. Its retreat exposed coastal areas to winter storms, speeding coastal erosion. Subsequently, there has been attention to the melting of the permafrost, which provides a basis for the piles on which Native houses are built. Its melting made both houses and trees precarious. The rate of change was unprecedented. The summer melting period is getting longer by about five days per decade; the sea ice has thinned by about a half from 1950 to 2005; and, on present trends, there will be none at the North Pole by the summer of 2080. In 2005 the ozone level over the Arctic thinned to its lowest level since records began.

The notion of controls on greenhouse-gas emissions, however, hit at the assumptions of powerful parts of the constituency that supported George W. Bush. At the same time, it suggested differences within this constituency. Legislation requiring car makers to cut emissions from vehicles sold in the state won support in Oregon, where the House is Republican, as well as from the Republican Governor of California, Arnold Schwarzenegger, while Republican-controlled states in the North-East expressed interest in emissions trading schemes, but there was far less support in the South. Similarly, a number of large concerns, such as Ford and DuPont, announced commitments to limiting energy consumption, but this was of scant interest to most suburban consumers. Nevertheless, the energy crisis of 2005 eventually led the President to urge energy conservation in the shape of driving less and more slowly, and using less electricity by turning down air conditioning and switching off lights. This repetition of the policies of the Carter administration, one that Republicans derided at the time and subsequently, indicated the extent to which ideology sometimes has to yield to circumstances.

Apart from global warming, conservation issues also pressed other buttons in the crucial field of rights. The most serious was that of land, and, specifically, control over its use. This led to local and national political struggles, not least Republican pressure for the development of the extensive public lands in the West and Alaska. In addition to underlining the extent to which the role of government was an issue, development pressures on land also created differences between citizens, which, in turn, helped to involve politicians and judges, competing, and overlapping, arbiters of disputes at every level. Property rights in the West were again contentious, with landowners challenging the split estate law that gave them only surface rights, and thus providing mineral companies with opportunities.

The sensitivity of controls was indicated in 2005 when, in giving judgement on *Kelo v. New London*, the Supreme Court interpreted the governmental power of eminent domain, the compulsory purchase of property for public use, to include the benefit of private interests that might yield indirect public benefit through higher taxes. Irrespective of the merits of the case, the outraged response to such a constraint on private property rights suggested that any attempt to use environmental causes to the same end would face major difficulties. In Oregon the state's attempts to use land-use planning in order to contain sprawl was challenged in 2004, when, with Measure 37, a referendum gave the right to those who owned land prior to 1973 to develop it or to receive compensation. The drift of American society was also indicated by the extent to which coastal sea-defences in the Gulf of Mexico were compromised by extensive building on offshore islands and marshlands, and the related draining of wetlands. Both allegedly helped to accentuate the devastating impact of Hurricane Katrina in 2005.

Discussing these issues with Americans indicates the very varied and contentious nature of opinions over development and the extent to which it pushes all sorts of buttons of concern and, indeed, outrage.

Much of the debate is not new, but that does not make it any less urgent. The debate also poses issues that question the value of accustomed political responses. Just as liberals are challenged by the extent to which concern for individual rights has hindered the struggle against the dangerous inroads of narcotic drugs, and may also be a weakness in the resistance to terrorism, so conservatives need to consider whether self-righting notions of economic responsiveness, and a hostility to the precepts and practice of government regulation, offer a sufficient remedy to environmental degradation. It will not be possible to sit aside and watch the results on television. The change is such that everyone, whatever their background, is affected. This is very much a shared experience, but one that many prefer to ignore or to blame on others.

Chapter 3

Changing People

POPULATION TRENDS

The American population rose considerably in the twentieth century: in millions, from 76 in 1900 to 106 in 1920, 132 in 1940, 179 in 1960, 203 in 1970, 226 in 1980, 239 in 1985, 249 in 1990 and 281 in 2000 (after the greatest rise in a decade), and 298 in 2005, with a projected 364 million for 2030, and 420 million by 2050, a remarkable increase. The percentage of the world's population living in the USA fell, however, due to much greater growth in some other areas, and also because the USA did not sustain the rate of population growth experienced in the 1960s. In contrast to the 18.5 per cent growth rate then, that in the 1970s was 11.4 per cent, that in the 1980s 9.8 per cent and that in the 1990s 13.1 per cent. Indeed, the percentage of the world's population living in the USA and Canada declined from 6.7 in 1950 to 5.7 in 1980 and 5.1 in 1996, while, in contrast, the figures for Asia were 55, 58.9 and 59.7.

Differential growth rates have also affected the American position within the West, at least in demographic terms. The US growth rates have been higher than in Europe (where the percentage of the world's population fell from 23.2 in 1950 to 16.5 in 1980 and 13.9 in 1996), but lower than in Latin America. The high rates of population growth in Latin America helped to drive the pressure for immigration into the USA, and thus the changing racial complexion of the USA.

The increase in the American population, however, was the overall product of very varied regional growth rates. In large part, these variations reflected the willingness of about 3 per cent of the population to move state each year. In the 1990s, 73 million Americans did so. A far greater percentage of the population moved within states. Migration within the USA, and the accompanying senses of loss and opportunity, played a role in individual, family and collective experiences, and was reflected in the arts, for example in Lisa Alther's novels *Kinflicks* (1976) and *Original Sin* (1981), in which characters repeated her move from Tennessee to the North. Migration was largely driven by economic opportunity, with retirement proving an important second strand. The major shift in population was from the Rustbelt of parts of the North-East and Mid-West to the Sunbelt of the West and South-West, as well as to Florida and North Carolina. The rate of job changes, which included the creation of more than two million jobs annually between 1994 and 2000, contributed to this movement. Earlier, in the 1950s–1970s, there had been major changes in the distribution of manufacturing, which became a more national activity, reducing the previous emphasis on the North-East and the Mid-West. Whereas New York had been the state with the most manufacturing employment in 1947, California (8th in 1947) held the top place in 1982. In the same period, Texas rose from 14th to 5th in manufacturing terms, North Carolina from 12th to 8th, Georgia from 15th to 12th, and South Carolina from 20th to 18th.

In California, which benefited greatly from the move of jobs, the population in millions rose from 5.7 in 1930 to 15.8 in 1960, 32.4 in 1996 and 36 in 2004, when it was the world's eighth biggest economy; it is due to rise to 48 million in 2030. In the years 1994–2003 there were about 10 million migrants into the state. Other states have seen significant growth, even if only in percentage terms, The population of Oregon, for example, rose from 2.2 million in 1973 to 3.6 million in 2004. Part of this growth stems from movement from California, a shift that has also affected Colorado, where the population of the Denver metropolitan area rose by more than 8 per cent in the years 2000–04, while Greeley, Colorado, was one of the fastest growing communities in the country.

Trends in manufacturing and retirement were not the sole issues at stake. The problems of agriculture, with its declining labour require-ments, and the crisis of many small towns, as warehousing, retail, food processing and light industry were centralized, further accentuated the population movements between and within regions. The general impression was of a movement to the coasts, although there were many exceptions, such as the growth in the Atlanta, Las Vegas, Phoenix and Raleigh-Durham areas. From 1960 the population of the greater Phoenix area grew by an average of 47 per cent each decade, while between 1990 and 2003 Austin's population grew by 63 per cent to 1.4 million. Austin's rise reflected its success in high-technology industries. One consequence was the growth in office construction and revenues. In 2005 projections for annual office gross-revenue growth over the next five years were 5.6 per cent for Austin. Predictions at or close to 5 per cent were also made for San Francisco, Orange County, California, Phoenix and San Diego; whereas, for the Rustbelt, projections for less than 2.2 per cent were made for Pittsburgh, Dayton, Cincinnati, Rochester and Detroit. Indeed, between the censuses of 1990 and 2000, Detroit lost 7.5 per cent of its population and Pittsburgh 9.6 per cent.

Despite growth in Phoenix, Austin and other cities, much of the hinterland suffered relative population decline and some of it, for example much of the Great Plains, particularly the Dakotas, absolute decline. Yet the cost of housing there was relatively low, and the Internet had lessened the inaccessibility of these areas. The movement to the coasts was the consequence of a number of factors, including the attraction of the knowledge-economics, economic opportunities and sense of buzz, in coastal California and New York City, and also the lure of living near the water, for example on the Gulf Coast. Between 1980 and 2003 the numbers living in the country's coastal counties rose to about 153 million, an increase of about 33 million. This led to a building boom in these areas, much of which was exposed to floods. Indeed, in 2005 approximately two million people left Louisiana, Mississippi and Alabama as a result of hurricanes Katrina and Rita.

Population changes fed directly into electoral politics, leading to shifts in representation at the federal and state levels. This provided opportunities for re-districting, and thus for the use of political power. For example, the census of 2000 was followed in Tennessee by a redrawing of district boundaries by the Democrat-controlled legislature in order to limit Republican representation.

The rise in the national population was caused by falling death rates, with their consequence in terms of rising life expectancy, as well as to birth rates higher than in Europe and to immigration. All of these factors were variable and interacting, and this affected population movements. For example, restrictions on immigration from the 1920s, and the impact of the economic crisis of the 1930s, was such that, between 1930 and 1950, the American population increased by only 14 per cent, its lowest percentage rate ever. In contrast, in the 1990s and 2000s growth rates were particularly high. As a result, by the early 2000s two-thirds of the population growth was natural increase, whereas, in Europe, it was largely due to immigration.

The American birth rate was also higher than that of many countries in the developing world, including economic rivals such as Brazil, China and South Korea. In 2000 the median age was 35, lower than that in most of Europe, a consequence of the birth rate and the fact that immigrants tended to be relatively young. By 2050 it is projected to be 41, far lower than European figures, and also those projected for China. These high birth rates reflected a degree of American optimism, as well as the opportunities for family formation presented by plentiful employment and relatively inexpensive housing, and the absence of any governmental anti-growth policy. To great domestic controversy, in 1973 the Supreme Court legalized abortion at the federal level, but, despite the frequent criticism of this policy, there was no equivalent to the demographic control attempted in India under Mrs Gandhi, let alone that in China, with its one-child policy, which led to the killing of many female babies.

The role of opportunity and optimism in age profiles is indicated by the extent to which states that attracted migrants, such as Colorado, a focus of migration from California, and North Carolina, a popular destination from further north, had lower median ages than the average. This, in turn, ensured both higher birth rates and a sense of the possible. In contrast, states and cities losing population saw their median age rise more rapidly and were characterized by less confidence. Ethnic differences also play a role in age profiles, interacting with a national trend towards a more varied ethnic balance. In 1960 whites made up 159 million of the population of 179 million, but by

2000 they were only 211 million of the 281 million. The Republican party, which has only limited representation among Hispanics, and even less among blacks, perceived this as a particular problem. As a consequence, under George W. Bush there was a major attempt to woo support from both groups, not least with symbolic appointments.

The Hispanic population has a particularly low median age, 26 in 2000, which reflects its high average birth rate compared to the rest of the population. In fact, in the years 2000-04, the Hispanic population was responsible for about half of the total population increase, and the Census Bureau suggests that this group will make up 20 per cent of the population by 2030. By 2005 Texas had a non-white majority, thanks primarily to Hispanic immigration (although Indians attracted by high-tech employment opportunities were also notable). California had already done so in the late 1990s. The Hispanic impact was particularly apparent in California, where in 2003 most babies were Hispanic, and, because of the number of recent immigrants, reading standards in many schools were low. After Los Angeles, the city with the greatest number of Hispanics is Chicago, where, since 1970, they have accounted for most of the population growth.

Immigration was eased under the Immigration Act of 1956, and the subsequent Hispanic influx helped to create a Hispanic population of 41 million in the USA in 2005. Hispanic immigration was largely from Mexico, including about 60 per cent of illegal immigrants, and by 2004 about 8 per cent of those born in Mexico lived in the USA, most legally. There was also an important flow from Central America. Furthermore, Castro's seizure of power in Cuba in 1959 led to large-scale immigration, mostly into southern Florida, in the years 1959-62, 1965-73 and 1980. Thanks also to immigration, most recently Vietnamese, Korean and Indian, the Asian-American population is due to rise from 14 million in 2004 to more than 22 million in 2025. In comparison, the Native American (American Indians) and Alaskan Native population is about 1.5 per cent of the total population.

Immigration figures are controversial because of the extent of illegal immigration, but, in the years 1991-2004, close to 14 million new immigrants arrived legally. As a result of this rise in immigration, particularly from Latin America, the number of those resident born abroad increased greatly, to 31.1 million people by the census of 2000 and to about 35 million in 2005. Many had been resident in the USA for less than a decade. The process of becoming American was a major theme in literature, for example in the novel *How the Garcia Girls Lost their Accent* (1991) by Julia Alvarez, who herself had moved from the Dominican Republic. At the same time, immigration ensured a major market for non-English culture. By 2005 Comcast was offering 90 non-English cable channels.

But insufficient visas for unskilled foreigners were issued. As a result, there was large-scale illegal immigration, providing a pool of cheap labour that assisted employers and challenged trade unions. By 2005 about 11 million illegal immigrants were living in the USA, most working at jobs that local people did not want, and another million arrived each year, many across the Mexican border. The rate of entry of illegal immigrants varied with the state of the economy, falling, for example, with the dotcom bust. Illegal immigration helped to meet demands for labour, particularly in agriculture, meat processing, nursing and construction, but also kept wages low. This labour was perceived as unacceptable to populists and to commentators concerned about the character of the country and the nature of society. Illegal immigration exposed the tensions within American society, and, more specifically, within both right- and left-wing constituencies. Proposition 187, banning illegal immigrants from benefits, was passed easily in California in 1994, although the courts later blocked it. That year troops were sent to Haiti, in part to restore the President, deposed by a military coup, but also to stop the flight of Haitian refugees to the USA. In 1996 the Illegal Immigration Reform and Immigration Responsibility Act expanded deportation powers.

In the early 2000s the issue became increasingly prominent. Books such as Victor Hanson's *Mexifornia: A State of Becoming* (2003) and Samuel Huntington's *Who Are We? The Challenges to America's National Identity* (2004) warned about a change of consciousness and a challenge to American-ness as a consequence of large-scale immigration. Huntington was concerned about the applause from Mexican-Americans for Mexican teams competing with Americans, although a more serious challenge might be seen in the shape of the political activism of

Cuban-Americans and their attempt to control policy towards Cuba. Environmentalists were also concerned about the implications of population growth. As a result, the influential Sierra Club, a generally liberal group, was divided in 1998 and 2003 over its policy towards immigration.

At a more immediate level, concerned about the situation and influenced by the beginning of vigilantism by 'Minutemen' in Arizona in 2005, the Governors of Arizona and New Mexico declared a state of emergency in August of that year. In November 2004 Arizona's voters had passed, by 56 to 44 per cent, Proposition 200, which required those applying for benefits to prove their identity and to establish their citizenship if they wanted to vote. Officials who failed to report illegal immigrants were threatened with penalties. In December 2005 the House of Representatives proposed a Bill providing for a wall along part of the border (700 of the 2,000 miles) and making it a felony to live in the country illegally.

In contrast, the federal government sought a long-term solution to immigration pressure, by means of stabilizing the economies to the south, first with the North American Free Trade Agreement (1994), and then with the Central American Free Trade Agreement (2005). Hispanic immigration also contributed to the more general situation of private prosperity (for many) and yet also widespread poverty. Low-wage jobs helped economic growth and provided employment, but also contributed to a rise in poverty. By 2004, 25 per cent of the population below the poverty line was Hispanic, compared to 12 per cent in 1980. In other words, approximately three-quarters of the increase in those below the poverty line are Hispanics. This presses on the social welfare system. In Texas, counties along the Mexican border had particularly high rates of poverty.

HEALTH AND MEDICINE

The fall in national death rates was caused by improvements in health and the availability of adequate supplies of food and clean water. These affected death rates across the age range, although there were major geographical and ethnic differences, due largely to differential prosperity and public provision. This was seen particularly in the case of infant mortality, which fell dramatically in the early decades of the twentieth century. In terms of deaths per 1,000 live births between 1890 and 1930, there was a percentage decline of 55, although that was only for the white population. For all Americans, between 1970 and 2002 the aggregate age standardized death rate from any cause fell by close to a third, and death rates from heart disease and strokes more than halved. In contrast, mortality from cancer fell by only 2.7 per cent. American researchers led the way in many of the improvements in medical knowledge that touched the lives not only of Americans but also of billions around the world. Indeed, the ability to identify and treat disease changed exponentially. For example, a vaccine against polio developed by the American epidemiologist Jonas Salk was first widely administered in 1956, while, from the 1950s, an antibiotic developed in the USA, streptomycin, helped to overcome tuberculosis.

The USA also played a crucial role in the dramatic development of transplant surgery. Although the technical skills were already present, the basis of rejection was not understood until the 1930s, and in any case patients were too ill for the operation. These problems were overcome from the 1940s. Kidney transplants became possible because patients could be kept alive on dialysis and thanks to antibiotics; the first was carried out in Chicago in 1950. More generally, a major increase in anaesthetic skills, due to greater knowledge and the introduction of increasingly sophisticated drugs, meant that complex surgical operations could be performed and once-serious operations became routine and minor. There were also major advances in the treatment of the heart. Bypass and transplant surgery were developed as an aspect of the growth of specialized surgery. The transplantation of human organs was transformed from an experimental, and often fatal, procedure into a routine and highly successful operation. Ovarian tissue was successfully transplanted in 2005. Open-heart surgery became possible, while major drugs for coronary heart disease were introduced. Medical technology developed in numerous directions. Invented in 1926, heart pacemakers were taken forward in the 1950s. Artificial hip joints were followed by knee joints. The pharmacological repertoire also expanded. From the 1980s anti-viral agents were used for the treatment of viral infections: antibiotics had been useless against them. The cost of medical treatment and insurance, however, became a major issue for family and company budgets, and also a crucial site of social differentiation, whether or not it is defined in class terms.

There was also a revolution in the knowledge and treatment of mental illness, which, indeed, was found to affect an appreciable proportion of the population. With greater recognition of the importance of psychological and mental processes, diagnosis and treatment both changed. The development of safe and effective drugs in the 1960s and '70s helped with major psychoses and depression, dramatically improving the cure rate. Psycho-pharmacology developed in parallel with psychotherapy. Prozac became a highly popular drug in the early 2000s. Tranquillizers, however, can be over-prescribed, and become addictive. This was a particular problem from the 1950s, and it encouraged the search for new drugs. The side effects of barbiturates led to the production, from 1953, of Miltown, later found to be addictive, from 1960 of Librium (chlordiazepoxide) and, from 1963, of a synthesized form of the latter, Valium. The success of Valium was such that, from 1969 to 1982, it was the country's biggest-selling drug, and its sales peaked at close to 2.3 billion pills in 1978, making vast profits for its makers, Hoffmann La Roche. From 1979, however, the danger of tranquillizer addiction became apparent, and Valium was replaced in the 1980s by the selective serotonin re-uptake inhibitors. The success of Valium was also a product of the openness of the USA to immigrant talent, since it had been invented by Leo Sternbach, a Jewish scientist who had fled Nazi-dominated Europe. He also developed the sleeping drug Mogadon, as well as Klonopin, a drug for epilepsy.

The misuse of drugs, discussed fictionally in Jacqueline Susann's novel *Valley of the Dolls* (1966) and factually in Elizabeth Wurtzell's *Prozac Nation* (1997) and Greg Critser's *Generation Rx* (2005; Rx for Prescription), reflected the interaction of consumerist pressures and changing views about safety. In the 2000s those in their twenties were increasingly using medicines and anti-depressants for attention deficit and sleeping disorders. Many were obtained from online pharmacies, although it is illegal to provide them without prescription.

The understanding of individual drugs has also changed. Meth-amphetamine (meth, crystal, ice, speed), which was sold in the 1950s and '60s as an anti-depressant and weight-loss agent, was, by the 1990s, seen as a dangerous drug linked to risky sexual behaviour. In 2005 it was estimated that 5 per cent of the adult population had used it at least once and that 600,000 people use it weekly. The latter statistic reflected the importance of self-medication to health-issues. This was taken further when Oregon, and subsequently Montana, permitted the use of marijuana for medical purposes.

One raft of tranquillizers was aimed at children, who became a focus of much public anxiety. Concern about the behaviour of children and about children as victims led to panics. Anxiety about what was held to be atypical behaviour for children encouraged the definition of attention-deficit disorder, which was held to characterize children seen as impulsive and easily distracted. As a result, by the mid-2000s, the relevant drugs, Adderall, Concerta and Strattera, were prescribed in their millions. The young are the most medicated generation ever, and this contributed greatly to a major rise in prescriptions: from seven per person in 1993 to twelve in 2004, the latter leading to about 3.5 billion prescriptions, at an annual cost of $180 billion. This is as part of a uniquely expensive healthcare system, which was costing nearly $2 trillion annually by 2005 ($6,700 per person), and absorbing about a quarter of economic growth.

Inappropriate prescribing was not only a problem with tranquilliz-ers. It was also an issue with antibiotics, where profligate pro-scribing had led to a rise in antibiotic resistance. By the mid-2000s fluoroquinolones were the most commonly prescribed antibiotics for American adults, but they were increasingly ineffective against *Neisseria gonorrhoeae*; there is a danger that they will become ineffective against *Mycobacterium tuburculosis*; and resistant strains of *Streptococcus pneumoniae*, *Escherichia coli*, *Klebsiella pneumoniae* and *Clostridium diffi-cile* have already appeared. There is a related problem in agriculture, where fluoroquinolone-resistant *Campylobacter* species have appeared in poultry.

Although developments in medical knowledge and practice had a major impact on individual and collective experience, and in decreasing anxiety, not all illnesses were, or are, in retreat. Death rates from chronic obstructive pulmonary disease doubled in the period 1970–2002 and continue to increase, while, by the mid-2000s, Americans were 45 per cent more likely to die from diabetes than they were in 1987. Despite childhood immunization, the number of reported cases of whooping cough among adults or adolescents doubled in the 1990s. Illness rates, however, are a difficult problem to assess, in part because reporting issues may give a misleading impression of the prevalence of particular illnesses. Nevertheless, a more thorough collection of statistics during this period led to a more comprehensive coverage of health problems. In turn, this fed into debates about the state of the people, which played a charged role in discussion about how far, and how best, to ensure healthcare. The debate encompassed contentious issues of personal and corporate responsibility.

In the early 2000s the former led to particular contention about obesity. This focused on diet, although exercise was also a factor. Concern about diet was particularly directed to burgers and fried food. Diet did not markedly improve, because adults consumed nearly as much saturated fat and cholesterol in 2002 as they had in 1988. Serum concentrations of total cholesterol, however, fell between 1988 and 2002, in part because of the turn to medical remedies. Between 1999 and 2002, 9 per cent of Americans over 20 took lipid-lowering drugs, including over a fifth of those aged 60 or over.

The percentage of the population defined as overweight rose from 47 in the late 1970s to more than 65 in 2002, and those judged clinically obese were 31 per cent. The percentage was considerably greater for women, particularly black and, to a lesser extent, Hispanic women, than men. Poverty also plays a role, since parks are uncommon in poor urban communities, while fast-food outlets are more common there than health food stores. There were also marked regional variations in obesity. A survey of the percentage of obese adults published in August 2005 by Trust for America's Health and the Centers for Disease Control and Prevention found that Mississippi (29.5), Alabama (28.9) and Louisiana (27.0) were in the worse situation, whereas Colorado (16.8), Massachusetts (18.4), Vermont (18.7), Rhode Island (19.0) and

Connecticut (19.7) were the states below 20 per cent. Only Oregon (21.2) showed no increase in the percentage over the previous year. By 2003 medical costs due to obesity were estimated as $39–$75 billion, and annual premature deaths at more than 110,000. Obesity is linked to the rise in diabetes. In late 2005 the US Centers for Disease Control and Prevention estimated that 20.8 million Americans had diabetes, an increase of 14 per cent in two years. About 90 per cent had Type 2 diabetes, which is commonly linked to obesity. The USA is the world's biggest diabetes-treatment market, but the ability to intervene early against diabetes and hypertension is constrained by the nature of healthcare, including the widespread lack of health insurance and also big social variations in access to relevant information. Obesity is also linked to problems with mobility, fractures, and bone and hip joint abnormalities, and, indeed, to the need to change consumer products, such as cars, in order to accommodate larger average sizes. The average large man grew 12.3 kilograms (27 lb) heavier and nearly 1.5 inches wider between 1962 and 2000. Public transport also responded, the seats on Chicago buses being altered from 16.75 inches to 17 inches wide in 1975, 17.5 inches in 2003 and 18 inches in 2006.

In turn, the undoubted crisis over obesity led to a discussion about the degree to which litigation and governmental action in this field would infringe individual rights and the practice of personal responsibility. This might include banning the sale of soft drinks and unhealthy food in schools. There was also concern about the role of companies, particularly in targeting soft drinks and other dispensers on children. As the pressure rose, consumer sensitivity led McDonald's, which had been heavily criticized by doctors and non-medical commentators for the calories on offer in its meals, to introduce a healthier menu. Similar comments could be made about some other chains. In turn, those who were large complained about discrimination, especially when, from the 2000s, they were expected to pay for two airline seats if they were unable to fit on a single seat.

Pharmaceutical research was another area of concern about company policies, but here again issues of personal responsibility also played a role. In 2003 the USA spent 49 per cent of the global total on research and development, discovering 45 per cent of the new molecular entities launched that year. However, popular expectations of ready cures and a reluctance to accept the nature of risk in all medical treatments interacted with the pushing of products through high-pressure direct-to-consumer advertising as well as off-label prescribing: urging doctors to prescribe drugs for conditions not in the original licence. In what is the world's most lucrative market for medical products, the high prices charged by the pharmaceutical companies, substantially higher than in other affluent countries, arose in part from government reluctance to control costs, and was a consequence of the absence of a national health service able to act as a monopoly purchaser.

The law, as ever, recorded contention over risk, and provided a crucial way of regulating the industry, a system that, more generally, led to the central role of lawyers in public life. Real or alleged corporate malpractice, which was encouraged by the high profits from the market, was also an issue. Alleged malpractice led to high-profile suits, such as those over silicone breast implants in the 1980s and '90s, and the suit against Merck in 2005 over the side effects of the Vioxx anti-inflammatory pain reliever, which had been withdrawn from sale the previous year. One suit alone led to an award (before appeal) of $253 million. High-profile product recalls, for example of pacemakers and heart defibrillators by Guidant in 2005, also affected confidence.

There has been evidence in recent decades of deterioration in some areas of health. Changes in lifestyle were responsible for the spread of some diseases. In particular, lack of exercise stemming from sedentary lifestyles, in both work and leisure, and an increase in food consumption led to a rise in diabetes and heart disease. This was an aspect of the extent to which medicine was expected to cope with symptoms rather than the underlying causes. The causes could be addressed only by public health measures and self-discipline, but this was made difficult by powerful social trends. For example, the popularity of video games has lessened the tendency to take part in sport. Indeed, for many, sport was increasingly a spectator practice, mediated through television, rather than a participatory activity, although skateboarding, which developed in Venice, California, in the 1970s, was an example of a new urban sport.

Social distinctions also played a role in avoiding ill health. The affluent are more able to afford the gym and golf (although the value of golf was lessened by driving round the course), and also to buy organic and natural foods. This in turn posed a problem for mass-market retailers and restaurants: did the greater individual profit that such customers represented justify gearing up to sell to them? The collective affluence of the mass market has been responsible for the success of many big retailers, most obviously Wal-Mart, which sells itself largely on value for its low-income clientele (claiming that in 2004 it saved consumers $263 billion); partly as a result, it has become the world's leading retailer. The extent to which the lifestyle and assumptions of the affluent can be more widely diffused has been an important aspect of market research and corporate speculation. It links with issues of fashionability, style and image, as, for example, in sales of particular types and preparations of coffee, and that reflects the extent to which the market involves more than simply groups defined by relative wealth.

Concern about diet was also responsible for fads, such as the Atkins Diet, which was hugely popular in 2003–4, and for a vast range of pharmaceutical and alternative medicines. Diets helped to dictate the success or failure of restaurants, and the popularity or otherwise of particular foodstuffs. The emphasis on protein in the Atkins Diet, which, at its height, was followed by 9 per cent of the population, helped the meat industry greatly. Concern with cholesterol, as well as with calories, led to further interest in lifestyle, diet and medicines. Drugs such as Zocor became household names. New surgical procedures were also tried. Gastric-bypass surgery developed, and became more popular: from 15,000 operations in 1994 to 103,000 in 2003.

A range of publications and television programmes also met this public interest in health, with news networks employing medical correspondents. The medical response to health issues was joined by lifestyle options, such as exercise and not smoking. The resulting practices helped to divide individuals from each other, as well as to provide common currencies of conversation, and also to provide ways to identify personalities and to define sexual appeal. In Mart Crowley's ironic play about homosexual life, *The Boys in the Band* (1968), Cowboy notes: 'I lost my grip doing my chin-ups and I fell on my head and twisted my back.'

Pollution is another health issue, with pressure on the environment also affecting humans. Increasing car-exhaust emissions and general pollution probably led to the increase in respiratory diseases, such as asthma, and subsequent mortality. This was combated by asthma drugs, clinics and nurses, but led to concern about the state of air quality. Uncertainty over the causes of asthma also fed into the 'culture wars' over health. Claims that pollution, and thus both manufacturing and consumerist lifestyles, were to blame were resisted. Asthma was an aspect of a major rise in the incidence and prevalence of increasingly diverse and dangerous allergic reactions. Allergies and food intolerances were more frequently reported and came to affect the food industry and, even more, restaurants, with about 1.5 million Americans seriously allergic to even the smallest trace of peanuts by the early 2000s, while eye irritation became a response to particles in the air. Asbestos poisoning proved a more serious problem. Just as the lead used in paint was a health hazard, so asbestos employed in insulation up to the 1970s caused cancer. More than 100,000 workers have died as a consequence, while the resulting litigation has bankrupted many firms, and is overhanging many more, as well as the insurance industry.

The variety of the environmental challenge to health was considerable. The massive increase in the movement, treatment and burial of hazardous waste led to concern about possible health implications. This also had an impact on the arts, as in Andrew Foster's play *Chemical Reactions* (1988), in which a toxic dump was a setting for the action, as well as an emblem of the society depicted. More generally, pollutants were linked to declining sperm counts and to hormonal changes, specifically the acquisition of female characteristics by men. Global warming, a consequence of pollution, was also blamed for the spread of some illnesses.

Other problems were not related to pollution. Increased use of 'recreational' narcotic drugs from the 1960s led to much physical and psychological damage, much of which became apparent decades later. Narcotic drugs also led to many deaths. In a report of 2005, the American Social Health Association estimated that one in two sexually active youths will contract a sexually transmitted disease by the age of 25. Concern about the frequency of sexually transmitted diseases focused on the most potent, AIDS, which developed as a new killer in the 1980s. It was first recognized as an infection in 1981. The origin of the HIV immuno-deficiency virus, the crucial prelude to AIDS, was (and remains) a matter of considerable controversy that, in part, throws light on cultural assumptions. The USA was not removed from global debates about AIDS, but they were given particular intensity by their relationship to tensions within American society. Some conservatives blamed promiscuity among homosexuals, while some black activists attributed responsibility to white doctors. Instead, it is likely that AIDS derived from the consumption of diseased primates as human settlement expanded into parts of Africa. The Centers for Disease Control and Prevention estimated that, from December 2003, between 1,039,000 and 1,850,000 Americans were infected with the HIV virus, with 47 per cent of those infected being black, 34 per cent white and 17 per cent Hispanic. At 45 per cent, homosexual sex was seen as the largest single risk factor for becoming infected, high-risk heterosexual behaviour coming next at 27 per cent, and injecting drug use at 22 per cent. More generally, the variations between racial groups and their relationships to social practices led to contention. Among young black males, there was a tendency to deny the prevalence of HIV, in part because of the stigma of homosexual sex among the black community. A political context for the racial contrast was provided by the higher incarceration rate among young black males and the extent of homosexual sex in prisons.

HIV and AIDS also demonstrated the prosperity of the USA. The expensive anti-viral strategies available there were absent in southern Africa, where, in contrast to the USA, life expectancies in the 1990s and early 2000s fell appreciably due to AIDS. In the USA (as in Europe), there was also a greater openness to public education in sexual health than in Asia, which led to a far higher use of condoms, including among prostitutes. This openness reflected a range of factors, including culture, affluence and education. Yet again, however, America's culture wars came into play, with the nature of public health education proving contentious. Many conservatives pressed for the emphasis to be on abstinence until marriage, and fidelity thereafter, rather than on contraception. This was taken up by the George W. Bush administration. Its international Emergency Plan for AIDS Relief (PEPFAR, President's Emergency Plan for AIDS Relief) devoted a third of its projected expenditure to abstinence and was reluctant about the use of condoms, affecting policy in states receiving American money such as Uganda. For fear of being seen to offend its core conservative constituency, the administration was also against needle-exchange projects for drug addicts. Conservatives feared that this policy, which is necessary to prevent transmission via contaminated needles, would encourage drug use. The Bush administration, backing a law passed by Congress in 2003, also required organizations receiving American money to declare their opposition to prostitution, even though prostitutes are a crucial group in AIDS prevention. The real world was to be ignored for it to be 'saved'.

AIDS indeed threw into sharper focus the extent to which the response to disease reflected social and cultural assumptions about personal conduct and the nature of society. Concepts of propriety and risk were re-examined. The arts were greatly affected, with AIDS becoming a major theme of discussion. If this discussion was disproportionate at the more serious end of the arts, at least with reference to incidence rates of the disease, AIDS, in contrast, was generally ignored at its more populist level, although *Philadelphia* (1993) was a successful film. As an instance of the less populist approach, Langford Wilson's short play *A Poster of the Cosmos* (1988) was a dramatic monologue account of a desperate relationship with a victim of the disease, while Jonathan Larson's rock opera *Rent* (1996) presented avant-garde New Yorkers facing AIDS. AIDS also drew attention to the issue of human ability to understand disease. It punctured the confident belief and expectation that medical science can cure all ills, a belief that had developed with the antibiotic revolution.

Less dramatically, but more seriously, the over-use of antibiotics threatened a more widespread calamity as their effectiveness lessened. Confidence in medical science will be hit further if avian flu hits the USA and mutates into the human population, since provisions to deal with it are inadequate. The lack of sufficient vaccines and antiviral medication is such that there would need to be an emphasis on surveillance and containment, which would probably reflect social and cultural fault-lines, and the roles of politics and litigation. In September 2005 the USA only had enough of the antiviral Tamiflu to treat 4.3 million people. The precedent of the swine-flu outbreak in 1976 is instructive. After lengthy delays caused by concern about litigation over side effects, it led to the immunization of only 40 million people. In the event, the outbreak proved far less virulent than had been feared, and vaccination was suspended because of side effects.

Food also gave rise to concern. Anxiety about the conditions in which animals were kept, and how the food chain operated, was related to worries about the impact on humans. There was particular anxiety about bovine spongiform encephalopathy (BSE), 'mad-cow disease', the first American case of which was reported in 2004, and which led to a Japanese ban on American beef, a ban that greatly angered producers, who saw it as disproportionate and lobbied successfully for diplomatic pressure on their behalf. Micro-organisms such as E coli 0157 also proved a challenge to food safety. At the same time, some changes in food processing were benign. In 1998 the USA and Canada introduced the addition of folic acid to flour, and this led to a fall in the number of neural tube defects, such as spina bifida, in foetuses.

Previously unknown diseases recognized during the period covered by this book include Legionnaire's Disease and Lyme Disease. These reflected the impact of hitherto unknown bacteria and viruses that, for some, challenged confidence in human progress. The rise in global travel aided the spread of disease, and this became more insistent as the speed and frequency of travel increased. This was a factor in the spread of AIDS and probably in the arrival of West Nile virus close to the major international airports in New York in 1999. This led to the aerial spraying of the city, a vivid demonstration of vulnerability, but also of the readiness to act. Such diseases, nevertheless, received far less attention in the 2000s than the threat from terrorism, which may have led to a lack of appropriate governmental preparedness in countering them.

As another example, both of the interaction of social trends with medical developments, and of the difficulty in charting and explaining links, it is possible that children who were bottle-fed, a practice that developed after World War Two, did not receive important vitamins and minerals to boost their immune system. It has also been suggested that, psychologically, they missed the important human bonding that comes from breast feeding, leaving them more detached and independent and susceptible to questioning authority. This has, in turn, been related to the 'protest' generation of the 1960s. Such suggestions may be far-fetched, but it is possible that bottle-feeding changed society in ways that are difficult to measure.

Although some illnesses are rising, the general picture remains one of an increase of average life expectancy for both men and women. This is true of all age groups, not least with the fall of infant mortality. Rising average life expectancy was linked to a change in the causes of death. Whereas infections were a major cause of death for the entire population in the first half of the twentieth century, by the 1990s they were far less significant. Instead, infections increasingly killed only those who were suffering from associated disorders and who were at the extremes of life. In their place, over the century as a whole, later-onset diseases, especially heart disease and cancers, became relatively far more important as causes of death. In 1999 circulatory disease, including heart disease, was responsible for 30.3 per cent of deaths and cancers for 23 per cent. By the early 2000s more than 300,000 Americans died annually of cardiac arrest. Overall figures, however, concealed many variations. Location, income, diet, lifestyle and gender all played interacting roles, to ensure, for example, that women in Alaska have a low incidence of heart disease. Furthermore, the relationship between data collection and disease indicators needs to be considered. For example, a study of melanoma (skin cancer) among those aged 65 and over in the years 1986–2001 showed a 2.4-fold increase in average incidence, but this was largely due to more biopsies, and not, in fact, to an increase in the incidence of the disease.

THE RISE OF THE RETIREES

Owing to higher fertility rates, the American population was younger than that of Europe or Japan, but the number of the elderly also increased markedly. By 2004 there were 36 million aged 65 and over (a number expected to double to 71 million by 2030). This led to less of a rise in the dependency ratio than might have been anticipated, because more of those over 55 continued working than had been anticipated, a process encouraged by the relative decline of manufacturing and agriculture, and the marked rise of the service sector. Furthermore, medical advances ensured that much of the elderly population were physically independent until close to death.

Greater longevity contributed much to the geographical mobility that was such a major feature of American society. Once retired, large numbers moved, particularly from the 1950s to Florida, which went from being the 27th most populous state in 1940 to the 17th in 1980, and, from the 1970s, to Arizona and Nevada. In the years 1970–79 the percentage increase of population by state was topped by Nevada (63.8), Arizona (53.1) and Florida (43.5). Less populous states with a modest base line followed (Wyoming, Utah, Alaska, Idaho), and the leading populous state to have a high percentage rise was Texas (tenth at 27.1). Of the North-Eastern states, only New Hampshire (13th), Vermont (22nd) and Maine (27th) were in the top 29 states for percentage population increase in this decade, and each had only a relatively small population. In 1975 to 1980 internal migration led to the South gaining 4.7 million people and the West 3.1 million, while the Mid-West lost 3.5 million and the North-East 3.1 million. As a result of such growth, in the years 1980–2005 Fort Myers and Naples in Florida, both popular retirement destinations, were the third and sixth most rapidly growing cities in the country. All this had political consequences. Furthermore, the sense of entitlement by retirees created demands not only on government but also for pharmaceutical companies. Companies that rose to the challenge profited greatly, as did Pfizer with its drug Viagra, the consumption of which reflected a sense of entitlement to sex. This was very much a new consumerism. Osteoporosis became an even bigger concern, leading to large-scale consumption of medicines such as Fosamax. For many, the nature of politics was measured in terms of the cost of such medicines to their own pocket and the ability to put off much of this cost onto the government.

At the local level, the role of retirees led to the development of retirement communities that reflected not only the distinctive interests and expenditure possibilities of the elderly, but also a desire for sameness and safety. Concern about crime also played a role, since these communities were generally gated. They might be ethnically mixed, but they were anything but mixed in terms of age and class. Retirement communities were also a practical consequence of the breakdown of extended families, which reflected not only the geographical and social mobility of the young, many of whom moved from the area of their upbringing, but also the extent to which many of the elderly had savings and pensions that permitted a degree of independence, including geographical mobility. Retirement communities, like youthful new suburbs with their high percentages of children, were crucial to an age-specific nature of settlement. This process became self-sustaining as communities acquired particular characters and the idea of living in age-specific tranches became more normative. Developers helped to encourage and sustain this process with distinctive advertising strategies for particular communities. This tendency added to the role of lifestyle enclaves, in which people of the same class tend to live in similar neighbourhoods, shop at the same stores, eat at the same restaurants and, if they can afford it, holiday at the same resorts.

Despite longer working lives, rising life expectancy meant an increase in dependency that represented an important new labour demand, not least because much of it was no longer handled within extended families. The resulting demand for support helped greatly in the expansion of the service component of employment, not least because the increased amount of pension wealth and savings held by many (but by no means all) of the elderly helped to fund the process. Part of the low-wage demand was met from immigrant labour, without which the care industry would have found it difficult to operate.

Age-related dependency also put major pressures on the public provision of social welfare, particularly after Medicare was introduced in 1965 to provide health coverage for the elderly. This was particularly a problem because many of the elderly remained within the political process, unlike marginal groups. Instead, they had a sense of entitlement and expectations of action on their behalf. In 2003 Medicare legislation, which came into effect in 2006, provided prescription-drug benefits for the elderly (a response to the persistent increase in their costs above the rate of inflation), a major expansion of social welfare that reflected popular pressure on Congress and the desire of the Republicans to outflank the Democrats and ensure support from the elderly; but in 2004 it was projected that Medicare's finances would be exhausted by 2019. As a result, some cuts were made in the budget agreed in early 2006. Political pressure from the elderly helped to ensure that Medicare became a programme more for the middle class than for the poor. Similarly, Medicaid was affected by pressure from the affluent elderly to join their poorer counterparts in not having to pay for nursing care.

Care for the elderly was a crucial aspect in the more general rise of health expenditure. This also affected employment, such that, in the 2000s, among the ten fastest-growing occupations listed by the Labor Department were medical assistants, physician assistants, social and human service assistants, home health aides, medical records and health information technicians, physical therapist aides and physical therapist assistants. This indicated the high labour requirements of healthcare, which were accentuated because these jobs could not be out-sourced abroad as some other service jobs could be.

Greater longevity also put real pressure on company finances, as pension issues became of greater importance for balance sheets. In the USA health costs are paid by companies rather than government, and this hit companies with older workforces, such as General Motors and long-established airlines, whose labour and welfare costs are disproportionately high compared to foreign competitors. Indeed, in 2005, the Pension Benefit Guaranty Corporation, a federal agency, calculated that General Motors' pension fund was $31 billion short of what was necessary to pay its workforce if the fund was terminated then. The company was responsible for health insurance to more than 750,000 current workers and retirees in America, a number that owed much to the combination of past scale and present longevity. In 2005 the company lost $8.6 billion and spent $5.2 billion on healthcare costs. An agreement between General Motors and the United Auto Workers Union reached in October 2005 that would cut its healthcare liabilities suggests that business had a better ability than government to rein in expenditure. In October 2005 Delphi, the world's largest maker of car parts, which had been part of General Motors until 1999, sought protection from its creditors in the bankruptcy courts.

Pension provisions also hit big public employers such as town councils. Health costs and workers' compensation for injuries were major burdens on employers, and, because regulatory regimes varied by state, an important source of difference in doing business. By the 2000s this was making California less competitive than many other states, including Texas. By 2003 Detroit car makers were having to pay pension and healthcare costs that exceeded $1,200 per vehicle sold (the estimate for General Motors' cars in 2005 was $1,500). Costs on those made in the South were less, which encouraged location there. By 2003 more than 295,000 workers worked in the motor industry in Kentucky, Alabama, Georgia and Tennessee.

While the growth of employment in areas with lower social welfare costs is, in the long term, a partial solution to the national issue of pension provision, this scarcely lessens the current problem created by inadequately funded liabilities, a problem that mirrors that of public finances. Lower costs to consumers, a crucial driver of economic growth, threatens established providers, since the lower costs, for example in airlines and communications, are often those of newer entrants (domestic, or foreign via imports) into the industry. The consequences for the government – that is, the public – are unclear. The liabilities of the Pension Benefit Guaranty Corporation, the government-supported insurer of company pension plans, are far greater than its assets.

CONCLUSIONS

More people meant more pressure on the environment, but rising living standards were also an issue, because average per capita consumption rose appreciably. Indeed, consumerism was a driving force in society, the economy and politics. This consumerism was very much a matter of individualism, increasingly unshaped by professional structures, but guided by corporate pressures, the latter present in particular in the role of advertising. This was seen, for example, in the active advertising made by personal-injury lawyers and pharmaceutical companies to individuals. By making direct appeals to consumers (which was approved for advertising medicines in 1997), the role of cartels, as well as of professionals such as doctors, was diminished. At a time of low inflation, promotional spending on medicines rose from $5 billion in 1995 to $18 billion by 2004. The low trust placed in governments and politics was, however, replicated by pharmaceutical companies (as well as lawyers). A Harris Poll of 2004 indicated that only 13 per cent of the public believed these companies to be 'generally honest and trustworthy'. Given such figures, it was scarcely surprising that alternative cures, religious faith, collective memory and communal rumour served for many instead of medical solutions or advice. All are under-reported and under-studied, yet social and regional differences in reliance on such approaches (as opposed to scientific medicine) were important to the individual and collective character of life, not least as they helped to shape local cultures.

The imaginative response to advances in medical science included a modernization of the horror genre with a concern about zombies, the living dead, as in George Romero's films *Night of the Living Dead* (1968), *Dawn of the Dead* (1978), a critique of consumerism, *Day of The Dead* (1984) and *Land of the Dead* (2005). The last was very much an account of affluent American society under threat, with the villain, Kaufman, running the equivalent of a gated community under threat from oppressed zombies. Less luridly, the idea of clones raised underground to provide perfect body parts for their donors in 2019 was the theme of the film *The Island* (2005). Such stories reflected the sense of a greatly changing people, one in which social and governmental factors helped to shape the consequences of technological change. Popular literature picked up the same themes. In his novel *The Sixth Commandment* (1979), Lawrence Sanders has a character remark: 'We are so close. You'll see it all within fifty years. Human cloning. Gene splicing and complete manipulation of DNA. New species. Synthesis of human blood and all the enzymes. Solution of the brain's mysteries, and mastery of immunology.'

Chapter 4

Social Trends

The Civil Rights Movement, the Women's Movement and the related changes, as well as the shift of employment away from agriculture and industry, helped to transform American society, but it is important first to consider the nature of the society that was changing. The ways in which Americans are described and categorized have frequently become sources of contentions – understandably so, since processes of identification, both of self and of others, affect the general sense of being, and are also at the root of political alignments and animosities. It is worth asking what primarily motivates people – their economic position, ethnic group, parental background, personal assumptions or peer-group pressures? To what extent does any one of these flow into the others? Do terms like 'class' mean much for the bulk of the American population, and, if so, what? Do such terms merely describe a situation (difficult as that is), or do they also explain it, and, if the latter, what guide do they provide to the future? The ambiguous nature of social categories, and the complexities of modern American society, of social formation, interaction and self-perception, all complicate the situation. Americans are chary of class-based analyses of society, far more so than Europeans. This indeed is an important aspect of American political culture, a perception of their society as without class divisions, and thus as inherently united. Patriotism and opportunity are linked in this account as aspects of being American. Outsiders, in contrast, are more apt to discern class divisions and to respond with amazement to claims that they do not exist, although these claims are a powerful testimony to the ethos and aspirations of American society.

A class is essentially a large group of people that shares a similar social and economic position. Much of the basis of class analysis is derived from Marxism, which, being both foreign and the root of Communism, helped to discredit it in American eyes. In Marx's analysis, class was linked to economic power, which was defined by the individual's relationship to the means of production, society being presented as an engine for the production of goods and for the distribution of tasks and benefits, directed by the dominant class. Society was divided between two self-conscious groups: the proletariat, or 'workers', who lived off the sale of their labour power, and the bourgeoisie, or property owners, who bought that labour power. These groups were assumed to be in conflict in order to benefit from, and control, the fruits of labour power; society itself was the sphere for this conflict, and was shaped by it.

Aspects of this analysis may indeed have been the case for the late nineteenth century, a period of rapid industrialization, but it was an approach that was far less credible for the late twentieth century. The focus on economic alignments did not capture the dynamic or the tensions of American society, while the division between workers and owners made less sense in terms of what was very much a property-owning democracy. By 2005 the rate of home ownership had risen to nearly 70 per cent, while fewer than 10 per cent of jobs were in manufacturing.

Nevertheless, this does not mean that economic analyses of American society are without value. Poverty, the theme of Michael Harrington's book *The Other America* (1962), is a persistent problem, although, because of economic growth and a major increase in government expenditure from 1965, the rate of poverty fell, to reach a 20-year low in 1999, while the real median income of households rose that year to a hitherto record high: $40,816. By 2003 it was $43,300. Furthermore, the official poverty line in 1999 – $17,029 for a family of four and $14,680 for a family of three – would have counted as riches across the world. It is partly in that context that child poverty has to be considered, since it is defined as being in a family with an income below 50 per cent of the national average. On that basis the USA (like Mexico) saw this indicator under George W. Bush rise to apply to more than 20 per cent of the population. In 2004 the numbers living below the poverty line, $19,300 for a family of four and $9,800 for an individual under 65, rose to 12.7 per cent of the population (37 million), an increase of more than a million over the figure for 2003. Comparative percentages were 22.2 in 1960, 12.6 in 1970, 11.6 in 1974, 13 in 1980, 15.1 in 1993, 11.9 in 1999 and 11.3 in 2000.

A range of social programmes lessened the impact of poverty. These included Earned Income Tax Credit (EITC), Medicare, Medicaid, Supplemental Security Income and food stamps. Under legislation of 1972 that became effective in 1974, Social Security payments were indexed for inflation, and a (similarly indexed) Supplemental Security Income programme was created to provide federal assistance for the elderly, disabled and blind who were poor. This helped to cut poverty dramatically among the old. By 2003 Medicaid, which provides health insurance coverage for poor children (although not all poor adults), had 51 million beneficiaries, while 19.3 million were covered by EITC. Medicare is healthcare for the elderly, although, in addition, about 70 per cent of Medicaid's spending is on the old and the disabled, particularly nursing-home care. Medicaid is likely to cost $329 billion in 2005, about 2.6 per cent of GDP, a marked growth (by a factor of 13) from 1966, its first full year of operation. A sense of the continued extent and social impact of poverty, however, was highlighted by the effects of Hurricane Katrina in 2005, which encouraged domestic and foreign critics to argue that there was a persistent and serious problem. Thus, Barack Obama, a black Democratic senator, was widely quoted when he told the Senate: 'I hope we realize that the people of New Orleans weren't just abandoned during the hurricane. They were abandoned long ago – to murder and mayhem in the streets, to substandard schools, to dilapidated housing, to inadequate healthcare, to a pervasive sense of hopelessness.' More presciently, John Edwards, the unsuccessful Democratic Vice Presidential candidate in 2004, has emphasized 'the two Americas', an approach that directs attention from complacent remarks about social opportunity and, instead, raises questions about the extent of social mobility.

Trends in benefits accentuate social contrasts. Workers are hit as defined-benefit pension schemes decline, while healthcare benefits are lessened. This is far less the case for employees at senior ranks. Furthermore, the wealthy have done well from a marked increase in corporate profits, which, as a percentage of GDP, have recently risen to 11 per cent, the highest percentage for 70 years, and one that contrasts with an average of 7–8 per cent in the 1980s. Income inequalities rose markedly in the 1980s, 1990s and 2005, and there are many surveys indicating that upward social mobility declined. Social contrasts are further accentuated by different attitudes towards savings, and by the impoverished institutional network accessible to the poor: fewer or no banking facilities, poorer schools, fewer work possibilities, social isolation and discrimination. The poor have fewer opportunities to get into universities, let alone good ones, than their more affluent counterparts, and that at a time when educational attainment has become increasingly important for income and, therefore, mobility. As a result, the possibility of working one's way up political or business hierarchies is lower than in the 1940s and '50s, particularly for poor whites lacking the benefit of the opportunities created by wartime and military-related expansion in the 1940s and '50s, and those offered racial minorities by affirmative action programmes.

The detailed mapping of income revealed marked geographical contrasts. This was particularly so in cities, including Atlanta, Boston, Miami and Washington, but is also the case in many non-metropolitan counties. John Mollenkof's *New York City in the 1980s: A Social, Economic and Political Atlas* (1993) showed how income, dividends, interest and rent all provided indicators of class differences. His maps indicated that the financial benefits of the decade were concentrated overwhelmingly in New York, in white upper-middle-class areas. Changing patterns of income inequality were seen more clearly in terms of income from dividends, interest and rents than in wages, and part of the 1980s boom took the form of higher returns on such assets. By the late 2000s the average selling price of Manhattan apartments had reached $1.3 million. In the years 1984–2004 the average annual return on shares, including reinvested income, was 13 per cent. Enormous personal gains affected politics, enabling the wealthy to fund their own campaigns. In 2005 Jon Corzine, a former Wall Street figure, spent more than $40 million of his own money to help finance his successful campaign for the governorship of New Jersey. His Republican rival, Douglas Forrester, made his money in healthcare.

In 2005, in contrast, when the Census Bureau reported that, in 2003, 12.5 per cent of the population were living below the poverty level (including 20.3 per cent of those aged under five), the highest poverty rate was in Mississippi (18.3 per cent), and Louisiana and New Mexico also had very high rates. Each of these states had high percentages of non-whites – blacks in the first two cases and Hispanics in the third. In contrast, the lowest rate (6.4 per cent) was in New Hampshire. As another index of geographical contrasts in wealth, in fourteen states 80 per cent or more of the privately held land was held by the largest 5 per cent of private owners, and, in another seventeen states, the percentage was 60 to 79 per cent. Only in eight states was the percentage less than 50 per cent. This trend in consolidation continued during the period. For example, from 1964 to 1982 the number of farms in Iowa over 500 acres increased by 118 per cent. Fiscal policy accentuated social contrasts. As in other countries, the wealthy or the relatively wealthy proved better able to gain financial benefits from the system than the poor. In the USA this was seen in particular in tax relief on mortgage payments, which cost $121 billion in 2003, whereas housing policies to help the poor cost only $36 billion. The tax relief largely benefited wealthy house-purchasers. House purchase and cost were important agencies of social differentiation, as were gated communities and private schools.

Non-Marxist analyses of class were less dominated by the notion of conflict, and were readier to present social structures as more complex. They were dominated by income and status (in part, market position) differences between occupational groups. They centred on a difference between the 'middle class' – 'white-collar' (non-manual) workers – and the 'working class' – 'blue-collar' (manual) workers. Consumer analysts further refined these differences in order to understand possible markets. At the same time, competing interests and identities fractured the goals of social groups. Contrasting regional interests were of considerable importance and were abundantly demonstrated in tariff disputes. The tariffs imposed on imported steel in 2002 were designed to help production in Rustbelt (heavy industry) states, particularly Ohio, Pennsylvania and West Virginia, all seen as electorally important, but they put up prices and hit steel-user states, such as Michigan, a major car producer. The tariffs were withdrawn in 2003 in the face of the threats of European Union retaliation aimed at goods from Republican states such as Florida (oranges) and the Carolinas (textiles). This aiming reflected an understanding of the role of sectional interests in American policy. In place of tariffs, a textile-trade agreement with China in November 2005 limited imports.

Moreover, the classification of society in terms of jobs had weaknesses, not least in its focus on male occupations. In addition, this classification ignored the particular characteristics of the youth society that became more important in the USA from the 1960s. This society was celebrated in the media, with films such as *Grease* (1978), and its willingness to embrace new sounds and fashions helped prompt new cultural waves. For example, the young who had made *The Twist* number 1 in the charts in 1960 and 1961 turned to the Beatles in 1964. Technology also enhanced the independence of youth, since mobile phones and blogging restricted parental monitoring. The independent role of youth was a crucial issue in the abortion debate, since opponents sought to ensure that parental notification and then consent was a necessary pre-condition for minors receiving abortions.

A stress on the distinctive lifestyles of youth, and particularly on youth independence, mobility and flexibility, underlines the more general fluidity of social life in the USA. Furthermore, to be 'working' or 'middle' class meant very different things at various stages of life, while families also increasingly contained individuals who were in different social groups. All this challenged notions of class coherence, let alone unity, and these themes were explored in American literature, television drama and film.

Indeed, social structure was not as rigid as much of the theoretical discussion might suggest. There was much fluidity in the concept of social status, while notions of social organization, hierarchy and dynamics all varied, and the cohesion of social groups involved and reflected much besides social status. This challenged class-consciousness and the discussion of society in terms of class, even suggesting that it was irrelevant. Debate over social structure was linked to that over political theory, with the emphasis on social equality in John Rawls's *Theory of Justice* (1971) challenged by *Anarchy, State and Utopia* (1974) by Robert Nosick, another Harvard professor, who pressed the case for a libertarian individualism that undercut any such collectivism. This individualism, indeed, was the crucial note in society in this period.

Whatever the criteria employed, there has always been social difference, but it is less clear how far this has led to division. American society, with its strong emphases on opportunity and mobility, both standard themes in family history, conversation and literature, has traditionally proved better than most other societies at overcoming the sense of separateness and division that may emerge from marked, and not-so-marked, contrasts in wealth. *The Beverly Hillbillies*, fictional television backwoodsmen who strike oil and move to Beverly Hills, offered a comic take on this mobility in the 1960s. In recent decades, however, there are indications that social mobility is becoming less common. This is certainly true of access to higher education, with the elite universities increasingly dominated by the children of the affluent.

More generally, a lack of opportunity for much of the population is confirming a degree of stratification. For example, the 1.3 million employees of the still-expanding Wal-Mart, many of whom lack health benefits, are not likely to be able to accumulate or borrow the capital that would enable them to afford housing in good school districts. Most workers have had to face downward pressure on their benefits, and, in 2003–4, this led to a strike at the California branches of the grocery chains Albertsons, Kroger and Safeway. The extent to which the 'ownership society' proposed by George W. Bush in his speech to the Republican Convention in 2004, with personal pension and health accounts, would work for a large tranche of society is therefore unclear. House-price inflation demonstrated the social divide, as, in 2003, the Urban Institute estimated that 800,000 people were homeless on any given day. Much of the problem reflected the failure of public provision in spheres such as mental illness and drug rehabilitation, although the mobile nature of society was also important at this level. The homeless do not necessarily seek institutional care and, therefore, constraints. As another instance of very varied opportunities, the 2005 United Nations report on global inequality demonstrated, unsurprisingly, that the infant mortality rate was highly skewed. Male babies from one of the wealthiest 5 per cent of families lived 25 per cent longer on average than their counterparts from the poorest 5 per cent. This was a reflection of the extent to which the nation with the world's highest expenditure on healthcare – 13 per cent of the national income – was socially slanted. Furthermore, far from there being a 'trickle-down', the fall in child mortality was reversed from 2000.

Novels captured, and suggested, a sense of contrasting opportunities corroding the social structure. In Sara Paretsky's Chicago-based novel *Guardian Angel* (1992), one of the characters asks 'What kind of benefits do guys get now? They have to negotiate pay *cuts* just to keep their jobs, while the bosses drive Japanese cars and laugh 'cause they're doing all they can to take more jobs away from more Americans'. Politically, this argument was voiced by Ross Perot, an independent Presidential candidate in 1992 and 1996, who claimed that, as a result of the North American Free-Trade Agreement (1994), there was a 'giant sucking sound' of jobs moving to Mexico. The potency of this argument, however, was reduced by economic growth in the 1990s: despite large-scale de-industrialization, there were, in fact, far more winners than losers. Nevertheless, the theme of villainous plutocrats was frequently captured in Hollywood, both in serious films and, more indicatively, in comedy, such as *The Dukes of Hazzard* (2005), in which Boss Hogg schemes to transform the county into an open-cast coal mine. The corrosive effect of money was more pointedly presented in the film *Indecent Proposal* (1993), in which a Las Vegas playboy offers a million dollars for sex with a happily married young woman whose devoted husband wants the money.

There is, in practice, a danger in ignoring the persistence of class differences in the USA and also the role of class or related criteria as an important prism for refracting views and identities. Many, for example, were apt to see the strong commitment to the public schools as reflecting an inclusive sense of equality, but there was no such inclusion or equality between school districts. Furthermore, this was related to senses of social and racial distinction that were encoded in spatial terms, and that led to great sensitivity about the busing of children to schools in order to achieve a measure of equalization within districts. Schools are funded by local property taxes, with the federal government in the early 2000s paying only 8 per cent of the costs of the public school system. Attempts to use the law to make states equalize expenditure failed until 1989 when, in Kentucky, a court established specific standards that children in public schools in that state had to reach. Since then judicial intervention in educational provision has increased, although with few beneficial consequences. In reaction to this trend, in 2005 the Texas Supreme Court struck down a state property tax for funding public schools on the grounds that spending more money does not improve provision and that 'the Constitution does not require a particular solution'. Across the country, white suburban school districts are generally better funded than metropolitan counterparts, where the pupils tend to be from poorer and non-white backgrounds, helping to ensure that whites leave the public school system, for example in Richmond. This is a national pattern, but the degree varies greatly both chronologically and geographically. Indeed, part of the local history and geography of the US can be written in terms of school funding, control and access. The results of these variations are readily apparent in terms of facilities, results and, indeed, the safety of schools. Apart from contrasts between public schools, education also revealed social and other divides through the varied role of private education, including the rise in 'home schooling' from the 1990s, principally by religious conservatives keen to reject what they saw as the values of public education.

RACE

Nevertheless, much else beside class was involved in self-identification. In the USA, ethnicity and religion were both particularly important. In spite of efforts in the first quarter of the twentieth century to check the influx of immigrants, the USA became increasingly Asian and Latino, especially in the last quarter. Most immigrants, however, wanted to learn English. This was an aspect of the extent to which migration contributed to a sense of greater ethnic consciousness and division, as well as to one of national identity transforming different ethnic legacies. Perceptions of ethnicity and race frequently provided the crucial element in the detailed cartography and dynamics of communities, leading to patterns of settlement, occupation, education and sociability, and to the success, or otherwise, of particular groups. As has been the case throughout much of American history, the dynamics of communities mean that the situation is far from fixed. This is true both of the inner cities and of suburbia. In South Central Los Angeles, for example, a largely poor area, successive tides of migrants have led to very different situations. In 1960 there were still parts of the area that were majority white, but by 1970 it was largely majority black, and it has since become increasingly Hispanic. This has led both to majority Hispanic areas and to more mixed sections.

This relationship between wealth and opportunity was amply suggested by the impact of Hurricane Katrina in 2005: the affluent could leave, but the poor lacked comparable mobility. In part, this was a matter of car ownership, but access to insurance or movable assets, such as money in bank accounts, was also an issue. There was also a related racial dimension, with blacks disproportionately present among the poor, both in New Orleans and in other coastal areas affected by the hurricane. In 2004 Louisiana ranked 48th among the states in levels of health insurance, 45th in public health spending and 50th in overall health, while in 2003 it had come second in the cost to the federal government of caring for its older and disabled citizens.

More generally, the particularly rapid rate of geographical mobility in the USA helped to ensure that social opportunity and mobility had swift consequences in terms of social differentiation by area of residence. Home ownership, in place of rent, helped lower the rate of mobility: in the 1960s approximately 20 per cent of the population moved annually, whereas by the mid-2000s it was about 14 per cent, albeit of a larger population, but this was still a very high percentage. More generally, the relative ease of house purchase helped in the integration of racial minorities and immigrant groups, while the decline in racial discrimination made it far easier for upwardly mobile blacks to move into previously segregated neighbourhoods. At the local level, there was a movement of blacks from inner cities to suburbia. The nature of suburbia varied greatly, encouraging movement within, and between, suburbs, but by 2005 about 40 per cent of blacks lived in suburbs.

The practice of local segregation, and how this changed, affected education as well as housing. The Supreme Court decision, in *Brown v. Board of Education* (1954), against school segregation led to a marked rise in white–black contact, particularly in the South. The potential represented by this step was to be lessened by white movement to suburban or private schools, as well as governmental steps, such as curbs on school bussing imposed in 1974, but nevertheless, there had been a major shift in the politics and cartography of race.

Focusing on the plight of the blacks, from the 1960s a strong governmental and public ideology developed that pressed for an emphasis on shared national concerns, and not on racial, religious or linguistic differences among Americans. Equality of opportunity became a more important goal, controversially so, particularly if pursued through positive discrimination and public action, such as the busing of children. Civil rights, a major theme of the 1960s, affected education and federal employment, but had less of an impact on public health and private housing. Increasingly, concern about *de facto* segregation and discrimination was added to action against *de jure* counterparts. Symbolism was also important. In 1990 Virginia elected America's first black governor, Douglas Wilder, a grandson of slaves; but at the same time there was considerable resistance in parts of the South to abandoning the Confederate flag, and other symbols of difference and defiance - symbols that, to critics, contributed to the intimidation of blacks. In 1998 David Beasley lost his post as Governor of South Carolina for supporting the removal of the flag from the statehouse.

Symbolic apologies were more commonly offered at the federal level. In 1999 Rosa Parks, the 'mother of the Civil Rights movement' (for her arrest in Montgomery, Alabama, after refusing to surrender her seat to a white man), was awarded the Congressional Gold Medal of Honor. She had received the Presidential Medal of Freedom from President Clinton three years earlier. The memorialization of the Civil Rights movement also led to the designation of the Martin Luther King

National Historic Site in Atlanta. Visiting Africa in 2003, George W. Bush went to Goree, a once-major slave-trading post, in an attempt to show his concern for black Americans. He declared that, with the slave-trade, 'Christian men and women became blind to the clearest commands of their faith . . . Enslaved Africans discovered a suffering Saviour and found he was more like themselves than their masters.' In 2005 the Senate formally apologized for neglecting to pass legislation in the late nineteenth and early twentieth centuries to make lynching a federal crime.

Sport and the media played a much greater role in encouraging reconciliation than politics. Black figures, such as the television presenter Oprah Winfrey, enjoyed strong cross-racial followings. In 2005 Muhammad Ali and Aretha Franklin were awarded the Presidential Medal of Freedom, but spectacular trials of a small number of black sportsmen, such as O. J. Simpson in 1994–5 and Mike Tyson, served to underline negative stereotypes. Blacks and Hispanics served disproportionately in the military, a point ignored by much of the media, both factual and fictional, which continued to focus largely on images of white heroism.

A spirit of reconciliation, however, could not prevent race playing a divisive role, particularly in terms of senses of local identity. Race was also used as an issue or mood in local politics, as in the opposition to Harold Washington, who in 1983 became Chicago's first black mayor, or in the 1993 mayoral race in New York between David Dinkins, the black incumbent, and Rudolph Giuliani, the successful Republican challenger, or the 2005 Detroit race, in which the unsuccessful black candidate was portrayed by his victorious black rival as pro-white. Furthermore, alongside the mainstream majority of black politicians, there were vociferous separatists such as Louis Farrakhan, who aroused considerable disquiet.

More generally, social indices revealed that blacks were worse off than whites, although the situation has improved. The percentage of blacks below the poverty line was 35.7 in 1983, 33.1 in 1993, 22.5 in 2000 and 24.7 in 2004, compared to percentages for non-Hispanic whites of 8–9. The percentage of whites in the population, however, ensured that the number of whites below the poverty line was greater than that of blacks. White poverty was most important, in percentage terms, in

Appalachia: in West Virginia, the state with the lowest median household income in 2000, and in eastern Kentucky. There was also a strong concentration of white poverty in the western Great Plains and northern Rockies, especially in Montana and the Dakotas. In these areas there has been no substitute for the declining profitability of agriculture. Partly caused by the concentration of poor blacks, Louisiana had the largest percentage of children in poverty in the early 2000s. The relationship between poverty and other indices was controversial but clearly a factor. Blacks were disproportionately numerous among those imprisoned, and therefore among the ex-prisoners who lacked a vote, which might have decisively affected the Florida result in 2000, and thus the Presidential election. At the national level, in the early 2000s black mothers were twice as likely as white counterparts to give birth to a low-weight baby, and their children were twice as likely to die before their first birthday. Louisiana and Mississippi had the highest infant-mortality rate in the early 2000s. To take another criterion, whereas 13 per cent of whites are uninsured, the percentage for blacks was 21 and for Hispanics 34. The UN estimated in 2005 that, if the gap in health between black and white Americans was ended, close to 85,000 lives annually would be saved.

Perceptions also played a major role in social location. That year, the readiness to believe false accounts of total social breakdown in New Orleans after Hurricane Katrina reflected a widespread association of blacks with criminality. In fact, little of the rumoured violence occurred. Nevertheless, this association lay behind support for private-school vouchers, an implicit form of segregation supported by Republican politicians, as well as the marked increase in gun purchases after Katrina.

The impact of Katrina illustrated the extent to which Americans revert to the same issues. Even as Americans dealt with its aftermath and the racial questions it raised, the nation was paying homage to Rosa Parks and noting the anniversary of the Birmingham Bus Boycott. In December 2005 an amphitheatre in Providence was re-dedicated, this time to Parks. At the same time, Rhode Island continued to face problems with racial profiling by the police and sought to settle a five-year-old case involving a friendly fire incident and the death of a black policeman.

More generally, the complexities of racial identity are increasingly understood, at least among those open to scientific advances: no race possesses a discrete package of genetic characteristics; there are more genetic variations within, than between, races; and the genes responsible for morphological features, such as skin colour, are atypical. Races were constructed as much as described. Furthermore, in the USA, biracial marriages and unions increased, becoming the subject of Hollywood comedy in *Guess Who* (2005), as well as a standard theme in pornography. This increase helped to underline the very fluidity of the racial situation, and at current rates the designation 'mixed' that has been added by the Census Board will encompass a large proportion of the population in 50 years time. Bi-racial marriages rose to nearly 7 per cent in 2000, with Hispanics and Asians being on average more likely to intermarry than blacks or non-Hispanic whites. Such a rate ensured that large numbers of Americans had in-laws of a different colour. Unless entrenched through endogamy (marriage within the clan), demographic developments undermined classification in terms of race. Instead, this endogamy is largely social and educational, although there are important caveats. In a lecture on social trends, I pointed out that, thanks to greater educational opportunities for women, doctors increasingly married each other, only for an Iowan Lutheran minister to respond that that was only true of the first marriage, and that, for the second, the (male) doctor always married the nurse.

Racial issues were very varied in character and impact. They were particularly charged, not only in terms of the geography of whites, blacks and Hispanics, but also in the very different ethnic geography of Hawaii, where, in addition to whites and Polynesians, there is a high proportion of Asians, particularly Japanese but also Chinese and Koreans. Frequently ignored in American history after mention of Pearl Harbor, Hawaii had both an important quasi-autonomous history and also demonstrated instructive aspects of general American trends. The complex interweaving of law and politics with the sense of ethnic distinction was amply displayed there. A strong sense of ethnic consciousness among much of the indigenous population led, from the 1970s, to political pressure: the assertion of cultural identity, especially from the 1960s, was followed, in the 1970s, by debate over land rights and self-determination. As with the mainland Native Americans (Indians), land rights were a major issue, and Native advocates argued that ceded land was in fact stolen. Pressure led to the State Constitutional Convention of 1978 creating an Office of Hawaiian Affairs. Furthermore, under the Carter administration, the US Congress created a Native Hawaiians Study Commission. The Reagan government that took office in 1981 changed the direction of policy, and the membership of the Commission. In place of the six Hawaiians and three Mainlanders, there were now three and six respectively. As a result, the Commission's draft report of 1982 denied that there was an issue, since it found American policy in the overthrow of the Hawaiian monarchy in 1893 acceptable. The majority final report, published in 1983, supported this view, but the three Hawaiians produced a conflicting version.

Tension continued, and 1993, the centenary of the overthrow, saw much public debate and dissension. The Hawaiian state's flag, that of the old monarchy, was widely flown without that of the USA, and the state legislature issued a resolution condemning the events of 1893, and thus the legitimacy of current arrangements. It declared that 'the United States military committed the first overt act to overthrow the independent nation of Hawaii, an overt act of military aggression against a peaceful and independent nation'.

These were not abstract issues. Claims of dispossession continue to serve as the basis for sectional demands on behalf of those of Hawaiian descent, for example for special educational provisions, that exclude the large numbers, in fact a majority of the population, with non-Hawaiian antecedents. Like other controversies about race, however, this issue at the same time highlighted problems of definition, which, in 2003, included the case of Brayden Mohica-Cummings, an 'Anglo' adopted by a Hawaiian. He was excluded on the grounds of race from Kamehameha Schools, Hawaii's well-funded guardian of indigenous culture and customs, but the US District Court of Hawaii overturned this decision. The court's earlier views on the issue of race and discrimination – a 1997 ruling – had been overturned by the Supreme Court in 2000, and in 2003 the District Court followed the Supreme Court. Apart from the relationship between federal and state courts, the dispute revealed the extent to which a perception of historical wrongs clashed with constitutional prescriptions for uniformity. One of the Kamehameha Schools trustees, Douglas Ing, declared that the Trust sought 'to rectify past imbalances to the Hawaiian people', and another that the 2003 court decision ignored 'centuries of injustice to the Hawaiian people', while the Supreme Court's minority in 2000 argued that the majority had failed to recognize 'a history of subjugation at the hands of colonial forces'. Notions of dispossession, however, had little purchase with the mainstream of American politics.

In Puerto Rico, which the USA conquered from Spain in 1898, and which is a Commonwealth, not a state, so that the inhabitants do not vote in Presidential elections and pay no federal taxes, pressure for independence from a small separatist movement has little popular support.

It is more appropriate for the USA than for most societies to argue that, in place of an account of society that presents human identities and choices as determined, or at least heavily influenced by, social structures, particularly class, it is possible to emphasize the role of human agency or activities. The resulting stress on the impact of human decisions, and on concepts and ideologies, in social formation and attitudes leads to a less clear-cut and more complex analysis. This is particularly so with the 'me' generation, when the individual, rather than the collective, is seen as the basic unit of decision-making. Patterns of social behaviour became less clear cut and processes of causation less easy to define. The growing emphasis in the USA in recent decades on self-identification as the major source of social location has limited both broad-brush approaches and the 'realist' analyses based on measurable criteria, whether related to the means of production, income or other factors. Self-identification itself was moulded, and provided with crucial signifiers, by consumerist pressures that were mediated by television and Hollywood. This has attracted criticism of both media, as in Richard Condon's *The Ecstasy Business* (1967) on Hollywood.

GENDER

Social location through self-identification involved a number of factors, including not only age, religion and ethnicity, but also lifestyle.

Gender was a crucial element and an important change in the period was the decline of the notion of 'separate spheres', in which women's special role was defined as that of home and family, an important theme in 1950s culture. It had been employed to justify the exclusion of women from other spheres and served to stigmatize the large number of women who had to work. At work, definitions of skills, which affected pay, were controlled by men and favoured them. Skilled women were poorly recognized. Trade unions, which were essentially male organizations, co-operated with management to this end.

From the 1960s, however, social changes combined with a self-conscious women's movement to produce, at least for some women, a gender revolution. The number of married women entering the job market escalated, and more women returned to work after having children. This led to a major rise in the workforce. By 1980, 52 per cent of Americans aged 16 or over were in the workforce, and, as a result of economic growth in the 1990s, the percentage rose to 67.3 in 2000, although, in 2004, it fell to 66 (with the unemployment rate at 5.4 per cent); for women the percentage was about 60. The harsher work requirements and benefit restrictions that constituted welfare reform in 1996 led to a marked increase in the percentage of never-married mothers working: from 46 in 1994 to 66 in 2002. The range of female activities also expanded. The growth in the commercial and financial sectors provided women with many opportunities. The appointment of the first female Supreme Court justice, Sandra Day O' Connor in 1981, was followed, in 1984, with the first female Vice Presidential candidate, Geraldine Ferraro, although she was unsuccessful. A greater assertiveness among prominent women was seen in the development of the role of First Ladies, from the quiet consorts of the 1950s and '60s to forthright feminists with Betty Ford and Hillary Clinton.

Most women, however, worked in far more limiting jobs, and background played a major role in helping to define the opportunities for women. In California in 2001, for example, 77 per cent of us-born white women worked, compared to 73 per cent of black women and 74 per cent of us-born Hispanic women, but the average hourly wage was 18.8, 16.0 and 15.1 dollars respectively. For Hispanic women born abroad the percentage fell to 58 and the wage to 10.4 dollars, indicating the role of education. The advantage of US education was also shown by the contrast between US-born Asian women (84 per cent and 18.3 dollars) and South-East Asian-born women (60 per cent and 15.8 dollars). This was more important than colour.

The legal position of women also improved, while equal rights were enshrined in institutional practices. This led to action against sexual harassment, although allegations of harassment did not prevent Clarence Thomas from joining the Supreme Court in 1991, or Arnold Schwarzenegger from becoming Governor of California in 2003. The prevalence of harassment was indicated by a series of scandals in the military and was also suggested by surveys. A survey of nearly 4,000 National Guard or Reservists serving between 1950 and 2000 conducted by the Department of Veteran Affairs and released in 2005 revealed that more than 27 per cent of males experienced some type of sexual harassment or assault, mostly from other men, but that the percentage for women was 60. As an indication of prevailing norms, fewer than a quarter of the women had reported the harassment and many who did were encouraged to drop their complaint. From the 1990s another aspect of harassment emerged clearly in, and from, the gangsta rap movement, Niggaz with Attitude, which centred on Los Angeles. The misogynist theme of many of their songs has been related to the failure of many fathers in black ghettos to support and guide their children. Having said this, the lyrics are also frequently homophobic. In the late 1970s conservative populism blocked an Equal Rights Amendment designed against gender discrimination, an amendment that had been pressed by Betty Ford. However, the judicial response to perceived harassment became much harsher, and the definition of harassment was greatly extended. In 2005 the California Supreme Court decided that an atmosphere of 'sexual favouritism' could be the basis for legal action, with employees able to claim harassment even if not approached for sexual favours.

Abortion was also an important and continuing field of political and legal contention. The sense of major change was noted by Ruth, a character in John Updike's Pulitzer Prize-winning novel *Rabbit Is Rich* (1981): 'I *did* have the abortion. My parents arranged it with a doctor in Pottsville. He did it right in his office and about a year later a girl died afterwards of complications and they put him in jail. Now the girls just walk into the hospital.' Far from being simply a case of the liberalization of the law at the national level permitted by the Supreme Court in 1973, there was also important subsequent legislation, litigation and judgement. In 2000, a year in which there were 1.3 million abortions, the Supreme Court rejected a Nebraska law that had banned 'partial birth' abortions, which remove a foetus through the cervix, only for Congress in 2003 to pass the Partial-Birth Abortion Ban Act outlawing such abortions, legislation twice vetoed by Clinton. Since this Act conflicted with the Supreme Court's judgement that abortion rulings include an exception for the mother's health, a district court and a federal appeals court invalidated it. Congress argued that the health exception was superfluous in this case because the procedure it claimed was unnecessary. In 2005 legal disputes over abortion included the case of whether Hawaii had the authority to allow counties to ban aerial advertising, since an anti-abortion group wished to pull banners showing aborted foetuses behind planes, as it had already done elsewhere without legal prohibition. In March 2006 South Dakota banned abortion except where the mother's life is at risk.

Female self-consciousness was partly a matter of views on legal issues such as abortion, and more generally on feminism, but there was also a more general interest in the distinctive position of women. In geographical terms, this led to works such as the *Women's Atlas of the United States* (1995) by Cathy and Timothy Fast. This mapped data such as the percentages of women living in shelters for abused women. The data itself, however, posed all sorts of problems in analysis. Lower rates, for example those in the South-East, may be a reflection of lower reported abuse, which may reflect socio-religious pressures to accept male headship of the family as entailing conduct that would be less acceptable elsewhere. Geographical data indicated marked variations in other indicators. For example, whereas in 1960, across the country as a whole, there were 97.1 males for every 100 females, in large part due to greater female longevity, the variation ranged from Alaska, with 132.3 males for every 100 females (due to the large number of young single migrant workers), to New York, Massachusetts and Pennsylvania, where the figure was under 95.

Lifestyle changes reflecting female wishes were also fundamental in social change, cohabitation and divorce being particularly important. Cohabitation before, and instead of, marriage became more common and ensured that more children were born outside marriage. The percentage of children thus born rose from 18 in 1980 to 33 in 1999, although it fell in the early 2000s. The rate was far higher for black children. Divorce had peaked after World War Two, but then fell and was stable in the 1950s and early 1960s. Thereafter it became more common, so that the percentage of children living with a single parent rose each year from 1960 until 1995, before showing a slight decline. Nevertheless, the overall trend was clearly upwards, for example from 12 per cent in 1970 to 27 per cent in 2003. The rate of divorce doubled between 1958 and 1976, and, by 2000, 40 per cent of first marriages were likely to end in divorce. Rates varied greatly, being highest in Nevada, a state with particularly liberal regulations (it is also the sole state where brothels are legal), and higher than average in the South. Some see this as an ironic comment on the region's social conservatism, but it is also a product of it, because the average age of marriage there is low. Divorce led to high rates of second and third marriages. The resulting family tensions led to a rise in contested wills. Subsequent marriages had higher divorce rates, contributing to an overall divorce rate of about 50 per cent.

Neil Simon stated that the basis for his very popular comedy *The Odd Couple* (1965) was a party he attended in California in which all the men were divorced, most sharing apartments with other divorced men because of the cost of alimony. Set in New York, the play depicts Oscar who is threatened with jail by his former wife Blanche because he is four weeks behind with child support. Replying that he would be better in jail, Oscar increases the stakes in the card game he is playing. Divorce was also extended to gay couples. In 2003 California's law required that all domestic partnerships be dissolved using the divorce-court system. The rate of remarriage, however, indicated the continued appeal of marriage, while the cult of the family remained strong, not least with Hollywood. In *True Lies* (1994), the secret agent Arnold Schwarzenegger was married and a father, unlike James Bond, the persona several of whose signatures he employed in the film. In 1987 the biggest hit at the box office was the film *Three Men and a Baby*.

Partly as a consequence of divorce, the percentage of households that were occupied by the 'nuclear family' – two parents and their children – fell from 45 in 1960 to 23.5 in 2000. This was a fundamental social shift, not least because of changes in resulting assumptions about what constituted normal behaviour, or the mismatch between conventional assumptions and current reality. Rising divorce figures challenged male norms about family structure, and led to an increasing number of families headed by women who were not widowed. This helped to ensure that the position of these women played a greater role in debates about social issues, and they were featured in literature and the media, as with the positive portrayal of Mrs Gump in the successful film *Forrest Gump* (1994). These women could no longer be treated as an adjunct of their husbands. Single-parent households, on average, commanded weaker mortgage opportunities than those in which two adults' incomes were at stake. This interacted with the geographical shifts and differentiation of the period, as indeed did the need for space. Thus, the outer suburbs and the exurbs with their large new houses had, on average, a lower rate of one-parent households, and an above-average percentage of nuclear families.

LABOUR

Changes in the position of women cannot be separated from other social shifts. Female identity and experience shifted within social, economic and political contexts that themselves altered. These contexts were not primarily structured by gender issues. For example, the economic shift from manufacturing to service industries, which was marked in the last quarter of the century, created more opportunities for salaried work for women, while the decline in traditional manufacturing accentuated the insecurity of older and relatively unskilled male workers. It also hit union membership, which not only fell from 23 per cent of the workforce in 1980 to 12.5 per cent in 2004, but was also increasingly found in weaker sections of the economy. By 2003 about half of union members were located in only six states: Michigan, Illinois, Ohio, California, New York and Pennsylvania, and unions were particularly short of members in the South. In the years 1983–2003 the United Auto Workers Union lost nearly one million members in manufacturing, as its heartlands in the Mid-West declined, while new car plants in the South were non-unionized. In 2004 union membership was only 8 per cent of private sector workers, and, in contrast, 36 per cent of public sector workers. As a sign of the changing composition of the workforce, the United Steelworkers of America lost 100,000 workers in the years 1998–2005, while the Service Employees International Union gained greatly in the same period. At the same time, the outsourcing of jobs to other countries challenged the rise in service employment in some spheres (banking but not nursing). Nevertheless, unemployment, at 4.8 per cent in February 2006, was lower than in Australia, Canada and the Euro area.

CONSUMERISM

Social location was not simply a matter of gender. Society was also shaped by expenditure patterns, and this gave great commercial and cultural significance to those who influenced them, such as the lifestyle guru Martha Stewart in the 1990s and 2000s. A combination of economic growth (although interrupted, particularly in the 1970s) and of readily available credit that fuelled the desire to borrow ensured that most of the population was left with more disposable wealth than their parents, and also with more leisure in, and on, which to spend it. Living standards were on average 82 per cent higher in 1973 than in 1948, a massive increase, and a greater one than in the war years, which themselves created the modern American economy. During the period 1948–73 median family income rose on average by 3 per cent per annum, while output per hour in the business sector rose by more than 3 per cent annually. Staples, in the shape of food, housing and heating, absorbed a smaller percentage of the average individual and family budget, and the latter was helped by the higher percentage of married female workers.

The ability of people to define themselves through spending accentuated the role of the money economy, which had itself increased with mass urbanization. Fashion, cost and respectability helped to determine choice, and consumer demands reflected the primacy of personal choice over public policy. Despite health warnings, taxation and restrictions, expenditure on alcohol and tobacco remained high, and the same was true of illegal drugs, leading to major criminal opportunities and providing subjects for Hollywood, as with *The French Connection* (1971) and *Traffic* (2000). As a consequence of greater wealth, so a range of activities became more common, which contributed to the consumer economy. Sports that had hitherto been the leisure of the wealthy became the resort of the numerous affluent. Retirement also became a more common option as a result of greater longevity, more statutory rights and better pension provisions.

However, whereas the growth after World War Two had benefited Americans of all social groups and provided a reasonably equable share of rising income, differences became markedly greater from the start of the 1980s, contributing to social differentiation. Poverty rates fell, but the percentage of the national income enjoyed by the poorest fifth declined and that by the wealthiest fifth increased greatly. If recent immigrants, who tend to lack capital and to be in low-income jobs, are excluded, the figures would be less divergent.

Consumerism and a sense of entitlement helped to drive the potent mix of economic growth and social expectation. This led not only to the hard work that helped to underpin social mobility, but also to the widespread anger that was a characteristic of many who did not benefit as they anticipated. Far from rejecting consumerism, as some hippies had done, they did not accept its terms and distribution of benefits. This anger was a characteristic of much of society, but it was reflected differently in accordance with the individual personality and social opportunities. Recourse to crime and/or drugs was the option of many. There was also a growing turning to therapies, counsellors and alternative medicine.

Each of these options in turn fed suppliers of the relevant hopes and substances. The different response of the law to these strategies was notable. Self-help through narcotic drugs remained illegal, despite becoming widespread. In contrast, therapy was not only legal but also actively encouraged by family courts as a way to categorize and improve problems and individuals. In part, this process reflected the culture of improvement that was so strong in the USA. Self-improvement might appear to be the main theme, but in practice this was heavily guided, both by religious groups and by therapeutic options. At the same time, individuals not only chose their option, but also changed options. The humanistic psychology that played a crucial role in therapism was a particularly attractive consumer option, and acted as a parallel to the fashion, in religious practice, for rebirth through faith during life, rather than for simply improving chances for salvation after death.

These varied tendencies have been accentuated in recent years, which have been a period of unprecedented liquidity, expenditure, borrowing, and debt. As an aspect of this problem, which, for many, constitutes a real or incipient or threatened crisis, the financial deficits of households have reached a record, and that after staying in surplus from the late 1950s to the mid-1990s. This shift was related to the wider politics, since low interest rates encouraged individual risk-taking. While attractive to entrepreneurs, this, in practice, meant borrowing to spend on houses and on imported goods.

As another crucial aspect of social change, the speeded-up quality of society reflected a number of factors. The consumption of stimulants, from coffee to narcotic drugs, was important, and, in turn, rapidly reflected new developments, such as cheap, smokable, highly addictive crack cocaine, which was invented in the early 1980s. Use subsequently declined, but in 2004 it was estimated that 5.1 per cent of those aged 15–34 used cocaine. The greater accessibility that followed the widespread use of computers and mobile phones was also important to the feeling of a faster pace. Although the size of the USA and the issue of coverage ensured that the use of mobiles was lower than in many smaller countries, by 2003, after a compound annual growth rate of 12 per cent in 2000–03, more than half the population had a cell (mobile) phone.

Consumerism is a major theme in the social trends of the period, seen, for example, in the extent to which residential choices reflect lifestyle assumptions and practices. Greater mobility has helped people choose locations that are defined by cultural attitudes. Consumerism is also one of the major aspects of integration referred to in the Preface, one, moreover, made more so by nationwide advertising. At the same time, the diversity mentioned in the Preface can also be seen as a pronounced character of these trends. This diversity takes many forms, with national trends, such as the impact of big-money, big-television sport, which, in part, are a sum of regional differences. Thus, particular sports are strong in specific areas, football, for example, in Nebraska, Oklahoma and Texas, and baseball in the South. This contrast, and others, can be taken further on the local level. The same is true of cooking. There are strong regional and local variations that reflect the combination of different environments, in the sense of varied climates and agricultural systems with the impact of ethnic patterning and class. In his *White Trash Cooking* (1986), Ernest Micler noted: 'If you live in the South or have visited there lately, you know that the old White Trash tradition of cooking is very much alive, especially in the country . . . what sets White Trash cooking aside from other kinds of cooking . . . saltmeat, cornmeal, and molasses.'

Both integration and diversity fed and feed into the cultural and political divisions, tensions and policies discussed in the next two chapters. There is no clear-cut divide between these categories, and it would be particularly unwise to treat their relationship as uni-directional. Instead, the cultural and political dimensions also helped to influence social practices and structures, leading to the situation of multiple feedbacks that made policy discussion so contentious.

Chapter 5

Culture Wars

Culture Wars concern memories and events, and how they are shaped
in terms of longstanding assumptions about identity and value. These
wars are ever-present within the USA and other countries, and are a
major theme in the perception and ordering of social developments, as
well as in the framing of political debate, with assumptions powerfully
feeding the senses of grievance that are so significant in American politics. The nature and role of these culture wars are an important aspect
of modern American history.

Stereotypes are misleading, yet they also capture realities, both in
terms of what they describe and because they reveal potent assumptions. One such stereotype is a belief in a major cultural discontinuity
or breach in the 1960s. In practice, the extent and impact of the novelty
of this period have been exaggerated, and, in this respect, the contrast
with the Cultural Revolution in China is particularly striking. Yet, there
were also important shifts. In this, the USA was taking part in an international development. Novel gender and youth expectations and roles
commanded attention across the world, and youth culture, as well as
feminism, drugs and sexual liberation, were international themes, as,
more generally, was the questioning of authority that was such a shock

to those of an older generation. The emphases, instead, in the 1960s, were on novelty, freedom and self-fulfilment. Design and the arts were fascinated with new forms, as with the geodesic dome designed by Buckminster Fuller in 1967. The 1960s was a period in which fashions, in clothes, popular music and much else, all stressed novelty. There was also an emphasis on the individual, and on his or her ability to construct their particular world, an emphasis that led not only to the cult of celebrity for performers, a fast-changing celebrity as Andy Warhol noted, parcelled out into fifteen-minute blocs of fame, but also to an attempt to translate it to consumers. Songs and films featured sexual independence. Hedonism focused on free will, self-fulfilment and consumerism, the last the motor of economic growth.

The net effect was a more multi-faceted public construction of individual identities, and a more fluid society. The stress on the individual did not lend itself to a classification of identity, interest and activity in terms of traditional social categories, especially class; or to any simple explanation of cultural, intellectual and artistic developments in terms of comprehensive themes. One cultural consequence of this, which continued a trend seen earlier in the century, was the creation of artistic works that deliberately drew on different forms and that transcended boundaries as an aspect of an attempt to discard established disciplinary classifications and conventions.

The changes of the 1960s reflected not simply long-established liberal causes, but also a more specific rejection of conventional social and cultural assumptions. In part, this arose from a challenging of earlier norms that, in turn, was to be opposed by a backlash that was characterized by conventional morality and patriotism. Tension between the radicalism of the counter-culture and the backlash led to the culture-wars of the last half-century. Radical intellectual influences contributed to a sense of flux, and also to established norms and values being seen as simply passing conventions. The chic fashionability of this liberal radicalism was satirized brilliantly in Tom Wolfe's *Radical Chic and Mau-Mauing the Flak Catchers* (1970). Social and cultural changes hit earlier taboos.

The women's liberation movement was particularly important to the sense of change. The movement was diverse, as can be seen by contrasting texts such as Betty Friedan's *Feminine Mystique* (1963) and Kate Millett's *Sexual Politics* (1970); but conventional assumptions and practices, including nuclear families, the authoritarian position of men within households and female sexual subservience, were all criticized, and there was a stress on 'consciousness raising' for women. Demands for the recognition of an independent sexuality included an assertion of women's rights to enjoy sex, to have it before marriage without incurring criticism, and to control contraception and, thus, their own fertility; and these, and related, issues were discussed in literature and film, as with Judith Rossner's novel *Looking for Mr Goodbar* (1975), which was made into a film in 1977. The introduction and rapid spread of the oral contraceptive pill from the late 1950s helped this shift towards an independent sexuality by making it easier to separate sexuality from reproduction. Furthermore, despite the refusal of some pharmacists to dispense them, later developments in contraception increased female control. These included the 'morning-after pill' and, from the 1990s, an injectable contraceptive that needed to be taken only once every three months. Religious conservatives sought to limit access to contraception. In 2005 the Food and Drug Administration proved reluctant to approve the emergency contraceptive Plan B for over-the-counter sale because it is an abortifacient.

Other aspects of technology that were of importance included the products of the consumer revolution in terms of labour-saving devices. Washing machines and prepared meals became far more common; they reduced domestic drudgery and encouraged higher female participation in the labour force. The decline in household service exposed more couples to confronting how best to handle the tasks that remained.

Shifting attitudes were not simply dependent on technology. Cultural shifts were also important. There was a readiness to embrace privately, and even publicly, what had hitherto been regarded publicly, and generally privately, as promiscuity, as well as greater interest in sexual experimentation. Furthermore, as an important aspect of female power, women played the crucial role in asserting and extending rights to abortion. In 1973, in *Roe v. Wade*, the Supreme Court by 7–2 struck down a Texas law banning abortions except where the mother's life was threatened and, instead, decided that women had such a right on demand as part of the right to privacy. This was a major extension of federal jurisdiction at the expense of the states, although one that was limited because of the continued impact of local opinion. As a result, few abortion clinics opened in areas that were hostile to it. Abortion, which, after 1973, was at the annual rate of about 1.5 million terminations, brought into sharp focus competing ideas, not only of judicial activism and the appropriate level of government activity, but also of social rights and responsibilities. Individual liberty, female assertion and sexual consumerism clashed with a moral authoritarianism that fixed on the womb and that was uncomfortable with libertarianism. The crucial element in choice was women's choice. In practice, this meant more choice for poorer women, since their more affluent counterparts had been able to use their greater mobility to travel in order to obtain abortions. Nevertheless, legal judgements in 1977 and 1980 respectively upheld state and federal bans on the public funding of abortion. The rise in the number of abortions has been linked to a fall in the crime rate from the 1990s, since fewer unwanted children were born, although the decline in the popularity of crack cocaine might have been more important.

Women's health also became a more significant issue, leading to screening for cervical and breast cancer, Well-Women clinics and elective Caesarian deliveries as a common method of childbirth.

There was also pressure for more radical or separatist feminist options, including an affirmation of lesbianism. This entailed not only private commitment, but also cultural assertion and legal demands, the latter a prime form of assertion in the USA. In 2005 the California Supreme Court decided that the custody and child-support laws of the state also had to apply to homosexual and lesbian couples, while, that year, the California legislature was the first in the USA to pass a bill legalizing gay marriage. The homosexual movement had become more assertive from the late 1960s, with an iconic moment in the Stonewall Bar in New York in 1969 when activists responded vigorously to police harassment. The previous year, homosexual life had been candidly depicted on stage in Mart Crowley's play *The Boys in the Band* (1968), which was set in New York. The idiom was fairly clear, Bernard remarking: 'You know why old ladies like poodles – because they go down on them.' The play was subsequently turned into a film in 1990. The end of the Hays Code in 1968 made it possible to provide a more overt depiction than hitherto of gays and lesbians in the cinema, and this played a role in greater assertiveness. At the same time, there was a contrast between fiction and the reality of discrimination. The film *Brokeback Mountain* (2005), which is based on E. Annie Proulx's short story 'Close Range', aroused criticism in Wyoming with its depiction of a homosexual relationship between cowboys there in the 1960s. The actual treatment of homosexuality in the state could be brutal, most clearly with the murder of a homosexual student, Matthew Shephard, in 1998. The normative role of homosexuality was suggested by family dramas, such as the film *The Family Stone* (2005), in which family members were presented as homosexual, in this case, the gay son being also deaf and having a black partner. Another form of homosexual assertiveness has been provided by Pride Festivals, of which the biggest, by the early 2000s, were, in order, in San Francisco, New York and Atlanta.

The development of gay and lesbian literature was not restricted to fiction. Instead, Queer Theory became a branch of literary studies, and influenced the academic coverage of English literature. The consequences can be gained, for example, by considering several of the essays in *Ian Fleming and James Bond: The Cultural Politics of 007* (2005). They indicate the extent to which cultural studies has scant grounding in the language, let alone experience, of most Americans. Among the gems that invite rearrangement in order to see if any meaning arises is the following by Judith Roof, also author of *A Lure of Knowledge: Lesbian Sexuality and Theory* (1991): 'The retro associations of Bond's style exploit and perform this nostalgia for Law, but as a measure of homeopathic resistance. Bond's efficacious style is a version of the same absolutist efficacy as that practiced by all world nemeses, who are themselves singular Mosaic figures delivering the word from on high.' Dennis Allen, in an essay on anal anxiety in *Diamonds Are Forever*, argues that Bond triumphs over the film's symptoms of this anxiety; Jaime Hovey claims that 'These "queer" aspects of Bond suggest that gender and heterosexual sexual expression in Bond novels and films are stylized to the point that they actually resist heteronormativity and respectability, constituting a recognizable queerness', and so on. Such language helped to constitute a cliquishness that was inherently divisive and the very opposite of educational.

Apart from demands for legal changes, and for shifts in the use of language to avoid male stereotyping, feminism also led to pressure for lifestyles and social arrangements that put women's needs and expectations in a more central position. Jobs and lifestyle became more important as aspirations for women, complementing, rather than replacing, home and family. These changes were faithfully recorded, and encouraged, in the soap operas that put family life on television screens.

Gender was also an important issue for men. The end of conscription affected notions of masculinity and also what academics referred to as gendered constructions of citizenship. Less emphasis than hitherto was placed on what had been seen as masculine values, and some of these were questioned, indeed mocked, as in anti-war literature and, very differently, the comedy film *40-Year-Old Virgin* (2005), which made fun of the pressure for sex rather than romance. This was part of a process of change in the images of masculinity, although it was a change that was greatly resisted. The cultural shadow included, alongside the cult of the muscly action hero, particularly in the Reaganite 1980s with Arnold Schwarzenegger, Sylvester Stallone, Bruce Willis and Chuck Norris, the frequent presentation of men as cut off by divorce from their families, and also the displacement of heroes. This was marked in the decline of the Western, and also left a comic form in the full-length cartoon *The Incredibles* (2004), in which comic-book heroes no longer have a place in society; although, according to the plot, this simply leaves the latter vulnerable. The decline of manual work and the growth in importance of women workers also contributed to the same sense of changing, indeed, in some contexts, imperilled, masculinity. Different attitudes to homosexuality contributed powerfully to this sense of contested masculinity. The gay rights movement presented homosexuality as normal, and as deserving equal treatment with heterosexuality.

The problems in personal relations, caused for both men and women by social and cultural changes, were the stuff of much television and cinema, as in the bittersweet comedy film *When Harry Met Sally* (1989). Television and cinema also engaged with the variety of personal relationships, so that *Tales of The City* (1993), *More Tales of The City* (1998), *Further Tales of The City* (2001) and *Desperate Housewives* (2004–5) presented same-sex as well as heterosexual relationships. At the same time, there were complaints about this presentation, and the nature of network priorities was shown with *Tales of The City*, which was produced for PBS and not one of the major networks. *Desperate Housewives*, like the film *American Beauty* (1999), was more shocking because the city of the *Tales* was San Francisco, which is widely seen as radical, while they, in contrast, were set in prosperous suburbia, and indeed were a satire on suburban complacency. This satirical theme became increasingly common in the 2000s, and, in part, was a hostile response to the social politics of conservatism in the George W. Bush years. Television soaps both reflect social trends and yet also present an opportunity for commentary. They are at once homogenizing, in that they make particular experiences and lifestyles seem all-American and part of the common currency of life, and also reveal difference. The former tendency is the most pronounced, since it enables the soap to work best as a commercial product.

Changing gender imaginings and roles fed into lifestyle choices, in matters such as clothes, hairstyles and food. Vegetarianism became more common, particularly among women. There were related changes in other consumer products, with a rise, in the 1990s, of toiletries and products linked to aromatherapy, while decaffeinated hot drinks became more popular, and the range of teas, coffees, soft drinks and bottled water all spread.

YOUTH CULTURE

Public culture owed much to, and interacted with, the social shifts that arose from consumer choice, and the need to shape and cater for it. One of the most striking was the emergence of the youth consumer, and the development of cultural and consumer fashions that reflected the dynamism and volatility of this section of the market, not least with related changes in popular music, drugs and sport. There was a widespread wish among young people to create a distinct adolescent identity – not to be younger copies of their elders – and to reject the opinions of their parents. Pop culture, which reflected the desire to focus the aspirations of youth on young adults, rather than on parents, was an important manifestation of this shift once the 'generation gap', itself an instructive concept, began to emerge in the 1950s. It is possible that youth culture reflected the more liberal post-war approach to raising children associated in particular with Benjamin Spock (1905–1998), a doctor whose *Common Sense Book of Baby and Child Care* (1946) was very influential. Before his death, Spock made a public apology, since he had come to believe that allowing children's intrinsic desires to develop, as he had earlier argued, only increased their egocentrism, leading to a decline in necessary discipline and the rejection of inherited values.

The widespread willingness to try different foods, to holiday in different places, to move away from parental religious beliefs, or to go on to higher education, were all part of the same process of youthful affirmation, as were subcultures of drug-taking and youth violence. The willingness and determination of the young to define themselves, frequently in opposition to their parents, greatly affected society and was also a means by which social change occurred. This definition was presented in terms of self-expression and freedom, but there was powerful peer pressure for consumer conformity, and a related exclusion of those unable to participate. Furthermore, adult tastes were extended onto teens and pre-teens and there was a reverse infantilizing of adults in their twenties and even thirties. The major rise in higher and further education was especially important in encouraging and facilitating social, geographical and cultural mobility. The Land-Grant College expansion of the late nineteenth century established the infrastructure for the GI legislation after World War Two that helped the USA to provide the educated workforce of the late twentieth century. Fresh generations of the young benefited from expanding provision. Youth itself gained more privileges, not least with the lowering of the voting age to 18 in 1971. Again, this was a trend that was not restricted to the USA, but nevertheless one that greatly affected its society.

The newly energized, demanding and distinctive youth culture of the 1960s drew on new technology, and the mass production of modern industrial society yet again provided the goods for popular culture. Artificial fabrics were employed more actively, leading to the use of modern plastics, such as PVC (polyvinyl chloride). Fashions changed rapidly, reflecting the mass marketing of consumer society and the concern of youth culture with novelty. This dominant theme was fashion appeal, not durability or other utilitarian goals (although the ubiquitous jeans were durable as well as reflecting a willingness of women to adopt and adapt male fashions). Consumerism had become the utilitarian end. This was not only a matter of youth. The enhancement of product range and possibilities through new developments was open to all consumers. Fashion became more insistent, due to the spread of colour photography, in magazines and newspaper supplements, as well as in film and on television. It became common to replace goods even when they were still functional.

From the 1960s massive open-air concerts focused the potent combination of youth culture and pop music. Pop, in turn, spawned subcultures such as punk and heavy metal. Youth demand also fuelled the drug culture that became more important from the 1960s, especially from the 'Summer of Love' in 1967. Drug use, however, remained illegal, and thus an appreciable portion of the population became familiar with breaking the law. The inability of the government to suppress the trade was a powerful demonstration of the difficulty of policing society and of influencing social habits. By 2000 about $60 billion of the approximately $150 billion world retail sales of illegal drugs occurred in the USA.

THE WORLD OF THINGS

Culture was a matter not only of social goods but also of the world of things, and of the expectations and experiences bound up in them. Revolutionary transformations in theoretical and applied science, and technology, underlined the nature of knowledge as a process of change. A comparable sense of human capability arose from the ability to synthesize new experiences, which culminated in the early 1990s with the development of virtual reality imaging. Technological application brought new capabilities within the scope of the bulk of the population. Communications satellites provided systems for transmitting words and images rapidly, while the silicon microchip permitted the creation of more effective communication methods. The miniaturization of electronic components made it possible to create complete electronic circuits on a small slice of silicon. The integrated circuit was invented in 1958, and the first hand-held calculator in 1966. The Intel 4004, the first microprocessor chip, was created in 1971. Gordon Moore, the co-founder of the company responsible, predicted a dramatic revolution in capability as the result of the doubling of the number of transistors on chips every eighteen months. Initially, in the absence of miniaturization, computers were an industrial product of great scale and cost, but, from the late 1970s, they became widely available as office and then household tools. Improvements in capability ensured that computing power became cheaper and thus more accessible, and, as was typical of the American economy, there were no political controls on access or content. Size, specifically miniaturization, was a crucial element in the popularity of new consumer goods, such as mobile phones, laptop computers and mini-disc systems. Fibre-optic cables, another advance of the 1970s, increased the capacity of cable systems, and the volume of telephone and computer messages they could carry. A single optical fibre could carry ten billion bits per second.

The capacity of the electro-magnetic spectrum to transmit messages was utilized, and thanks to computers and electronic mail, more messages were sent and more information stored than ever before. The growing number of company and personal computers facilitated the use of electronic mail and access to the Internet. Companies such as Apple, founded in 1976, and Microsoft created and transformed the industry. Specifications changed rapidly. In 1984 the Macintosh, a computer with a graphical interface controlled with a mouse, was launched, and in 1999 a range of iMac computers in different colours. In 1998 nearly half of the 130 million people in the world with Internet access were Americans. Their companies had played a crucial role in the development of computing. Since the Internet only really became efficient when there were sufficient users to create a widespread system, the take-up rate was particularly important. It also indicated that the lapse factor in technological advance between innovation and widespread use had greatly diminished. Affluence and a sense of need fuelled the quest for the new and more powerful in technology, and this was linked to a discarding of earlier models. By 2004 more than 130,000 personal computers were replaced in the USA daily. Miniaturization was to be followed with the development of nanotechnology, which was based on Richard Smalley's discovery of a new form of carbon molecule in 1985. By the early 2000s this new technology was in receipt of substantial government backing.

Successive improvements in technology enhanced not only communications but also other aspects of organizational activity, such as information storage and analysis, and accounting systems. This contributed to governmental and economic activities, making it easier to exercise control and to engage in planning. Technology was an enabler of new notions of efficiency, effectiveness and control, spanning society from individuals to companies and government, and characterizing in particular organizational culture. Cybermetrics, the study of information systems, developed. It was applied to both brains and computers, an instance of the extent to which analogies between humans and machines were pressed. However, the overload, management and accessibility of information became major problems for both individuals and institutions. Fiction provided clues to other anxieties that were not realized. Although by 2004 the USA had 115,000 robots in operation (third in the world after Japan and Germany), there were neither the humanoids seen in films such as *The Terminator* (1984) nor the super-intelligent computers of *2001: A Space Odyssey* (1968) and *The Forbin Project* (1970) that seized control from humans.

The rise in telecommunications made the production of the necessary equipment and related electronics an important field of manufacturing and trade. It also greatly affected the world of goods. There was a marked fall in the centrality of paper products and records, and in the need for cash transactions. Credit cards facilitated telephone purchases and therefore helped to limit the importance of face-to-face commercial transactions in the 1990s. By 2000, 21 per cent of consumer spending was by credit card. Purchasing was increasingly divorced from shops and other retail premises, a tendency taken further with the success of such companies as Amazon and eBay. The same shift affected other economic sectors. Telephone banking was introduced in the 1980s and Internet banking in the 1990s.

Pornography, an industry in which the US leads the world, thanks to its wealth, sexual licence and freedom of expression laws, became more accessible as a result of the Internet, while, in addition, computer fraud spread. As another aspect of technological opportunities, and their link to consumerism, individuals were assailed by unwanted phone calls, faxes and e-mails, but also benefited from the new technology in order to assert themselves. Video cameras added to this, a process that played a role in Steven Soderbergh's film *Sex, Lies and Videotape* (1989), and also in the production of home pornography. The spread of videos and of pornography had been synergetic in the 1970s, leading to the success of *Deep Throat* (1972), which became one of the country's most popular videos.

More generally, the USA was increasingly a knowledge society. Culture, economics and politics were each seen as dynamic, with information a crucial item and 'messaging' a major form of interaction, work and opinion-forming. By 2006 about 70 per cent of Americans had mobile phones. The emphasis on information technology was important in the world of work. Among the ten fastest growing occupations in the 2000s listed by the Labor Department were networks systems and data communications analysts; computer software engineers, applications; and computer software engineers, systems software.

For the elderly at the close of the period – and the aged were becoming more numerous – it was not only the individual major technological innovations of their lifetimes, whether atomic energy or contraceptive pill, television or microchip, jet engine or computer, bio-technology or artificial hip, that were of importance in affecting, directly or indirectly, insistently or episodically, their lives. There was also the cumulative impact of change. The past ceased to be a recoverable world, a source of reference, value and values for lives that changed very little, and became instead a world that was truly lost, a theme park for nostalgia, regret or curiosity. The period covered in this book saw research into biotechnology, fuel-cell technology, information technology, artificial intelligence and the use of outer space, all designed to increase the capacity of human society to overcome problems, and each a product of applied knowledge.

Part of the process of change was glimpsed through the television. Its rise was seen in more sets, more channels and longer periods of broadcasting. From the 1950s television succeeded radio as a central determinant of the leisure time of many, a moulder of opinions and fashions, a source of conversation and controversy, a cause of noise, an occasion of family cohesion or dispute, and a major feature of the household. A force for change, a great contributor to the making of the consumer society and a 'window on the world', which demanded the right to enter everywhere and report everything, television became, increasingly, both moulder and reflector of popular taste. It took over from radio the function of providing common experience. Television became central to the trend-setting and advertising that were crucial to the consumer society, and to politics. It also increasingly set the idioms and vocabulary of public and private life. By 1986 there were 195 million televisions in the USA, compared to 26 million in Brazil, 10.5 million in India and 6.6 million in Indonesia. Television became more moulded to the consumer with the video and then the DVD (digital-video discs). By 2005 close to 70 per cent of homes with televisions also had DVD players.

Technology also influenced cultural possibilities. The capabilities of writers, designers and others were enhanced by computerized systems. Sound was changed with the development of electronic music. The analogue synthesizer, invented by Robert Moog, replaced, in 1964, the physical bulk of previous synthesizers. This possibility was taken up both by avant-garde classical musicians and popular counterparts, and, in turn, was taken further as synthesizers became smaller, less expensive and cheaper, with computer-based digital synthesizers being used from the 1980s. At a very different level, computer animation transformed film-making, particularly cartoons, and the American company Pixar was at the centre of this. Technological application was an aspect of the world of mixed media, which also, for example, saw jazz poetry, such as the work of Jane Cortez, which was best grasped through recordings and videos, for example *Celebrations and Solitudes* (1975).

An emphasis on change, however, has to be tempered by awareness that change itself was not a single option but had several, often competing, strands. Furthermore, there were aspects of continuity. The strength of established assumptions in at least some spheres was shown, for example, by the continued role of gun culture. Personal ownership of guns remained higher in the USA than elsewhere in the developed world, and this contrast became particularly marked as ownership of guns declined in Europe. Guns were bought for children as presents, as were gun lessons. At the same time, gun ownership in the USA recorded social change, not least in the marked growing rate of female ownership in the latter decades of the century. Gun ownership was seen as affirming individual rights and self-reliance, and was vociferously defended on these grounds and with reference to the Constitution; but it was also a facilitator of criminality. Furthermore, rioting, as in Los Angeles in 1992, or simply the use, or reported use, of guns in a situation of precarious control, as in New Orleans in 2005, underlined the dangers that gun-ownership posed to social stability and political order. The killing of others, including the prominent, by those enabled to act out their fantasies by gun ownership was an aspect of the democratization of violence that was a characteristic of American society, and one that interacted with individualism. The prominent killed included not only politicians, including John and Robert Kennedy, but also major cultural figures, such as John Lennon in New York in 1980. Attempted assassinations included Ronald Reagan and George Wallace. Guns and shooting also played a powerful, frequently iconic and pivotal role in the arts, as in 1980, when the character J. R. Ewing was shot on the television series *Dallas*. As an instance of the global grip of American culture, this shooting was reported in Britain on BBC television as an item of news.

RELIGION

Themes of continuity overlapped and interacted with aspects of change. This was most prominently the case with the powerful strand of religious conservatism. Throughout the period, most Americans had a religious affiliation (the number denying any was only 14.3 million in 1990 and 29.4 million in 2001), and the leading religion was Christianity. In accordance, however, with the constitutional ban on an established church, this was a Christianity fractured among a variety of creeds as a reflection of the individualistic and regional nature of American society. For example, the Southern Baptists are particularly strong in the South-East, the Catholics in the North-East, the South-West, southern Louisiana, southern Florida, Hawaii and Alaska, and Lutherans in the Northern Plains. The individualistic context of American religion ensured that new denominations were easily founded there and that they flourished more readily than in other countries. This context was taken a long way in Pentecostalism, with its notion that individuals could receive the gift of 'speaking in tongues', and furthest in the creation of messianic cults. Furthermore, there was a major role for faith communities as a whole, and this ensured that other religious groups, such as Jewish communities, readily found a place in American society. Immigration ensured that the number of non-Christians increased, although the dominance of immigration by Hispanics, who are Catholics, was such that there was no comparable impact on percentages. In particular, there was a marked increase in those following East and South Asian religions such as Buddhism. Some religious practices challenged or tested American laws. In 2005–6 the Supreme Court had to consider whether the Religious Freedom Restoration Act of 1993 obliged the government to permit the import of hoasca, a hallucinogenic tea for use by the O Centro Espirita religious group, a Brazilian movement that had spread to the USA.

Evangelical Protestantism and millennialism flourished in much of American society, and could have an uncompromising, if not intolerant, character. Protestant fundamentalism was a strong presence throughout the century, encouraging Prohibition (the banning of alcohol), as well as creationist attacks on the theory of evolution, support for school prayers and opposition to homosexuality. At the same time, state regulation constrained behaviour. The polygamy that was distinctive to the Mormons proved unacceptable, and was officially forbidden in 1890 in order to promote Utah's claims to statehood, although some 30,000 polygamous relationships still continue there today. The Fundamentalist Church of Jesus Christ of Latter Day Saints caused problems in 2005, not least because its members openly practice polygamy.

The religious situation was far from constant. In the late nineteenth century Protestantism had in part defined itself in opposition to the Catholicism of recent immigrants, especially Irish, Italians and Poles. This remained important in the first half of the twentieth century. In part as a result, local and national differences between the Democrats and Republicans frequently related to religious divides. The Democrats were more open to minorities, both Catholics and Jews, particularly in the big cities where both were important sections of the electorate. The first Catholic Presidential candidate (Al Smith) and later, in 1960, the first Catholic elected President, John F. Kennedy, were both Democrats.

Although anti-Catholicism continued to play a role among some religious groups, there was a full integration of Catholics into American public life, such that George W. Bush's second nomination for the second vacancy in the Supreme Court in 2005, Samuel Alito, led to a Catholic majority there. This integration was followed by a religious reconfiguration. In this, many Catholics, alongside the Evangelical Protestants, sought to resist and roll back what they presented as the irreligious and destructive social revolution of the 1960s. As such, religious values were defined against what was seen as a tide of pernicious secularism.

This trend was given added force by a shift in Protestantism that saw the long-established and more liberal denominations – the Episcopalians, Methodists and Presbyterians – lose support and energy in the 1960s to 1980s. In particular, their ability to respond to geographical and social changes declined. Instead, the 'born-again' conservative churches, particularly the Southern Baptists, the largest Protestant body, and the Assemblies of God, became more prominent. By the early 2000s there were about 50 million Evangelical Christians in the USA. Americans were drawn to a 'fundamentalist' Christianity that focused on a direct relationship between God and worshipper, without any necessary intervention by clerics and without much, if any, role for the sacraments. Certain aspects of this Christianity, especially its charismatic quality, which was epitomized by the evangelist Billy Graham, had considerable appeal for other Christians. The theme of choice – of individuals choosing to turn to God rather than God choosing individuals – reflected an emphasis on personal belief and redemption. The language of choice and, indeed, consumerism was reflected in the sign outside the Emmanuel Baptist Church in Manassas, Virginia, in September 2005: 'Try God'. More generally, the increase in individualism and the erosion of hierarchical religions led to a Christianity that was custom-made by each individual.

Yet there was also an emphasis on orthodoxy. In reaction against the growing liberalism of the Southern Baptist hierarchy in the 1950s to 1970s – a liberalism that led to an interpretative, rather than a traditionalist, exegesis of the Bible and to a questioning of conventional Christian moral issues – there was a reiteration of traditional views, particularly after Adrian Rogers was elected President of the Southern Baptist Convention in 1979. Liberals lost their positions in seminaries; the literal truth of the Bible was emphasized; a harsher line on abortion and homosexuality was followed; and there were calls for the conversion of the Jews and for women to submit to their husbands. Rogers abhorred the idea of women clerics as well as the 'influence of postmodern culture', and he declared that Baptists reject 'inclusivism and pluralism in salvation, for these compromise the Gospel itself'. He was invited by both Jimmy Carter and Ronald Reagan to preach at the White House.

Other important trends included the growth in popularity of non-Trinitarian religions (which do not regard Jesus as the Son of God), such as the Christadelphians and Jehovah's Witnesses. Furthermore, the long-established Mormons expanded outside Utah, becoming, for example, one of the major religious groups in California. Scientology was a more recent success. Islam has also grown markedly, so that there are now about eight million American Muslims, although the potential political impact is lessened by the fact that only one in eight are of Arab origin (others come from Iran, South Asia and Indonesia). Conversely, 70 per cent of Arab Americans are Christian. Religious themes also played a major role in popular culture, as with *Raiders of the Lost Ark*, the most successful film of 1981, *The Passion of the Christ*, an unexpected major film success in 2004, and Dan Brown's novel *The Da Vinci Code* (2004), a leading bestseller. The theme of spiritual danger was also a potent one, as in the film *The Exorcist* (1973), and this and other horror films in part drew on a widespread concern about black magic as a direct challenge to Christianity. Black magic was not so explicit in many horror films, but the location of many plots, for example *Poltergeist* (1982) in suburbia, created a sense of menace as a normal part of life.

Television evangelists, such as Jerry Falwell, Jimmy Swaggart and Pat Robertson, used modern technology and became prominent and influential figures, just as Billy Graham had been. Indeed, in August 2005, when Robertson publicly called for the assassination of President Chávez of Venezuela, his call made a considerable splash. Accepting no barrier between religious conviction and public politics, the Evangelical groups pushed hard to back particular causes and candidates: Carter in 1976 and Reagan in 1980 and 1984, although Reagan turned out to be more socially liberal than they wished. Christian conservatism led first to the 'Moral Majority' movement, founded in 1979, and then to the Christian Coalition.

Opposition to abortion and other social policies linked Evangelicals to the Catholic Church. Pope John Paul II (1979–2005) was wooed by the Republican leadership, particularly Reagan, who saw him as an important ally in the Cold War, and George W. Bush. This has been linked to the Catholic hierarchy's policy in the Presidential election of 2004, in particular its criticism of politicians, such as John Kerry, willing to support abortion. The Catholic hierarchy had shown itself more forgiving of clerics who covered up sexual abuse by fellow clerics, but, as a sign of major shifts in American society, there was far less public willingness to accept such cover-ups by the early 2000s. The deference that the Catholic Church had relied on has greatly lessened. Furthermore, as an indicator of the tendency to contest issues in the courts, and also to relate causes to compensation, one of the major consequences of this shift was a series of high-profile settlements in sexual abuse cases that put successive dioceses under serious financial strain. The travails of the Catholic Church were of greater importance because, with the rise of the Hispanic population, it was of potentially growing significance in the USA.

The election of Bill Clinton as President in 1992 and, even more, his re-election in 1996, was a major blow to the political cause of Evangelicalism. More generally, the movement failed to achieve many of its goals. It also, however, contributed to, and reflected, a powerful sense that religion was normative in public life, as was a strong private faith. Both separated the USA from Western Europe. In the Presidential election of 2000, candidates vied to assert their born-again piety in a fashion that did not characterize, for example, Australian, British, Canadian, French or German politics. Naming the political philosopher who had most influenced him, George W. Bush replied 'Christ. Because he changed my heart'. As President, Bush backed the White House Office of Faith-Based and Community Initiatives, although, in assisting religious bodies to obtain federal money for social services, it was accused of a political agenda, not least trying to win Evangelical and black support for the President. Other politicians, and not just Republicans, also emphasized their personal faith, including Tim Kaine, who won the Governorship of Virginia for the Democrats in 2005. That year, there was considerable agitation about the alleged failure to celebrate Christmas as a Christian feast, and religious Conservatives pushed this issue hard, as in the 'Friend or Foe Christmas Campaign'.

Religiosity contributed to a situation in which many Americans were happy to describe themselves as conservative, the percentage describing themselves thus rising from 29 in 2000 to 33 in 2004, while those describing themselves as moderates fell from 50 to 45 per cent, although most were also religious. At the same time, polls indicated that, while many saw themselves as having become more conservative, they also thought that they were more liberal than their parents, and increasingly willing to support the legalization of homosexual unions and the use of marijuana, and opposed to the death penalty, even though there was also greater opposition to trade unions.

Convictions of a Christian worldview did not differentiate between religion and other forms of public and private opinion and conduct. As a result, Christian commitment was a major cultural impulse, and, as such, there was popular pressure to allow prayer on public occasions, for example, in schools, at graduation ceremonies and at school sports games. This was in response to one of the more proactive judicial deci-

sions of the liberal 1960s and '70s, *Leoman v. Kurtzman* (1971). In a determined attempt to maintain the constitution's separation of church and
state, the Supreme Court came out against anything that might suggest
a theocracy. Indeed, the three provisions then decreed for government
measures – that they should serve a secular end, accordingly have
largely secular consequences, and not lead to an 'excessive entangle-
ment' of church and state – provided the background for moves against
school prayer, school Bible classes and similar public provision of religion. The Supreme Court was responsible for such moves as prohibiting
the display of the Ten Commandments in schools and preventing
public-school teachers from providing remedial lessons at religious
schools. The local implementation of the Supreme Court's rulings
across the country proved a slow fuse for long-term dissension. For
example, it was in 1985 that the Court rejected the Alabama practice of
a minute of silence in which pupils could pray if they chose. In 2004
the Court listened to submissions on whether 'under God' should be in
the Pledge of Allegiance, but decided not to pontificate on its constitu-
tionality. In 1984, in *Lynch v. Donnelly*, it had been argued that such a
phrase made the non-religious feel less than full members of the
community.

Given the importance of such decisions, it is unsurprising that the
composition and attitudes of the Supreme Court proved contentious.
This was accentuated because of the liberal direction of the Court from
1953 to 1969, when Earl Warren was Chief Justice. During this period
the Court became much keener to extend its interpretation of the law, a
policy made particularly controversial because of its concern with civil
liberties, a field that bore directly on issues of segregation and freedom
of speech. The latter was extended, in particular by the *Brandenburg* decision of 1969, while in 1989 free speech was interpreted as protecting
those who burned the Flag.

The politicization of Supreme Court choices, in particular Republican
attempts to produce a more conservative court, formed the background
for bitterly contested nomination hearings, especially over Robert Bork
(1987) and Clarence Thomas (1991), the latter an appointment linked
to the Republican attempt to woo black votes. As part of a more general
shift in the judiciary, the Court became more conservative in the 1980s

and '90s, although it maintained the autonomy of the law and did not automatically find for governmental or Evangelical views. The importance of membership was shown in 2005, when Sandra Day O'Connor retired and William Rehnquist died, leading at once to promises of expensive lobbying. Culture wars played a role in the response to particular nominations. In 2005 conservative criticism of the nomination of Harriet Miers led Bush supporters to argue that she was a good choice for them because she was an Evangelical Christian. This made a mockery of the Constitution, with its provision that public officials should not be subjected to religious tests, but it captured the popular political assumption of the religious right that the Constitution, and indeed conservatism, was a matter for religious conviction, not judicial thought. After she withdrew, Bush nominated a more explicitly conservative candidate, Samuel Alito, who was subsequently confirmed.

The strength of religious commitment did not mean that Christians all acted en bloc, felt under pressure or even shared the same values. If more committed Christians voted Republican than Democrat, and their activism, including among the black community, helped to give George W. Bush victory in 2004, there were still many who voted Democrat. Nevertheless, however diverse in configuration and varied in impact, Christian commitment played a major role in society, politics and culture. Far from being episodic in its influence, this role was a structural component. Moreover, it played a part at local, state and national level. This part grew in the period under discussion, even though church attendance did not increase at the rate that might be suggested by some foreign presentations of Americans as a nation of Bible-thumpers. Indeed, church attendance does not appear to have risen in the early 1980s and early 1990s, even though it has been increasing since. Furthermore, the particularly ostentatious role of Christianity in the South, and the growing role of the latter in American politics, has made the issue of religion more prominent. So also has been the attempt by conservatives to use religious arguments when justifying the attempt to reverse what they present as the agenda of the godless sixties. This is not only an issue for Christians. Concerned about signs of serious social problems in the black community, the Nation of Islam emphasizes the supremacy (and responsibility) of men in the home and is opposed to abortion.

The conservative agenda was less static than might be imagined. At the same time that particular issues recurred, in part because they spoke to the powerful sense of grievance that provided much of the impetus behind the particular socio-cultural imagination of the conservatives, so others arose. New issues reflected both technological developments, such as the 'morning after' pill and stem-cell research, and social shifts, for example gay marriage. Embryonic stem-cell research and gay marriage both became particularly controversial in the early 2000s. Stem-cell research offered the possibility of major advances in the treatment of diseases, and in 2004 Ronald Reagan's widow, Nancy, actively backed it for the hope it might bring to Alzheimer's sufferers. The research was unacceptable to religious conservatives, however, because it involved the destruction of human embryos. They thus related it to abortion, a touchstone of evil on the religious right, and one that had totemic power for both sides. Stem-cell research was one facet of the desire for perfectibility that was a major theme in national culture; the popularity of plastic surgery and much advertising were other facets.

George W. Bush responded to the view of religious conservatives. In 2001 he confined stem-cell research to current stem-cell lines, which dramatically limited the prospects of research in the USA. A less rigid House of Representatives agreed to relax these guidelines in 2005, and to create new embryonic stem cells, only to meet with the threat of a Presidential veto. Some states, particularly California and Massachusetts, decided to press ahead with funding such research themselves: in a state referendum in November 2004 California agreed to spend $3 billion.

GAY MARRIAGE AND OTHER ISSUES

Gay marriage is another recent addition to the culture-wars battlefield. In 2004 it became a major issue when it was legalized in San Francisco and Massachusetts (the Massachusetts Supreme Court rejecting the compromise 'civil union' proposal). Large numbers welcomed it, but the conservatives sought to reverse the decisions, initially at the local level. The targeting of civil unions by conservatives led to hostile state Defence of Marriage Acts, as in Washington in 1998 and Texas in 2003. Some, however, pressed for a constitutional amendment to outlaw legalized gay marriage, which was presented as a defiance of God's law. This campaign helped the Republicans, while the Democratic candidate, John Kerry, was subliminally linked with gay marriage because he was a senator for Massachusetts. Votes in eleven states (Arkansas, Georgia, Kentucky, Michigan, Mississippi, Montana, North Dakota, Ohio, Oklahoma, Oregon, Utah) at the same time as the Presidential election led to a ban on gay marriage. After the election, George W. Bush continued to exploit the issue. He favoured a Federal Marriage Amendment designed to ban gay marriage and thus to supersede state law. This reflected Bush's personification of the country's polarization, although, in the event, he decided not to push for a constitutional amendment. In November 2005 Texas also voted against same-sex marriage.

Tension over homosexual rights had also led to disagreements between federal and state levels over the legality of same-sex sodomy between consenting adults. In 1986, in *Bowers v. Hardwick*, the Supreme Court decided that states could ban this, but it overruled this decision in *Lawrence v. Texas* (2003), and also rejected a Texan law that did so, and this was the ruling cited by the Massachusetts Supreme Court in 2004. Gay marriage was succeeded as a crisis by the Terri Schiavo case. Schiavo's husband wanted her feeding tube removed, arguing that she had no hope of recovery from her vegetative state, a view backed by doctors. Her parents disagreed and, from 1998, the case went to the courts, which found for discontinuation, despite opposition from the Florida legislature and Governor Jeb Bush. Outraged religious conservatives in Congress persuaded it to ask the federal courts to intervene, but they refused to do so, leading to political threats against the judiciary by Republican legislators. Schiavo died. To critics, the episode reflected a fetishization of life itself, as opposed to concern about its quality, a situation related to some of the views expressed in the abortion debate. This fetishisation reflected the widely-held belief that humans were directly created by God, a rejection of evolution. The right to die was also at issue in Oregon, where the Death With Dignity Act permitted doctors to assist terminally ill patients to die, a policy opposed by religious conservatives and the Bush government. The Supreme Court considered the issue in 1997 and 2005, when it was settled for Oregon.

Other issues in 2005 included the legality of retaining framed copies of the Ten Commandments on the walls of two Kentucky courthouses (the Supreme Court decided no) and of a monument inscribed with the Decalogue outside the Texas capitol in Austin (yes). The Supreme Court also decided in June 2005 that the medical use of marijuana was illegal, although laws in eleven states permitted its use, that in California based on a proposition (referendum) in 1996. Rhode Island became a twelfth in late 2005.

Religious issues were often closely interleaved with other sources of tension. For example, the use of public money for education vouchers at religious schools was in part seen as a way to subsidize the opting out from public school districts where ethnic integration had taken place. It was an aspect of the hostility to public education that is a major theme in particular constituencies.

CONTESTING THE PAST

Conservative religious views also rested on a more general critique of science. Fundamentalist Christians had rejected the theory of evolution from the outset. Their stance enjoyed considerable popular support, particularly, but not only, in the South and Mid-West, and, because of the democratic nature of local government, a measure of institutional backing. In 1925 John Scopes had been convicted for teaching evolution in Tennessee, where it was forbidden. Although the fundamentalists were castigated for intolerant ignorance, the state law was not changed for several decades. The Scopes trial itself was the basis of *Inherit the Wind*, a Broadway hit of 1955 that was made into a Hollywood film, and *The Great Tennessee Monkey Trial*, a radio play of 1992 updated in 2005. The issue was treated as a litmus test by liberals who, in turn, had their own paranoia, as shown by Edward Kennedy, a member of the Senate Judiciary Committee, when, in 1987, he opposed President Reagan's nomination of Robert Bork to the Supreme Court.

He anticipated 'a land in which women would be forced into back-alley abortions, blacks would sit at segregated lunch counters, rogue police could break down citizens' doors in midnight raids, children could not be taught about evolution'.

That year, the Supreme Court determined in *Edwards v. Aguillard* that teaching creationism (the biblical account) in the science classes of public schools was an unconstitutional erosion of the boundaries between church and state. In 1999 the Kansas Board of Education decided that creationism should be taught alongside evolution, although the guidelines were repealed in 2001 after considerable public protest had led to changes in elections in 2000. The topic nevertheless remained a live one. A creationist majority was put back in place in Kansas 2004, and in November 2005 it voted to introduce criticism of evolution into science lessons. George W. Bush seemed willing to support the notion of intelligent design, although not the strict creationism banned in state schools by the Supreme Court decision in 1987.

Intelligent design argues that an intelligent being shaped development, and is thus a form of creationism that does not mention God. This is seen as the form of creationism most likely to survive legal challenge, and has therefore been actively pushed in the 2000s, for example by the Discovery Institute. The intelligent design debate became one of the most prominent issues in American intellectual culture in the mid-2000s, appearing frequently in the op-ed pages of major newspapers. Attention focused on Dover, Pennsylvania, where the School Board required that teachers explain intelligent design alongside evolution. This led to a federal court case brought by parents claiming that this violated the constitutional separation of church and state. In November 2005 most of the Board was voted out in a local ballot.

Less distant history was also a source of major controversy. The culture wars involved the presentation of the past, and this became increasingly vexed as an important strand of political disagreement focused on the content of education at school and university. This was an aspect of a more general debate about the value of multiculturalism in American society. Bilingual education was a related issue, with the Bilingual Education Act of 1968 increasingly opposed from the late

1970s, leading, in the No Child Left Behind Act of 2001, to support for English-only teaching. Already in California in 1998, Proposition 227 had ended bilingual education, while, two years before, Proposition 209 had ended affirmative action for minorities. Supporters of multiculturalism in history lessons referred to recovered voices, and critics to a fragmentation that denied any sense of unity, and that made it difficult to produce more than a series of histories of minorities.

This debate acted as a background to the controversy over the release in 1994 of the draft National History Standards, which were intended to act as a voluntary system of guidance to state Boards of Education and other bodies. The Standards concerned outlines and study guides for the teaching of American and world history. The pressure for these Standards reflected widespread public and professional anxiety about the limited knowledge of history of many young Americans, including students at good universities, and the belief that this was largely the result of failing to teach much history at high-school level. History indeed had been largely replaced on the curriculum by social studies. This pressure led to the establishment of the National Center for History in the Schools at the University of California, Los Angeles. Their work on formulating the Standards was funded from 1991 to the tune of $2.2 million by the National Endowment of the Humanities (NEH, a body established in 1965) and the Department of Education.

In response to fashionable norms among educators, the emphasis in the draft Standards was on social, not political, history. More specifically, it focused on groups held to have been underrated in American history and public culture, especially women and African Americans. The draft Standards conformed to the new multicultural agendas that many academics (and others) were advocating. They led to a controversy that was touched off in 1994 by Lynne Cheney, a Republican, who, as head of the NEH under George H. W. Bush, had supported the project and allocated management of it to the Los Angeles Center. She condemned the draft Standards for 'their unqualified admiration for peoples, places, and events that are politically correct', a term of abuse designed to draw on populist hostility to insiders and received values. Cheney saw their consequence as anti-American, in that they focused on negative aspects and individuals, such as the Ku Klux Klan and Senator Joseph McCarthy, and not on praiseworthy ones, such as George Washington and the Wright Brothers. She alleged similar double standards in the treatment of world history, specifically a running down of the value and values of the West, and an account of the Cold War that placed the two sides (the West and the Communist world) on an equal footing. The Cold War was presented in the draft Standards as leading

> to the Korean and Vietnam wars as well as the Berlin airlift, Cuban missile crisis, American interventions in many parts of the world, a huge investment in scientific research, and environmental damage that will take generations to rectify. It demonstrated the power of American public opinion in reversing foreign policy [a reference to the abandonment of American participation in the Vietnam War], it tested the democratic system to its limits, and it left scars on American society that have not yet been erased.

There was no comparable critique of the Soviet Union and China. The Standards also ignored the established pantheon of heroes, both because the authors contested the interpretations that led to these choices and because they were opposed to the emphasis on great men in history.

The controversy over the draft Standards in part reflected the sensitivity of the Native Americans issue. It presented them in positive terms and criticized their treatment at the hands of the colonists. This approach failed to do justice to the complexity of Native cultures, which included much that would now be found undesirable or limited (for example, illiteracy and the absence of the wheel). It also neglected to point out that their relationship with colonists was not simply adversarial. What has been termed the 'middle ground' of shared cultural space between colonists and Natives involved intermarriage, as well as trade and military co-operation. Intermarriage is not a subject that fits with the notion of coherent ethnic blocks, let alone with relationships that were not adversarial, but it was important.

There was also a clash in the draft Standards between the essentially static values offered by an emphasis on – and praise for – Native Americans and the changeable nature of American (and not only American) society, especially in the individual striving for betterment and the collective pressures for change flowing from democracy and purchaser-consumerism. These, however, were not seen in positive terms. In contrast, there was a stress on working-class solidarity expressed through popular activism.

The National Standards rapidly became a subject for political controversy. Two Republican senators – one, Robert Dole, later the unsuccessful Presidential candidate in 1996 – introduced amendments to ban the employment of federal money for the implementation of these draft Standards. They also required that the money should be spent only on those who 'have a decent respect for United States history's roots in Western civilization', which was a critique of the search for other roots, for example African-American ones, and also of cultural relativism. Lynne Cheney had put the issue squarely in a political light. She argued that the election of Clinton in 1992, which led to her fall from office, had caused the Standards project to go wrong, and that it had spurred radical historians to drive forward their agenda. Other conservative columnists, such as Charles Krauthammer and Patrick Buchanan, and radio commentators, such as Rush Limbaugh, a prominent figure of the Clinton years and a bitter critic of the President, followed suit. Conservatives could not be expected to warm to being asked to assess Reagan as 'an agent of selfishness'. Such commentators were increasingly prominent in the 1980s and '90s as conservatism displayed increasing intellectual energy and a greater ability to challenge not only liberalism but also middle-of-the-road positions.

In January 1995 the Senate condemned the draft Standards as irresponsible and malevolent by a vote of 99 to 1 (the latter, Richard C. Shelby, a Republican senator from Alabama, sought even stronger action). Later that year the Secretary of Education also attacked them. In turn, Gary Nash, Director of the Center and President of the Organization of American Historians, claimed that the critique was an assault on a cohort of scholars, and both the American Historical

Association and the Organization of American Historians approved them. Once the controversy broke out, many prominent historians supported the draft Standards, as did liberal publications such as the *New York Times*, although some major historians who were not right-wing, such as Diane Ravitch and Arthur Schlesinger Jr, offered important criticisms of particular interpretations. Eventually, after the Standards were revised under the auspices of the Council for Basic Education, not least to provide a different account of the Cold War, and then released in 1996, the controversy became far less heated, although its legacy was divisive, bolstering the convictions of both sets of protagonists.

These and other debates were not restricted to academic circles. Instead, the culture wars in the USA took on much of their energy because of the large degree of public participation, which was often vitriolic. This ranged across American history, from relations between colonists and Native Americans to the treatment of recent events. Military history proved especially contentious. Many foreigners were surprised that the military records of the Presidential candidates during the Vietnam War played such a major role in the 2004 campaign, but this reflected a long-term political engagement with such issues. This was multi-faceted, relating not only to specific conflicts, particularly the Vietnam War, but also to their commemoration.

The controversy over the World War Two Memorial provides a good example. Congresswoman Marcy Kaptur had proposed it in 1987, but it was not officially opened and dedicated until 2004, significantly on Memorial Day, 29 May. Meanwhile, there had been serious disputes over location and funding. The Memorial was designed for the central axis of the National Mall in Washington around the Rainbow Pool and between the Lincoln and Washington Monuments. The use of so much of the Mall's open space for this purpose was controversial. An opponent, Judy Feldman, President of the National Coalition to Save our Mall, declared: 'if we don't have our public space and our commons, where do we go to celebrate, to demonstrate?', and the Coalition mounted a successful lawsuit to prevent construction of the Memorial. Under political pressure, however, Congress overturned this decision. The funds raised for the Memorial indicated the extent of popular support for the project. The first $7 million were raised through the sale of government commemorative coins, but the remainder of the $175 million required came from private donations, as did another $20 million for a trust to cover maintenance costs. The design of the Memorial also reflected the nature of the Constitution. The columns bear the name of every state and American territory, while the bronze rope linking them signifies the bond between the states.

The treatment of World War Two is bound up with the concept of the 'Greatest Generation', those Americans who came of age in the 1940s and fought the war. They have been widely honoured, not least as part of an implicit, and often explicit, critique of the '1960s generation', which is held to have abandoned their values, with damaging cultural and social consequences for the USA. Politics plays a role in this controversy, with the Republicans particularly keen to appropriate the myth of the 'Greatest Generation' (which is ironic because the war was waged by Democratic administrations). Military history, in the sense of the popular portrayal of World War Two, is thus directly linked to present-day 'culture wars'.

More generally, there has been tension over how to present American history as a whole. 'Consensus historians', such as Daniel Boorstin and Richard Hofstadter, were influential from World War Two until the mid-1960s. They offered an attractive, in the sense of both positive and readable, account of the national past, presenting a teleology in which a benign element was discerned. This was true of books such as Boorstin's *The Americans: The National Experience* (1965) and *The Americans: The Democratic Experience* (1975). In turn, revisionist radicals in academic circles challenged these accounts, keen to present them as complacent and to draw attention to tensions within American society.

This could also be seen in interpretations of particular issues, for example work on the origins of the Cold War, a crucial issue as far as the legitimacy of American foreign policy was concerned. Whereas scholarship in the 1950s had stressed Soviet aggression as the cause of the Cold War, in the 1960s there was a revisionist reaction that emphasized American responsibility, the expansion of American capital being allegedly linked to that of American power. This was a reaction to the perception of the USA as an imperial state, and was linked to bitter criticism of participation in the Vietnam War. In turn, in the 1980s, the post-revisionists returned to the themes of the 1950s, although this time with the added benefit of archival research. This shift was related to the renewed concern about current Soviet policies seen from the aggressive Soviet intervention in Afghanistan in 1979 and associated with the Reagan presidency. In the 2000s debates over responsibility for the Cold War and its consequences continued, although, in public policy terms, the conservative interpretation of it as a necessary and successful struggle was taken for granted by the Bush government. Indeed, a defence of the Cold War, and a view of American participation in it as successful, helped to vindicate current government policy. On the left, however, critics remained unconvinced, and continued to hold the USA responsible for the Cold War. The perception in the early 2000s of the USA as an imperial state also controversially affected accounts of earlier American history.

Controversies in the USA are often bitter, especially when they relate to ethnic issues. The treatment of black history is particularly contentious, and the emphasis on race and ethnicity certainly seems to be changing the way it is taught. For example, in 2000, in response to discussion of the Interior Appropriations Bill, the National Park Service submitted to Congress a report assessing the educational information at Civil War sites. It recommended that much be updated, not least to illustrate the 'breadth of human experience during the period, and establish the relevance of the war to people today'. Representative Jesse Jackson, Jr, and other Congressmen had complained that many sites lacked appropriate contextualization and, specifically, that there was often 'missing vital information about the role that the institution of slavery played in causing the American Civil War'. The treatment of the Civil War is particularly contentious, with the issue of slavery (rather than states' rights) highlighted in order to criticize ante-bellum Southern culture, and to present the South as 'un-American' or 'anti-American'. Thus controlling and defining the past becomes an aspect of current politics.

Charges of exploitation and of historic wrongs explaining present circumstances are contested, especially from the 'white South' with its sometimes aggressive and self-righteous sense of historical grievance. This situation is exacerbated when other issues such as gender are involved. Thus, the charge that Thomas Jefferson had had an affair with a black servant, Sally Heming, led to contention in the 1990s and early 2000s. The charge was seen by some as an assault on the integrity of the Founding Fathers, associating them with sexual exploitation. The emphasis on the relationship certainly seems to obscure Jefferson's achievements and is nearly always taken out of context.

The controversy also reflected the degree to which a strong sense of identity held by many (but by no means all) ethnic groups in America could lead to contention over historical issues, or, more usually, symbols. In the 2000s Italian Americans did not take kindly to ahistorical criticism of the consequences for Native Americans of the voyages of Christopher Columbus, since Columbus Day celebrations were important to their sense of self-identity. Some commemorations, for example Santa Barbara's 'Old Spanish Days', were not particularly contentious, but they all underline the variety of American public culture. In the American tradition, these particular celebrations are designed to complement the inclusive theme of national memory, seen most particularly with the Fourth of July celebrations.

Members of different racial and ethnic groups found their voices readily in the late twentieth century. These voices were frequently more radical than hitherto, reflecting, in particular, the opportunities created by higher education and by alternative publishing. A good example was provided by Paula Allen, who taught on the Native American Studies programme at Berkeley and sought to fuse the Native American tradition with feminism, arguing, for example in *The Sacred Hoop: Recovering the Feminine in American Indian Traditions* (1986), that Native American women benefited from women-centred values before white conquest. Controversy in 2004 over the position of Native Americans focused on the contents of the newly opened National Museum of the American Indian in Washington, DC. Some Native activists, such as members of the American Indian Movement, criticized it for downplaying the role of violence in the European and European-American conquest of the Americas, although a tour of the Museum indicates that the disruptive nature of European contact is clearly discussed. The public theme of the

Museum is one of reconciliation, the Director, W. Richard West Jr, a member of the Cheyenne and Arapaho tribes, declaring at the opening: 'At long last the culturally different histories, cultures and peoples of the Americas can come together in new mutual understanding and respect.' Earlier in 2004, at the annual Independence Day Celebration and Naturalization Ceremony at Monticello (where the oath of citizenship is taken on the steps of Jefferson's house), West offered a version of the official account of multiculturalism past, present and future: 'The demographics of the United States will change dramatically and materially within a generation, requiring that all American citizens respect and honor anew cultural difference and the vast benefits that diversity can bring to America's future – just as it has in enriching this country's past cultural heritage.'

Other Native Americans, however, contested this consensual approach. That year, they objected to an attempt made by a group of re-enactors to follow the Lewis and Clark overland expedition of 1804 to the Pacific Ocean, arguing that this marked the start of the end for traditional culture. The re-enactors alleged that they received threats of violence, while the Native leader, Alex White Plume of the Pine Ridge Reservation in South Dakota, the poorest reservation in the country, declared: 'Lewis and Clark brought the death and destruction of our way of life.'

Public contention over this and other issues was a background to legislative discussion and action. On 20 June 2003 the American History and Civics Education Bill passed the Senate by a vote of 90 to zero. The Bill created a National Alliance of Teachers of American History and Civics, and founded summer residential academies for students and teachers. Its prime sponsor, Senator Lamar Alexander, declared: 'This legislation will help put the teaching of American history and civics back in its rightful place in our schools, so our children can grow up learning what it means to be an American . . . When our values are under attack we need to understand clearly what those values are. And second, we should understand what unites us as Americans.' Education was linked to values, the legislation being intended 'to inspire better teaching and more learning of the key events, documents, persons and ideas that shaped the institutions and democratic heritage of the United States'. Those who received grants should plan programmes stressing the theme of 'unity amidst variety and diversity'. Alexander, a Republican, was open about his support for what he termed 'the traditional kind' of history: 'the study of the key persons, the key events, the key ideas, and the key documents that shape the institutions and democratic heritage' of the United States. History and 'civics' were therefore to be linked, with history used to support civic awareness and national identity.

CULTURAL SPACES

These issues may seem far distant from culture as generally defined, but they help provide the multiple contexts within which the arts operate and are perceived. The patronage both of institutions and the directly paying public is defined in terms of social and cultural preferences that vary greatly. This is true not only of regional and ethnic distinctions, but also of the spatial configuration of America. In particular, there is a contrast between city centres, which tend to see more self-consciously progressive and experimental artistic work, and suburbia and small towns, where the emphasis is rather on an artistic life that conforms to inclusive and unchallenging cultural notions. The former tends to focus on the individual consciousness, while the latter offers something for the family. This contrast can be glimpsed in differences in film and concert programmes, and in the types of plays staged, or public sculptures commissioned, or books stocked in bookshops and libraries. Theatre repertoires in suburban areas tend to be conservative in character and the individual works are generally unchallenging. Increased suburbanization was in part a product of the cult of the home, a marked revival of 1950s tendencies that reflected not only the appeal of suburban living but also a reaction against the real and perceived drawbacks of metropolitan life.

The cult of the home interacted with convenience and the problems created by the sheer size of the suburbs to encourage domestic and neighbourhood activities. The latter were seen with local sport, leading to the classification of 'soccer moms', and the former led to the major expansion of home entertainment. Hollywood was now brought more easily to the television screen, first with video cassettes and then, from 1997, with DVDs. The latter offered technological improvement – better pictures and sound and greater durability – as well as consumer convenience in smaller and easier use. The enhancement of home systems with big-screen televisions and surround-sound systems added to this trend. In 2003 only $9.2 billion was spent at cinemas compared to $22.5 billion on DVDs and (to a lesser extent) videos.

The extent of difference between metropolitan and non-metropolitan culture and society became a theme in culture wars. Metropolitan areas were seen as liberal, individualistic and lacking in values, while their non-metropolitan counterparts were presented as dull. In each case, the depiction was overly clear, if not smug. Thus, in 1985, Manhattan audiences could thrill to the opening of Horton Foote's comedy *Blind Date*, which was set in a small town in Texas. The plot centres on finding a suitor for Sarah Nancy, a visiting niece. One, Felix, proposes games: 'let's see who can name the most books of the Bible'. Dolores recommends to her niece a list of topics for conversation:

> One: Who is going to win the football game next Friday? Two: Do you think we have enough rain for the cotton yet? Three: I hear you were a football player in high school. What position did you play? Do you miss football? Four: I hear you are an insurance salesman. What kind of insurance do you sell? Five: What is the best car on the market today do you think? Six: What Church do you belong to? Seven: Do you enjoy dancing? Eight: Do you enjoy bridge?

In practice, question six would come earlier or the answer would already be known, since church membership helped to establish social links and aspirations as well as to define marital parameters. The idea of common interests was given a television focus in a passage in Anne Tyler's Pulitzer Prize-winning novel *Breathing Lessons* (1988): 'Today's question on *AM Baltimore* was: "What Makes an Ideal Marriage?" A woman was phoning in to say it was common interests. "Like if you both watch the same kind of programs on TV".'

Another set of regional stereotypes was presented in *The Dukes of Hazzard* (2005), a comedy film that presented rural Georgia in terms of rednecks, illegal moonshine and dirt roads. It was not only the South that was depicted in stereotypal terms. In Gary Braunbeck's short story *Safe* (1998), he presented Cedar Hill, Ohio, with blue-collar America seen as insecure more than aspirational:

> He managed through hard work and good solid horse sense to build the foundation of a decent middle-class existence; who works to keep a roof over his family's head . . . But never ask him about anything that lies beyond the next paycheck . . . Because this is a person who feels inadequate and does not want you to know it, who for a good long while now has suspected that his life will never be anything more than mediocre.

In contrast, playwrights and film-makers offered metropolitan sophistication or amorality, as in Neil Simon's comedy *Plaza Suite* (1968) and Woody Allen's films, such as *Annie Hall* (1977) and *Manhattan* (1979), all set in Manhattan.

At the same time, it is necessary not to reify suburban or inner-city areas. Each were, and are, very varied; and at the crucial level of individual choice, rather than organized provision, the variety helps to defy ready distinctions. This can be seen, for example, in magazine subscriptions. New technology and organizational practices also worked to challenge spatial distinctions. Living, for example, in an area without a good bookshop or an arts cinema became less important when books could be purchased, and music listened to, over the Internet, and films viewed on cable, video or DVD. In 2001 the iPod proved an easily used and successful hand-held digital music player, while in 2003 the launch of the iTunes Music Store revealed the large size of the market for downloading music.

Popular taste was generally at variance with critical guidance, but neither were monoliths and some distinguished works were well received. The dependence of high on popular culture was suggested by the importance of book-club recommendations from Oprah Winfrey, the most successful of the daytime talk-show hosts. Modern writers pressed her to pick books by current rather than earlier novelists, since her choice allegedly affected sales.

More generally, there was a sense of cultural volatility. Novels such as Joseph Heller's *Catch 22* (1961) encouraged a challenging of values and, in particular, deference. The Western, a crucial iconic source of cinematic myths, was reinterpreted to show a bleaker account of the West, as in *Unforgiven* (1992), and indeed of American history, with the US Cavalry responsible for atrocities in films such as *Soldier Blue* (1970) and *Little Big Man* (1970). The decline of the Western has been discussed in terms of the rise in popularity of a different form of frontier film, that of science fiction. The range of that genre precludes easy characterization, but a number of films challenged the notion of human superiority. This was particularly seen with *E. T.: The Extra-Terrestrial* (1982). Science fiction writers, such as Ursula Le Guin, similarly used other societies in order to comment on the USA.

At the same time, science-fiction films frequently presented adventure stories based on the idea of fundamental hostility between humans and aliens, and thus on the need for human vigilance. For example, in *Independence Day* (1996) the potent aliens destroy all they can, beginning in Los Angeles with those gathered to welcome them, and stop only when they are in turn destroyed. In the television series *Dark Skies* (1996–7) the advanced powers of the aliens are again deployed for destructive purposes and the seizure of control. In the satirical film *Mars Attacks* (1997) the Martians are revealed as particularly homicidal, delighting in their destructive capability and implacable until their explosive demise at the sound of American popular music. The Presidential science adviser explains that the approaching Martians are bound to be peaceful, because no advanced culture would wage war, but he is revealed to be a fool.

NEW VOICES

In artistic terms, the rejection of existing canons went further in some genres than others. Thus, in painting, Pop Art sought to conflate the comic-book character of popular culture with established methods. Similarly, Abstract Expressionists, such as Jackson Pollock, broke with conventional methods, not only of representation but also ways of painting. John Adams did the same in opera, as in *Nixon in China* (1987) and *The Death of Klinghoffer* (1991), while Wynton Marsalis took forward the fusion of jazz and classical music with his symphony *All Rise* (1999). Underground poetry was particularly important in the 1960s, associated especially with the Beat Generation, a group that had become notable in the 1950s. They rejected commercialism and searched for new rhythms and vocabulary, which led them to look to jazz music and Eastern philosophies, particularly Buddhism. Allen Ginsberg coined the term 'flower power', and the hallucinogenic drugs he and others used had an influence on his writing. Drug overdoses, however, were to lead to the death of leading musicians and actors, including Jim Morrison (1971) and River Phoenix (1993).

Other challenges to existing canons came from the deliberate cultivation of distinctive voices by members of groups that had hitherto enjoyed fame only by integrating with the consensus, particularly blacks, feminists and Native Americans, not that any of these groups was uniform in character. Writers such as Toni Morrison explicitly engaged with racism and won recognition, winning the Nobel Prize for Literature in 1993. August Wilson co-founded the Black Horizon Theater Company in 1968 and produced a series of plays in which he depicted aspects of the recent black experience, portraying white-dominated society as a largely uncaring background. The long aftermath of slavery plays a role in several of his plays, for example *The Piano Lesson* (1988). Many of the characters he depicted survived by resorting to crime, and the overlap between that and 'normal' life was a central feature, as in *Fences* (1987), which won a Pulitzer Prize. Set in Pittsburgh in the late 1960s, *Two Trains Running* (1990) presented an ex-crap-game runner newly wealthy from selling coffins to families bereaved by murder. A different black voice was provided in Spike Lee's *She's Gotta Have It* (1986), a film centred on a male image of black female sexuality. The black and Native American experience also inspired writing by whites, as in William Eastlake's *Dancers in the Scalp House* (1975), an attempt to present Native thought that engages in particular with their holistic view of the environment, and Arthur Kopit's play *Indians* (1968), which linked the Vietnam War to the destruction of Native life. The latter was given a wider audience when it was made into a film,

Buffalo Bill and the Indians; or, Sitting Bull's History Lesson (1976). Hollywood also provided the perspective of women who reject and seek to escape a male-centred society in *Thelma and Louise* (1991). Immigrant groups varied in the degree to which the processes of acculturation and ethnic definition led to the adoption of particular cultural voices that affected the mainstream. Their character in part reflected the nature of the culture from which they sprang. Thus, Cuban Americans tended to be more affluent and educated than many immigrants from Mexico, and this was reflected in the vitality of their culture.

At the same time, the elision of difference was crucial for the success of many blacks, women, Hispanics and Native Americans, most obviously in the 1980s with the singer Michael Jackson, who sought to make himself less black, and with another singer, Madonna, who happily played to standard male fantasies. However, much black music attracted white backing precisely because it contrasted with established patterns. This was true of rap music, which developed in the Bronx in the 1970s, and which provided a way for white children, both then and later with the hip-hop generation, to irritate their parents. A similar attack on norms is seen in the violence of video games such as *Grand Theft Auto* (1998).

A reiteration of the norm, however, characterized many of Hollywood's offerings. It is always dangerous to read too readily from individual works and their reception to general social currents, but it is notable, for example, that the highly successful film *Fatal Attraction* (1987) depicted a career woman as unhinged and murderously demanding. Five years later, *Basic Instinct* (1992) offered another dangerous modern *femme fatale*.

At the same time, it is the variety of popular cinema that is so notable. Alongside the comedies, with their general theme of a benign order made awry by misunderstanding, there is the persistent adventure theme of heroism challenged or undermined by corrupt hierarchies or dishonest colleagues, themes in films as varied as *Dirty Harry* (1971) and *Mission Impossible* (1996). In *Sin City* (2005) the figures of authority, the Cardinal, Senator and policeman, are all corrupt. The themes of *film noir* can be applied all too readily to adventure films, as well as those about politics. To fit these and other approaches, as well as particular artistic genres, into political shifts is questionable. It is possible to suggest a dark pessimism in response to particular conjunctures, but it is also notable that the conflation of film and television viewing indicates a consistent preference for escapism, a situation similar to that in other national audiences. Culture as relaxation, however, does not preclude culture as stimulus, and for many this stimulus involves reflection about social values. This was true, for example, of the delineation of class in Tobias Picker's opera *An American Tragedy* (2005).

The overwhelming characteristic of American culture and artistic life is that of variety, although freedom of expression is constrained by parameters, as in other societies. Thus, the singer Janet Jackson briefly displaying a breast on prime-time television became a cause of contention and penalty in 2004, and the claim by a rap artist, Kayne West, that the government did not care about New Orleans' blacks was similarly contentious in 2005. As a reminder, however, of the cultural variety of the country, one of the most popular films of 2004 was *The Passion of Christ*, an attempt to recreate the last days of Christ's life that was designed to elicit religious fervour, and which, to the surprise of Hollywood, indicated the breadth of the audience for a religious film. Religious publishing is very big business. In opera, alongside experimental work there were representational operas with clear plots. This was an aspect of the reaction against the break with conventional approaches that had characterized the 1960s. Thus composers rediscovered melody, as with Joan Tower's *Made in America* (2005).

The economic importance of film indicated its wider role in both American society and that of much of the world. Hollywood's share of the world market increased greatly during the period, with the worldwide production and distribution interests of the American film industry becoming more important in the 1990s, although this was as part of a global industry in which crucial American icons were bought by foreign companies. In 1985 the Australian Rupert Mudoch bought the loss-making Twentieth-Century Fox and in 1989–90 the Japanese electronic conglomerates Sony and Matsushita took over Columbia Pictures and MCA/University respectively. Much of the world judged the USA through Hollywood films and they were a crucial aspect of 'soft' power, as opposed to the 'hard' power of military strength. This soft power was very varied in its message, with some popular entertainment exports, such as the television cartoon series *The Simpsons* (1987), providing a critical account of corporate America. Nevertheless, thanks to its entertainment industry, the reach of America into the imagination of the rest of the world is unsurpassed.

Chapter 6

Politics

It is all too easy when discussing politics to focus on Presidents and to provide an account that is structured by administrations and punctuated by elections. This provides, however, a narrative that implies that the analysis should be in terms of the interaction of politicians and electors. While important, that is not the sole narrative, or the only analysis. Like environment, demographics, society and culture, politics is a product of multiple contexts and wide-ranging interactions. Social and cultural shifts and expectations are particularly important in providing dynamism to this equation. So also are economic and fiscal developments and pressures. Because they tend to be underrated, this chapter will begin with them, echoing the comment made in 1992 by James Carville, Bill Clinton's successful campaign strategist: 'It's the economy, stupid!' The economy indeed played a crucial role in political popularity. Growth, employment and fiscal strength were far from constant during the period, and their variations were very important to the political narrative.

ECONOMIC DEVELOPMENTS

Buoyed by domestic demand and export markets, the economy grew rapidly for much of the 1960s, maintaining the expansionist trend of the 1950s. Annual real (i.e., calculated for inflation) GDP growth averaged

4 per cent between 1963 and 1972, but in the late 1960s economic problems increased markedly. In part, this reflected inflationary pressures that owed much to the decision to pay for the Vietnam War and the 'Great Society' programme of social improvement by borrowing, rather than taxation. Loose money policies led to an inflation that spread through the global economy. In addition, it was in any case increasingly difficult to control financial flows in what was a larger world economy. Whereas liquidity had been restricted to the USA in 1945, and the American government had then extended it to other governments in small packets, especially the reconstruction scheme known as Marshall Aid, by the late 1960s liquidity was widely distributed and therefore difficult to control, while balance of payments deficits contributed to a fall in American gold reserves. Furthermore, employing Keynesian demand management, the USA, under both Johnson and Nixon, was more prepared to tolerate inflation and price pressures than Germany and Japan. The different levels of inflation in particular economies made it very difficult to manage the international economy and exchange rates, and eventually shattered the Bretton Woods system of fixed exchange rates established in 1944: in August 1971 Nixon suspended the convertibility of the dollar into gold, allowing the dollar to fall. In addition, it had proved difficult to sustain earlier rates of American innovation and productivity growth, while, as a result of rapid German and Japanese economic development, the USA faced increasing problems, first in some export markets (not, however, computers, film or aircraft) and then in the domestic market. Much of the American economy was dominated by large corporations closely linked to major unions in a corporatist system in which the unions were bought off and the costs passed on to consumers. Innovation was stymied, not least because there was no wish to change working rules that would upset the unions. In contrast, the Japanese were far more innovative on the production line. In 1971, helped by rising oil imports, the USA ran the first trade deficit of the century, and this greatly hit confidence in economic management, and thus in the dollar.

Difficulties were turned into crisis in 1973 when the major producers in the Middle East grouped in the Organization of Petroleum Exporting Countries (OPEC) pushed up the price of oil dramatically.

They were angry at American support for Israel in its war with Egypt and Syria that year, but also keen to exploit growing world dependence on oil. The price per barrel rose from $3 in 1972 to $12 at the close of 1974. This hit oil importers, which included the USA, and fuelled inflation, damaging economic confidence. The prosperity, and thus politics, of the USA ultimately depended on unfettered access to large quantities of inexpensive oil. The price of oil was raised again in 1979, from $14 to $25 a barrel in six months, as a consequence of the successful Iranian revolution against the Shah, a crucial US ally. The crisis of the 1970s did not match that of the 1930s, but the USA suffered from 'stagflation', a combination of stagnation and inflation, which led to a sense of uncertainty and malaise.

The economy, however, returned to significant growth in the 1980s, and in the 1990s even more. It was helped by a marked fall in real energy prices in the mid-1980s, a fall that resumed after a spike in 1990 as a result of Iraq's invasion of Kuwait, and also by the continued capacity of the economy for innovation, not least by moving into new areas of demand, such as personal computers. The USA had the requisite resources for economic development, which focused more on the skills and investment required for increasingly complex manufacturing processes than on the raw materials needed for basic processes. The ability both to contain wage inflation and to raise productivity significantly was also important. It reflected, in particular, the social politics of the Reagan years, the limited role of organized labour in the American economic and political systems, and the influx of the post-1945 'baby boomers' into the workforce. The economy was subsequently to benefit from the important structural reforms of the late 1970s and '80s, since the Reagan years in particular saw a move away from the corporatist state. Capital invested per worker remained high, and the openness of the internal economy and market, accentuated by deregulation, encouraged the speedy diffusion of most efficient economic practices and capital flow to whatever seemed profitable, and, in the event of it not being successful, to other investments. The development of Silicon Valley near San Francisco reflected the strengths of the American system, not least the extent to which entrepreneurship was not dependent on bureaucracy.

America's position in the global economy was indicated by the rise in its share of global exports, from 15.7 per cent in 1993 to 17.7 per cent in 1999, and that in a period of major growth in world trade. There was a marked slowdown at the start of the new millennium, but economic growth then resumed. Trade policies, such as export subsidies for crops, helped in American economic growth, but so did the entrepreneurial and organizational strength of American business. There was a major development of multinational companies and a large number of these were American, 24 alone of the world's 50 largest in 1974. This pattern remained the case in the 1990s, but this was a decade in which the new economy of, in particular, information technology recorded major growth, while the old economy had to change its production systems and respond to markets with innovation and not the maintenance of former working practices. Intel became the world's largest chipmaker, Cisco Systems the foremost manufacturer of Internet networking equipment and, after a long battle, Google the leading Internet search engine. Some companies, such as Microsoft and IBM, had networks and annual turnovers greater than those of many states, and a small number of very large companies controlled much of the American GNP. Citigroup, America's most profitable bank, declared profits of $9.87 billion for 1999. In 2000 the world's largest drug company, GlaxoSmithKline, itself the result of numerous mergers, had a market capitalization of $172 billion, while in 2005 Wal-Mart, the world's biggest retailer, had sales of $312.4 billion, and 1.3 million employees and 3,800 stores in the USA. In 2004, the oil giant Exxon Mobil made more than $25 billion profit on about $300 billion sales. Its market capitalization was about $360 billion. AT&T is the world's largest telecom firm, with a stock-market value in early 2006 of about $110 billion. If its bid for BellSouth succeeds, the figure will be around $170 billion. Launched in 1972 as the world's first financial futures exchange, the world's trading of financial derivatives is dominated by the Chicago Mercantile Exchange. At a smaller scale, many American companies are world leaders, FedEx being the largest air-express carrier and Starbucks the largest chain of coffee outlets.

American economic activity, consumerism and openness to imports also helped to drive production elsewhere. This was especially true of

East Asia. By 1987 the trade deficit with Japan had reached $60 billion, and in the 1990s this was followed by a marked rise in imports from other developing Asian economies, particularly South Korea, Taiwan and China. In 2000 close to 40 per cent of Japanese car exports went to the USA. In 2000 the USA and Japan were responsible for 46 per cent of world output. In 2005, based on data for 2003, the Canadian Fraser Institute ranked the USA third in the world, behind only Hong Kong and Singapore, in its assessment of economic freedom, which was understood to be a function of institutional support for competition, property rights, personal choice and sound money. In contrast, China ranked 86th, a consequence of its state-directed pattern of growth. Nevertheless, the comparative advantage of cheap labour ensured that China became very important as a source of manufactured goods. The resulting contrast was readily apparent in the computer industry, with the USA concentrating on higher-end machines, and China on the cheap production of lower-end counterparts. As a result, in 2004 China was the leading world exporter of small, labour-intensive computers. Low costs led to major American investment in China, while by 2004 overall imports from China were responsible for 2 per cent of the US gross domestic product. The trade deficit with China, which in effect imposed a tariff on imports by undervaluing its currency, was a record $202 billion for 2005. This helped China to manage its transition away from Communist economics, but at the cost of a heavy burden to the USA.

Economic growth was not a constant across sectors. Acute competitiveness ensured that comparative advantages on the part of other producers rapidly affected American concerns. This hit heavy industry particularly hard; it suffered from a number of problems, including the impact of the value of the dollar in export markets and relatively high wage rates. As a consequence, there was recession, closures and unemployment in traditional areas of heavy industry, which were concentrated in the North-East and the Mid-West. This played through into the detailed configuration of political loyalties and issues, and also affected internal migration patterns. National policy was also affected, as with the pressure for quotas on steel imports in the early 2000s, which was successful in the short term.

Trends in the world of finance were also a crucial backdrop to political developments. In particular, generally cheap money eased borrowing and helped the USA to weather economic problems without shifting too much of the burden onto middle America (not that those made unemployed would have agreed). Since the dollar was the world's principal reserve currency within the period covered by this book, the USA has not had to hold official reserves as large as other states; in fact, in 2005 it held only 2 per cent of world reserves, a small percentage given the size of the economy. Japan, China, Taiwan, South Korea, Hong Kong and Singapore each held considerably more. This situation helped to increase sensitivity to financial, as well as economic, relationships between the USA and East Asia. In July 2005 China not only revalued against the dollar, but also announced that the yuan would no longer be pegged to the dollar, instead floating it against a number of currencies.

The USA was a major beneficiary of net capital inflows throughout the period ($102 billion alone in September 2005). This lessened the money available for other states, with detrimental consequences for their economy. From the 1970s the greater yields enjoyed by oil-producing states, particularly Saudi Arabia, were invested in the USA, a crucial aspect of the relationship between the two economies and states. Similarly, the beneficiaries of East Asian economic growth, particularly Japan, invested in the USA, thus helping the Americans to finance imports from East Asia. The inflow of foreign capital was encouraged with the ending in 1984 of the withholding tax on interest on income paid to non-residents. This inflow led to the large-scale purchase of Treasury bonds, which reduced bond yields and ensured that the federal government could borrow in order to cover expenditure.

The practice of coupling large budget deficits with tight monetary policy, a policy particularly obvious in the 1980s, helped to keep interest rates attractive in the USA relative to other parts of the world. Attractive interest rates kept the demand for the dollar strong in foreign exchange markets, since the rest of the world saw the dollar as a ticket to high interest rates. In the late 1990s and early 2000s, in contrast, interest rates were kept low in order to encourage growth, but foreign central banks still bought dollars in order to keep their own currencies low and thus aid exports. A strong dollar kept imports cheap, holding down the price of oil, and cheap imports kept workers content with lower wages, paving the way for a rejuvenation of capitalism. Thanks to the capital inflow, banks and other institutions could lend money for housing and personal expenditure, both readily and at low rates of interest. This helped to maintain economic growth and restore confidence after crises, such as the NASDAQ stock bubble burst in the spring of 2000; it also cushioned politicians and people from the consequences of their own profligacy. Having fallen below 11,000 in June 2001, and below 8,000 in 2003, the Dow Jones Industrial Average stock-market index rose above 11,000 in January 2006. The inflow of capital was also a product of the credit-worthiness of the economy and its underlying strengths; there was a sense too that financial management was more open, and less susceptible to political pressures, than the situation in other large economies. This openness encouraged confidence in American assets.

Government was dependent on easy money in order to sustain the borrowing booms that kept consumers happy; they also helped to fuel demand and thus both growth and imports. Consumers (in work) also benefited from the weakness of protectionism, for inexpensive imports – in the 2000s increasingly from China – helped to limit price and wage inflationary pressures. By 2005 imports were responsible for about 37 per cent of domestic purchases of goods. Wal-Mart is a particularly prominent customer for Chinese goods. As a result, the USA benefited from cheap Chinese labour, which acted as an alternative to greater American productivity in limiting inflation. American trade unionists, in turn, saw the poor conditions of Chinese workers, in terms of pay, social welfare and working conditions, as a cause of unfair and damaging competition. The trade deficit with China doubled in the years 2001–5. This had very different consequences in terms of local economies. Imports from China hit the textile industry particularly hard, but sustained activity in West Coast ports such as Los Angeles.

Even excluding China, the USA still faced major competitive issues and problems. In the car industry, which had a totemic significance to the economy, in addition to its considerable real economic importance, both direct and indirect, the American share of the total production of the USA, Japan, France, Germany and Britain fell, in percentage terms, from 87.1 in 1960 to 37.7 in 1970, 29.9 in 1980, 24.1 in 1990 and 23.5 in 2000; total production also fell, particularly in the 1980s and '90s. These figures omit Chinese and South Korean production, both of which grew. Furthermore, by February 2006, the General Motors' share of the American market was down to 23.4 per cent and that of Ford to 18.2 per cent, while Toyota's share rose to 13.3 per cent and Honda's to 8.5 per cent. There were also problems in the aircraft industry. In 1988 Boeing and McDonald Douglas (which later merged) recorded 877 firm orders for aircraft, but thereafter orders declined, although in 2005 the appeal of the Boeing 787 Dreamliner led to a recovery to 806 firm orders.

Nevertheless, the marked rise in American labour productivity, as well as organizational efficiency within business and finance, was important to the success of much of the economy. They permitted major growth in the 1990s in a tight labour market without inflationary pressures. By aiding profitability, productivity and efficiency encouraged fresh hiring of labour, which contrasted with the situation across much of the European Union. Low unemployment, which in August 2005 fell to 4.9 per cent, with the monthly average gain of 194,000 jobs in the year to August, further contributed to high personal expenditure and to the borrowing seen in a negative savings rate. Expenditure and borrowing led to the failure of George W. Bush's hope of reviving thrift so as to reduce the future burdens on social security expenditure, including Medicare. Nevertheless, he benefited from strong economic growth. Even bad news had a silver lining. The need for extensive rebuilding after Hurricane Katrina led to a surge in new orders in September 2005, although this, in turn, produced inflationary pressures, while the disruption to oil production led to a rise in oil imports, to $23.8 billion for September and $17.1 billion for October, which put heavy pressure on the balance of payments: the current-account deficit, which had been a record $668 billion in 2004 (5.7 per cent of GDP) was $805 billion in 2005, 6.4 per cent of GDP; and $225 billion, 7 per cent of GDP, in its last quarter alone. This rise of the world's biggest current-account deficit exposed the dollar to pressure, and the risk of it falling led to greater investor sensitivity to interest rates. Furthermore, in the last quarter of 2005, GDP increased at an annual rate of only 1.1 per cent.

The economy provided a crucial, and variable, context for political activity, at both the governmental and popular level, but it was not alone in providing such a context. Technology was also important, although its role attracted less comment. Major shifts in communications practice created problems as well as opportunities for politicians. At the outset of the period there was already pressure from public politics on that world of intimacy in which politics was controlled by bosses, in smoke-filled rooms far from public scrutiny. This was an aspect of the more general tension between democracy (government as a result of the exercise of the vote within a system of mass-franchise) and democratization (a system in which government and institutions are readily and regularly responsive to popular views). Democratization, however, was limited by ideological and practical factors, by structural features of the Constitution, and by aspects of political practice. These responded both to the oligarchic tendencies of politics and the inegalitarian nature of society, and to the practical difficulties posed by democratization. The difficulties included the variety of views expressed and the practical problems of rule by referenda, although these drawbacks did not prevent the replacement of the Governor of California, Gray Davis, in October 2003. His vanquisher, Arnold Schwarzenegger, declared: 'For the people to win, politics-as-usual must lose.' Davis, who had done nothing particularly wrong, was recalled (dismissed) because he was seen as part of an unresponsive political elite that devoted its energy to its own interests. The success by an outsider who presented himself as a non-politician was striking. Populism weakened party affiliations, enabling Schwarzenegger, a Republican, albeit a relatively liberal one, to win in a generally Democratic state.

Widespread popular hostility to the idea – and even more the cost – of government affected the possibilities for both populists and oligarchs, although there were still high expectations of its services. Hostility to government was a major theme of the Republican right in the 1960s, and from then became a more mainstream theme. This was caused by widespread hostility to the legacy of the 'Great Society', particularly welfare for others, and related taxation, as well as a suspicion of the probity of politicians and bureaucrats that was enhanced by the legacy of Vietnam and Nixon. Conservatives and liberals each liked the aspects of government (critics would say the military and social welfare respectively) that reflected their ethos and the constituencies they served, but both were able to criticize government, although the conservatives tapped this theme more effectively. When in power, they did so by directing criticism at agencies run by their opponents. Reagan was a particularly vigorous critic of government. The nature of general popular assumptions about government led politicians seeking support to propose a constrained role for it. This was particularly true of Republicans, but it also became a part of the Democratic repertoire, particularly with Clinton. In his convention speech of 1992, he proposed a government that 'expands opportunity, not bureaucracy', managing change, not controlling society. In his comparable speech in 2004, George W. Bush announced: 'Government should help people improve their lives, not try to run their lives.' For Bush, the emphasis was not on help but on the tax cuts that were seen as a desirable correlate of smaller government. The fiscal agenda was clear in his speech, which called for 'restraining federal spending, reducing regulation, and making the tax relief permanent'.

Technology and other measures that seemed to bring politicians and government closer to the public enhanced the possibilities for democratization in American politics. Ironically, however, the technological exercise that had the greatest specific impact was Nixon's taping of discussions in his office. This provided investigators with vital guidance to his knowledge of illegal acts. Their disclosure was a crucial issue in the closing of the net round him in the Watergate affair.

Television was very important in creating a sense of closeness, not least because its scope was greatly expanded with the televising of the proceedings of public bodies, including Congressional debates and hearings, as well as trials. On 8 August 1974 Nixon announced in a televised address that he was resigning the following day. Television also exposed politicians and the public sector to public scrutiny, most significantly with the televised debates between Presidential candidates and between Vice Presidential counterparts. In 1960 Kennedy famously was seen to draw an advantage over Nixon from the debates, while in 2004 George W. Bush was able to avoid serious blunders. As another instance of the impact of television, the images of Los Angeles police officers beating Rodney King in 1991 had a potent impact, underlining a sense of discriminatory policing; this made the officers' acquittal in 1992 a particularly sensitive issue, precipitating a major riot in the city.

Television also offered politicians major advantages in disseminating messages or, at least, images, and in reaching and affirming constituencies of support. This was more important than converting voters, since most elections, including that of 2004, were won as a result of mobilizing already existing support, rather than persuading opposing voters to change sides. Political programmes, speeches and advertising were drafted accordingly. Politicians happily played to the cameras, but stage-managed their appearances, whether in press conferences, interviews, mass-audience programmes and, overwhelmingly, advertising. Indeed, advertising expenditure helped to push up the cost of elections, and thus the oligarchic dimension to politics. The special election held in California in November 2005 to consider four proposals by the Governor, Schwarzenegger, is reported to have cost $300 million, with the hostile trade unions alone spending $100 million on critical television advertisements: the proposals included a curb on union powers, for example spending such sums without consulting members, and an extension of the probationary period for teachers. The furore over the cost helped to defeat Schwarzenegger.

Fund-raising also made electioneering a continual process for politicians. This provided important opportunities for lobbyists and those for whom they acted. Thus, in 2002, when the Republicans gained control of the Texas statehouse, for the first time in 130 years, they benefited from large-scale corporate financial support. The legality of this led, in 2005, to the indictment of Tom DeLay, the Republican leader in the House of Representatives (he resigned as leader, first temporarily and then for good); but the Texas redistricting in 2003 (an unprecedented step prior to a census) made possible by this shift in control, helped the Republicans to gain five Congressional seats in the 2004 elections. The Democrats were far from exempt from dubious conduct; 'politics as usual' also involved them in activity judged criminal.

The conflation of society and politics through the focus of consumerism led the devices of marketing and market research to encompass policies and votes. Politics fully entered the world of consumerism. This was accentuated from the 1960s, when the value of new design, as a device to enhance the image of a good or service and improve sales, was widely recognized. The impact of design consultants spread widely through society and affected political presentation. Like exposure on television, this moulded the norms of political appearance and behaviour. So also did the presentation of fictional accounts, such as *The West Wing*, a long-running series starting in 1999, with the fictional President Bartlett serving as a liberal counterpoint for George W. Bush, a point made by commentators.

The role of television also made the real, supposed or alleged affiliations of television channels, and particularly television anchors, matters of concern to politicians and also of public controversy. Thus, in 2003, conservative commentators derided the liberal *New York Times* when its editor and ethos were blamed for (a few) failures in journalistic integrity, while in 2004 Dan Rather of CBS became a news item when he seemed over-keen in his support of an inaccurate report about George W. Bush's unwillingness to fulfil his National Guard commitments as a young man, a mistake that led to Rather's fall. Other anchormen, such as CBS's Walter Cronkite, NBC's Chet Huntley, David Brinkley and Tom Brokaw, and ABC's Peter Jennings, had all become household names. The rise of Fox News to become the leading cable channel in the late 1990s and 2000s was seen as important to Republican fortunes, since it was more conservative and partisan than the other national networks. This conservatism applied not only to news reporting, but also in the general approach to social issues, not least law and order.

The rise of other communication systems, however, challenged the dominance of these networks. Cable and satellite technology led to the proliferation of television channels, which weakened the role of national networks and permitted the dissemination of more opinions, as well as gearing advertising to particular sectors of the population. The Internet also provided a challenge, not least as its bloggers became increasingly active as opinion formers. The NGOS (non-government organizations), which became more prominent in political and social activism in the 1980s and '90s, benefited from the extent to which new technology and its capacity for enhanced organizational capability, was not limited to government. New social, economic and political networks and groupings were created, and this established new patterns and hierarchies of communication.

Politics converged with economy and society, with voters also consumers, and each appealed to, in an increasingly searching fashion, as individuals. Technological application made this possible. Users were the crucial figures in the computer revolution, with systems designed for the benefit of individuals, and for linking and reaching out to them. In response, the targeting of voters became more sophisticated, and also more able to link individuals to national campaigns. If targeting was one response to the willingness of voters to act as consumers, so also was the determination to shape policies in order to secure votes. This, however, discouraged expenditure in areas not seen as likely to attract support, such as mental health. One consequence was seen in the aftermath of Hurricane Katrina. A report commissioned by the Office of Secretary of Defense from Stephen Henthorne, a Pentagon adviser who played a role in the relief efforts, argued that 'corruption and mismanagement within the New Orleans city government . . . diverted money earmarked for improving flood protection to other, more vote-getting, projects. Past mayors and governors gambled that the long-expected Big Killer hurricane would never happen.'

The shaping of politics did not determine its contents, but it helped to ensure that politicians had to respond within rapidly changing contexts. At the same time, one of the major responses was affirming or clinging to traditional assumptions and interests. This is a remark frequently directed against conservatives but can also be applied to liberals. Indeed, the process of political change encouraged this practice in both camps.

FEDERAL AND STATE GOVERNMENTS

One of the crucial elements of political history was the relationship between federal and state government. This formed both a background and a theme in the political history of the period covered by this book, and it matched a wider tension over the extent of central control. This was seen, for example, in banking, when the Depository Institution Deregulation and Monetary Control Act of 1980 both deregulated important aspects of the banking industry and extended Federal Reserve authority over the state banks, particularly in the area of reserve requirements. Prior to this legislation, the state governments set the reserve requirements of the state banks (banks with charters from the individual state governments), and these were usually much lower. Funds held as reserves earn no interest. Since reserve requirements are one of the tools that central banks use to control money stock growth, the Federal Reserve felt that it needed control over the reserve requirements of state banks.

Apart from disagreements over policy, the role of the states underlined the extent to which government was very much a coalition activity that required continual negotiation and compromise. Different assumptions about the responsibilities of government played a major role in the tension over state–federal relations. This had a range of manifestations. For example, in 1982 Congress permitted the reservations of Native American tribes to issue tax-exempt bonds for 'essential government functions', which were defined in a Congressional report as 'projects like schools, streets and sewers'. This, however, left room for contention over investments for economic development, a policy increasingly defined in terms of gambling after the Supreme Court in 1987 restricted the power of states to regulate gambling on reservations. This led to a surge in activity in the 1990s that highlighted the question of appropriate government activity, as well as the problem of competing local interests: states were worried about tax exemptions. Again, to follow the money, the financial benefit of federal government varied greatly by state. In 2003, for example, whereas New Jersey received from the federal government only 62 cents for every dollar levied in federal taxes, and California 76 cents, New Mexico obtained $2.37.

Tension over state authority also involved other issues. For example, the energy legislation of 2005 included a provision that enabled federal regulators to override local and state opposition to the construction of facilities to take imports of liquefied natural gas. These imports were predicted to rise, because electricity power stations were increasingly powered by gas, but in 2005 only four such facilities existed. None was on the West Coast, primarily due to environmental anxieties. The issue therefore fused energy and environmental policies and federal and state power. Another environmental issue reflected plans for the disposal of nuclear waste. From the 1970s these focused on a site under Yucca Mountain in Nevada. Several billion dollars have been spent on the site, but the state government has repeatedly delayed progress through the courts. More specific energy issues also affected, and were affected by, relations between federal and state governments. For example, Texas has kept most of its transmission system and power plants as a separate grid, since that keeps it under state control. In contrast, interstate commerce is subject to the Federal Energy Regulatory Commission.

THE 1960S

Although much of politics revolved around local issues of control, with the opportunities and problems they posed for financial benefit and expenditure, there were also major issues. The Civil Rights controversy of the 1960s was, in part, a matter of states' rights. This linked the issue to that of slavery in the Civil War, which helped to provide both sides with a sense of historical positioning and therefore legitimacy. The rejectionist Southern position was, in the end, overcome in the 1960s, because the Democratic coalition of Southern populism and Northern city politics that had long underlain the Party collapsed. In the 1960s this coalition was first put under strain under Kennedy, although he was less willing to support legislative action and support judicial and other administrative action than his language of hope might suggest. This reflected both his innate conservatism and the narrowness of his Presidential victory in 1960: by 34.2 to 34.1 million. This made his re-election in 1964 vulnerable. Northern liberals and black activists were both justifiably disappointed in Kennedy's conduct, although in June 1963 he used federal troops to desegregate the University of Alabama, successfully outmanoeuvring the State Governor, George Wallace. Kennedy went on to introduce a Civil Rights Bill, but his assassination in Dallas on 22 November 1963 led to a hiatus.

The Warren Commission concluded that the assassination was the work of a single individual, but the number of conspiracy theories that circulated testified not only to the strength of paranoia but also to a sense that the barrier to an alternative world, in which violence played a major role, had been surmounted. This was partly a matter of bridging the division between international conflict and domestic politics, most obviously with reports that the Cuban government or anti-Castro Cuban exiles, disillusioned by a lack of support, had been responsible. There were also reports suggesting that domestic politics were themselves more complex, with Kennedy the victim either of organized crime, or, in contrast, of sections of the military or intelligence world that wanted a tougher anti-Communist stance. In practice, it is far harder to organize conspiracies than to allege their existence, but the murder began a decade in which assassinations or attempted assassinations (Malcolm x, 1965; Martin Luther King and Robert Kennedy, 1968; George Wallace, 1972) played a role in politics. Partly as a result, it became easier to think in terms of conspiracies. The assassinations certainly indicated the consequence of one aspect of the broader context of politics: the prevalence of guns.

Kennedy was succeeded by his Vice President, Lyndon Johnson. In 1964 he won the Presidential election convincingly, defeating Barry Goldwater by 43.1 to 27.2 million votes, the largest margin, and highest percentage, achieved up to then. He also won the largest majority in Congress since that of Roosevelt in 1936. Johnson's subsequent reputation has been far more mixed than Kennedy's. This is partly caused by American participation in the unsuccessful Vietnam War, but also because, in hindsight, his looks and personality proved unattractive in a television age that gave posthumous plaudits to Kennedy. Yet in domestic politics Johnson was willing, and able, to engage with profound inequalities that Kennedy had largely proved willing only to talk about. This reflected the legacy of his particular Texas Southern populism, one that was far less geared to ethnic exclusion than that represented by Southern segregationalism, let alone the Ku Klux Klan. Indeed, one of his election advertisements in 1964 associated the Klan with Goldwater.

Johnson, instead, tapped into powerful iconic language with his talk of frontiers and society, affirming a possibility of national greatness, and being willing and able to link this to government action. The notion of social betterment through legislation bore testimony to Johnson's early start as a protégé of Roosevelt and an agent of the New Deal, and also to his long experience in Congress: in the House of Representatives from 1937 to 1948 and in the Senate from 1948 to 1960, from 1955 as majority leader. Another election advertisement in 1964 attacked Goldwater for threatening the Social Security system, adding: 'President Johnson is working to strengthen Social Security'. At the same time, he was not seen as a challenge to big business, much of which had a corporatist character, and Henry Ford II even endorsed his candidacy.

As an agent of the New Deal, Johnson looked back to Progressivism, declaring 'unconditional war on poverty' in his first State of the Union address in 1964. His 'Great Society' programme entailed a marked rise in expensive social programmes. As a result of this, and of the Vietnam War, public debt per capita rose from $1,585 in 1960 to $1,811 in 1970 (as a result of World War Two, the figure for 1950 had been $1,697, but there had been a fall in the 1950s). Furthermore, the balance of payments deficit put pressure on the dollar, leading to a crisis of confidence in its value. There was major speculation in 1968 that it would be devalued, although in the event the official redemption rate of $35 per ounce of gold was eventually maintained.

More than legislative fiat was involved in the 'Great Society' programme. Johnson was also committed to betterment, and understood social mobility to mean the improvement of the entire population, not the enhancement of just part of it. As such, he looked back to his experience as a teacher and also to the wider progress, and social problems, of his Texan homeland. Johnson declared of the blacks in 1965: 'Their cause must be our cause, too . . . And we shall overcome'. Desegregation, which Johnson had earlier supported in the Senate, was moreover seen as a way to improve America's international reputation at a time of global competition with Communism, as well as to end a potential route for Communist subversion. The early to mid-1960s were subsequently to be praised by Clinton as a time of hope, and indeed they helped to shape him.

Johnson isolated the Southern segregationalists in Congress, ensuring that they no longer possessed the voting numbers to use the blocking device of filibustering. The weakness of the segregationalists owed much to the degree to which the moderate Republicans in Congress were unwilling to ally with them in order to thwart the Democratic leadership. Under Nixon, the Republicans were later to begin an alliance with the South that was to help give them considerable electoral power, but that policy first required the dismantling of *de jure* Southern segregation achieved under Johnson; as opposed to the *de facto* practices that were common in the Northern cities, where particular school districts were white or black. The Civil Rights Act, passed in 1964 with Johnson's eager support, banned employment discrimination on the basis of race, religion and gender; decreed an automatic end to the funding of discriminatory federal programmes; and beefed up the federal administration in order to fulfil these goals. An Equal Employment Opportunity Commission was created, and the Justice Department was authorized to be proactive in order to help the desegregation of schools. The segregationists termed this federal oppression; for them, it was a resumption of the unwanted Reconstruction of the 1860s and '70s. In light of the brutality of the Chinese Cultural Revolution of these years, talk of oppression was laughable.

A top-down legislative account of desegregation does less than justice to the pressure for change arising from direct black action, which had played an important role from the mid-1950s. Direct action took the form of demonstrations in the North, but, more dangerously for segregationists, there were attempts to breach and discredit segregation in Southern strongpoints, such as Birmingham, Alabama. Revisiting Alabama in 2005, Condoleezza Rice, the black Secretary of State, declared: 'I remember a place called Bombingham, where I witnessed the denial of democracy in America and where blacks were terrorized by rebel yells and nightriders', the first a reference to a Birmingham racist bombing of 1963 that killed four black girls. The willingness of local and state bodies, such as the Birmingham police in May 1963, to suppress any protests or breaches of segregation violently, and to do so in full view of the national media, now more immediate and potent due to television news, ensured pressure for federal intervention, which in fact was one of the main goals of the anti-segregationist activism. Federal Marshals were dispatched to the South, while

National Guardsmen were federalized in order to end state control over them. Protests involving buses and facilities at bus terminals, mounted by 'freedom riders', were particularly effective in encouraging federal intervention, because the regulation of interstate travel was a federal matter. The range of discrimination and the determination for reform were such that success in one sphere was followed by pressure in others. Demands for an end to methods used to prevent blacks from voting led to demonstrations and a violent response to them, most clearly in Selma in March 1965, and to the passing of the Voting Rights Act that year.

These episodes might suggest that the issue was a sectional one, but there was also to be a series of large-scale riots in black neighbourhoods in cities outside the South, particularly in Los Angeles in 1965, Detroit and Newark in 1967, and Baltimore and Washington in 1968, but also in Chicago, Cleveland, New York, Pittsburgh and many other cities. These riots indicated that a sense of lack of opportunity, and indeed an alienation that could, at times, be pointlessly destructive, were not only an issue in the South, but also affected black neighbourhoods more generally. Ironically, the major riots in Watts (Los Angeles) in 1965 occurred within a week of Johnson signing the Civil Rights Act of that year. Most blacks in the urban ghettos were stuck in poor housing, and their areas were generally short-changed in terms of metropolitan and state expenditure on infrastructure, as well as on new industrial and retail investment. Many of the riots reflected a particular sense of police oppression of blacks. The situation had not greatly changed by the time of the Los Angeles riots in 1992, touched off when an all-white jury acquitted the police officers who had brutally beaten Rodney King, a recalcitrant speeding motorist. The riots of 1965–8 produced potent images of the underside of the American Dream, prefiguring the very different Hurricane Katrina in 2005, and were exploited by Soviet apologists to argue that the USA was a fundamentally oppressive society riven by conflict. Radicals also suggested that the rioters were in some way part of the same struggle as the Viet Cong. This was a seriously flawed analysis. So also is any attempt to remove the more general rise in crime rates in the 1960s from a political context.

The political impact of the riots was to undermine 'Great Society' liberalism; it eased the reconciliation of the Republicans with the

South and gravely weakened the Democrat 'big tent' approach. At the local level, the riots encouraged whites to flee from the inner cities into suburbia, and also made it harder to maintain social and political cohesion in black neighbourhoods. Radicals – such as Malcolm X, the head of the separatist black Nation of Islam; Stokely Carmichael and H. Rap Brown of the Student Nonviolent Coordinating Committee; Floyd McKissick of the Congress of Racial Equality; and Bobby Seale and Huey Newton, who founded the Black Panther Party in 1966 – rejected the hitherto dominant influence of leaders (many, such as Martin Luther King, driven by Gospel values) who favoured gradualism rather than separatism, and who were keen to ally with white liberals. The Black Power movement, with its interest in separatism and willingness to turn to violence, was not generally representative of the black population, most of whom continued to support integration, but it helped to drive forward a divisive assertiveness and empowerment.

More than federal action and black activism were involved in the changing position of blacks. The degree to which the South was integrating with the national economy, which was dominated by Northern markets, manufacturing and finance, was also important. It created a sense of opportunity, particularly in such 'New South' centres as Atlanta, but of opportunity on terms. National employers were far less prone to adopt segregationist practices than local or regional counterparts.

NIXON

The 1960s are often remembered in terms of pop festivals and the alternative culture, but the politician who emerged victorious from them was Richard Nixon. This would have seemed surprising in 1963. Eisenhower's two-term Vice President, Nixon, had been the Republican choice for President in 1960, but he had been defeated by Kennedy in part as a result of fraudulent electoral practices in Illinois and Texas. Nixon did not challenge the result in the courts because he said the country was too divided: the election had indeed been very divisive. In 1962 his attempt to stage a comeback was thwarted when he was heavily defeated for the Governorship of California. This seemed the end.

An angry Nixon told newsmen 'You won't have Nixon to kick around any more', and ABC broadcast as a special 'The Political Obituary of Richard Nixon'. In 1964 the Republican choice for President was Barry Goldwater, a vocal hawk, who famously declared that 'Extremism in the defense of liberty is no vice'. Goldwater was backed by Nixon, and his principal opponents within the Party were the more liberal Nelson Rockefeller and William Scranton, both representatives of the North-Eastern wing of the party. In a clear sign of the way in which Republican politics was going, Rockefeller was booed off the stage. Nixon's return reflected both Goldwater's inability to sustain his position after his failure in 1964 and the growing weakness of the North-Eastern wing. Rockefeller was again unsuccessful in 1968, as was Ronald Reagan, since 1966 the conservative Governor of California. Instead, Nixon easily won the nomination, in part because he told Southern Republicans unhappy with integration that he sympathized with their views, and in large part because he was more of a coalition candidate: less liberal than Rockefeller and less conservative than Reagan.

The Democrats, in turn, were weakened by association with the Vietnam War. This led Johnson to pull out from standing for re-election and also hit his Vice President, the eventual Democratic nominee, Hubert Humphrey. The Democratic coalition fractured over the war and the pace of integration. Opposition to the war tended to be strongest among liberals, and they also backed welfare and integration to an extent that the pro-war camp was increasingly unwilling to countenance. By 1968 the war was clearly going badly, while conscription ensured that it was a direct issue, not least for the articulate and demanding middle class. The volatility of the political atmosphere also owed something to the new-found assertiveness and radicalism of large sections of the young. Their illegal drug culture demonstrated the breakdown of established social and political practices.

The Democrats were also hit in 1968 by the ending, by an assassin's bullet, of the liberal hope for President, Robert Kennedy, and by the leaching of support in the South (but also in Northern cities) to the segregationalist third-party candidate, George Wallace, the Governor of Alabama, who was to carry Georgia, Alabama, Mississippi, Louisiana and Arkansas in the Presidential election. Wallace's populism hit hard at the Democratic coalition and was given added political direction by his opposition to the anti-war movement and to the counter-culture. He brought together important strands on the American right, not least an ardent patriotism, including firm support for the war. His running mate, Curtis LeMay, was a bellicose former Air Force general, and critical demonstrators chanted 'Bombs Away. With Curtis LeMay'.

Nixon was elected in 1968 with 43.4 per cent of the votes (31.8 million), compared to 42.7 per cent for Humphrey (31.2 million) and 13.5 per cent for Wallace (9.9 million). Outside the North-East, Humphrey carried only Washington State, Hawaii, Texas, Minnesota, Michigan and West Virginia. The election reflected the increased conservatism of the South, although that partly arose from there being a Southern candidate in the shape of Wallace.

Nixon was less rigid in office than might have been anticipated. Apart from abandoning South Vietnam and ending the draft, he was responsible for a reconciliation with China, including a visit to Beijing, that was a striking contrast to the long legacy of Republicans accusing Democrats and the State Department of 'selling out' (Nationalist) China, which after 1949 controlled only Taiwan. Furthermore, although Nixon was keen to win over the South, there was no prospect of any resumption of segregation.

In fiscal policy, he had to cope with inflation, which had gathered pace from 1965, fuelled by a major loosening of the money supply by the Federal Reserve. The Consumer Price Index rose from 2.9 per cent in 1967 to 5.4 per cent in 1969 and 5.9 per cent in 1970. In response, Nixon, authorized by Congress, which, in 1970, had given the President authority to impose wage and price controls, struggled to maintain continuity. The reality under this bland remark was a fiscal policy of some confusion, with Nixon imposing, in August 1971, the wage and price controls that he had promised, in 1969, he would never turn to. This was the first time such controls had been imposed in peacetime. Phase One froze wages and prices for 90 days, followed by a Phase Two, from November 1971 to January 1973, that set standard rates for labour contracts and price increases, to be administered by the Pay Board and the Price Commission respectively. In 1971 Nixon also imposed a 10 per cent surtax on imports, in a desperate attempt to tackle the deficit.

Rising prices and unemployment contributed greatly to a sense of uncertainty. Hitting savings, inflation rose to 12 per cent by 1974, having been only a quarter of that in 1967, while unemployment rose to 6 per cent in 1973.

Pressure on the fixed value of the dollar had led West Germany, which was exporting heavily to the USA, to allow the Deutsche Mark to float upwards against the dollar in May 1971. This was a major challenge to the Bretton Woods system, although the West Germans sought a realignment of fixed exchange rates, not the end of the system. Throughout the 1960s the USA had outpaced money stock growth in most other countries, kindling inflation in the USA. To keep the dollar from depreciating in accordance with the fixed exchange-rate regime, other countries bought up excess dollars with their own currencies, adding to the growth of their money stock. They could have forced the USA to redeem excess dollars in gold, but everyone knew that there was insufficient gold to redeem all the dollars. This fixed exchange-rate system was forcing other countries to accelerate their own money stock growth, keeping inflation rates in other countries growing in step with US inflation rates. Thus, the fixed exchange-rate system led to the US exporting inflation to the rest of the world. France was the least happy about this situation, and in 1971 began demanding that the US redeem dollars held by France into gold, which forced the world to abandon the Bretton Woods fixed exchange-rate system. In August 1971, in the face of the massive foreign holdings of dollars that arose from a negative balance of trade, and the obligation, if required, to redeem them in gold, Nixon suspended the convertibility of dollars into gold, the crucial element that had anchored fixed exchange rates. In turn, the Smithsonian Agreement reached that winter created a new system of fixed rates, with the dollar devalued against the Deutsche Mark, the yen, the Swiss franc and gold, but the agreement collapsed in 1973, in part because of a loosening of price and wage controls after Phase Two came to an end. As a result of a flight from the dollar, the USA devalued it by 10 per cent in February 1973, but West European governments now preferred to float their currencies against the dollar, and the Smithsonian Agreement collapsed.

Despite the problems of government, Nixon was helped politically by his ability to define his constituency in terms of a 'silent majority', a term he used in 1970, which summed up the idea that the consensus was naturally conservative. In practice, however, Congressional activism on social issues revealed that there was a path between left-wing radicalism and Nixon's definition of appropriate stability. This activism extended to environmental policy with the Occupational Safety and Health Act (1970) and the National Air Quality Control Act (1971). It was matched by the Supreme Court, most prominently in the *Roe v. Wade* decision of 1973, which established abortion as a right by constructing the constitutional right to privacy to cover abortion. A cynic, Nixon, however, had little time for activism, in particular if it challenged his constituency. He saw big business as a crucial interest, and had scant interest in environmentalism. In 1970 Walter Hickel was sacked as Interior Secretary after he had alienated oil interests by his concern about pollution. In 1971 Nixon responded to opposition from the motor industry and stopped regulations that would have required the installation of air bags in cars, an expensive way to save lives.

Serious divisions within the Democratic Party eased Nixon's position as it struggled to respond to the more radical agenda of the late 1960s, and to make its liberalism more broadly popular. This policy challenged support from blue-collar constituencies, particularly in the Northern cities, support that was already qualified by the association of the Party with racial integration. Indeed this had hit the Democrats badly in the mid-term elections of 1966. The resulting tension was seen during the Democratic National Convention in August 1968, when the police force of Chicago, a corrupt Democratic fiefdom under Mayor Richard Daley, set about radical demonstrators with alacrity. In 1972 the Democrats chose a liberal candidate as their Presidential candidate, George McGovern, a noted critic of the Vietnam War, who defeated Humphrey for the nomination. Nixon, however, easily beat him, with one of the largest margins of the period: 47.1 million to 29.1 million votes. McGovern carried only Massachusetts and the District of Columbia. The Democrats had lost much of their middle-class constituency, although the blacks still gave them firm support. Most voters saw McGovern as too radical. He changed the system of Democratic primaries, increasing female and minority representation, and made the party more of a radical and less of a coalition-building force.

Before being shot, badly wounded and withdrawing from the race, Wallace again acted as a spoiler, in another hurrah for third-party politics. Wallace represented a Southern separatism that, however, was to be replaced by a determination to become powerful within the major political parties. This saw Jimmy Carter (Georgia) and Bill Clinton (Arkansas) become the only Democratic Presidents after Johnson, and Al Gore (Tennessee) come closer to victory in 2000 than John Kerry (Massachusetts) in 2004. Furthermore, in the 1990s Newt Gingrich (Georgia), Phil Gramm and Tom Delay (both Texas) and Trent Lott (Mississippi) became crucial Republican Congressional figures.

Nixon's political dominance did not assuage his paranoia, and indeed these were years of radical opposition to the state, most prominently with the terrorism of the left-wing Weathermen movement and also with widespread anti-war protest, which revived markedly in 1969. Most of the demonstrations were peaceful, but the government focused on what it saw as subversion. Indeed, this divisive notion entered the mainstream with a hostile classification of the anti-war movement and liberals in general as damaging, unpatriotic and un-American. Instead, there was praise for those presented as true Americans. In 1970 anti-war activism was taken further, in part in response to the breaching of Cambodian neutrality. Unable to cope with the resulting disruption short of using force, state governors reacted harshly, most prominently on the campus of Kent State in Ohio, where the poorly controlled use of National Guardsmen left four students dead. In Berkeley another student was killed when Governor Reagan sent police against a people's park created on unused ground. There were also pro-war demonstrations, and the war played a stronger role in polarizing opinion in 1970 than it had for much of the 1960s. Nixon sought to use his call to patriotism to detach Democratic voters from their party.

Convinced that he and the government were the target of conspiracies, Nixon displayed some of the phobias seen earlier with J. Edgar Hoover, but translated them to the particular circumstances of the radical fringe of the period and the challenge from the anti-Vietnam movement. This involved Nixon in encouraging a systematic campaign of illegality, including telephone tapping and break-ins. The CIA kept files on about 10,000 Americans, while the Committee to Re-elect the President (CREEP), and a group organized in 1970 known as the 'plumbers', were active in dirty tricks and illegal acts against those defined as enemies of the President. The break-in on 17 June 1972 at the headquarters of the Democratic National Committee, in the Watergate Building in Washington, was only part of this process, but it was the act that brought the edifice down. Ironically, discovering Democratic plans, as part of an illicit campaign to weaken the Democrats, was unnecessary because Nixon was in a strong position to win the 1972 election. Before this landslide victory, the FBI had already investigated the break-in and had linked it to Nixon's re-election campaign. There were suggestions of malpractice by John Mitchell, the Attorney-General, but not yet by Nixon.

The long aftermath of the discovery of the break-in, however, over-shadowed the second term. Nixon's scorched-earth policy towards the investigation, first by the press and then by the Senate investigating committee, took the form of political and legal obstruction, but, in the end, he was forced in August 1974 to resign for his conspiracy to obstruct justice, thus avoiding impeachment. The House Judiciary Committee had voted to impeach him on three counts, including viola-tion of the Constitution. Since his Vice President, Spiro Agnew, a bitter critic of radicals, had also had to go for tax evasion in 1973, the new President was Gerald Ford, a more moderate Republican Congressman who had replaced Agnew.

The Watergate scandal led not only to the fall of Nixon, but also to a crisis of confidence in national leadership, one that left a powerful legacy in terms of the role of conspiracy theories in fiction and on the screen. Nixon's paranoid response to opposition and his obsessive concern about security were in truth more a personality problem than a sign of breakdown in the American political system, but that was unclear to many contemporaries. It is easy to understand why the Democratic majority in the Senate in 1973 decided to investigate the Watergate issue. Not only did this provide an opportunity for partisan action, but, in addition, the willingness of Nixon to break the law raised the prospect that he would use practices such as threatening not to renew federal licences for businesses, for example television broadcasters, in order to hit the Democratic Party and its contributors. The episode also raised issues of Presidential power, particularly as the Senatorial Special Committee on Presidential Campaign Activities faced obstruction to its investigations. An increasingly stressful Nixon tried to stop his aides testifying, and to prevent access to the tapes of his conversations with his aides, while the sacking of the independent special prosecutor, Archibald Cox, in October 1973 was seen as a serious abuse. This pressure, however, did not succeed. The Supreme Court voted unanimously in 1974 to force Nixon to hand over the tapes. The Senatorial Special Committee's televised hearings ensured that the public was given access to information about governmental misdemeanours, and allowed to make up its own mind, to an unprecedented extent. In response to Nixon's policies and his ability to sustain himself in office for so long during the crisis, Congress sought to put limits on the presidency, particularly with the War Powers Act. Congressional investigations of the CIA and FBI in 1975 led to the establishment in both houses of permanent committees to oversee intelligence operations.

If Watergate overshadowed Nixon's second term, for most Americans it was recorded in a growing sense of economic crisis. Inflation had been driven up by a bad harvest in 1972 (and food prices continued to rise at more than 10 per cent for 1973 and for most of 1974) and by the rising price of oil, which led to a 39 per cent increase in retail fuel prices between September 1973 and May 1974. This pressed hard on Phase Three of wages and prices policy, a quasi-voluntary phase that began in January 1973 but that had to be suspended in June 1973 in favour of a 60-day freeze. Phase Four, which began in August 1973 and lasted until April 1974, maintained controls in some industries, but, by early 1974, annual inflation was rising at a rate of 15 per cent. Inflation, which Ford referred to as 'public enemy number one', pressed on a society that was not enjoying its customary growth. Far from it: average annual growth in real GDP fell to minus 0.06 in 1974 and minus 1.2 per cent in 1975. Whereas real hourly compensation for workers had increased at an average annual rate of 3.4 per cent in the years 1962–9 and 2.7 per cent in the years 1970–73, it then fell to minus 0.3 per cent in the years 1973–5. The Dow Jones Industrial Average, which had risen to over 1,000 in November 1972, fell to 577.6 in 1974. The fall in stock-market shares was such that there was a real loss of 35 per cent in the years 1964–74. These statistics meant the wreckage of the aspirations of many individuals.

FORD AND CARTER

Ford suffered from the economic consequences of the 1973 oil-price hike and from the legacy of the Vietnam War. The full pardon he gave to Nixon in September 1974 was also politically inopportune. It contributed greatly to the sense of national cynicism and disillusionment, hit Ford's approval rating and helped the Democrats win the 1974 midterms. Ford had tried to draw a line under the recent past, also offering those who had evaded military service under the draft a form of leniency. Congress sought to respond to the economic crisis by turning to traditional remedies, increasing expenditure on job creation and welfare, only for much of the legislation to be vetoed by Ford. Standing against Jimmy Carter in 1976, Ford lost by 47.9 per cent (39.2 million) to 49.9 per cent (40.8 million) of the popular vote, in a vote against the greying of the American dream and also for the outsider. If Carter's majority was a modest one, it was larger than that of Nixon in 1968, although he had also had Wallace to contend with. A combination of stagnation and inflation led to a widespread sense of malaise. This was accentuated by what was presented as a breakdown in the social fabric, as seen in particular with rising crime rates. Cities were the maelstrom of this crisis, and New York neared bankruptcy in 1975. Problems were not restricted to the North-East and the Rustbelt. In the Los Angeles area, the cost of living rose 10.4 per cent from June 1973 to June 1974, while the wages of the average factory worker rose by only 3.3 per cent. Bombs contributed to an unsettled political atmosphere in the city. There were bombs in Los Angeles in 1974, including in the downtown industrial area and at the airport.

An anti-authoritarian theme, critical of government, was seen in many films, such as *All the President's Men* (1976), an account of Watergate. Authority, at all levels, was also seen as corrupt and dangerous in a range of films, ranging from *Chinatown* (1974) to *Apocalypse Now* (1979). The vacuous quality of affluent society was a theme of *Shampoo* (1975), and a wider alienation in films such as *Taxi Driver* (1976). An emphasis on crisis has, however, to be set in context. Compared to the failure in the Algerian War that had led to the fall of the Fourth Republic in France and to the crisis of governability and public finances in Britain in the years 1973-6, the USA was not particularly in difficulties as a governmental and political system. It proved possible to remove Nixon by constitutional means and to end the Vietnam War without a major political breakdown. The economic crisis, however, was more serious.

Due to the onset of serious problems during the Ford presidency, Carter was the short-term beneficiary of this sense of malaise, but it then came to characterize his presidency. Carter's progressivism did not win him continuing support, and was unable to overcome important differences between sectional interests. Carter also seemed a less than competent director of the government. Monetary policy was loosened in 1977, contributing to inflation and hitting the value of the dollar, which also fell because growth after the recession of 1974-5 fed into imports (including oil) rather than comparably increasing exports. The dollar fell in the second half of 1977 by 10 per cent against the Deutsche Mark and 10.3 per cent against the yen. There was also a fresh combination of the problems of the early 1970s, not least the major hike in oil prices in 1979 as a result of the Iranian revolution. Prior to that, the economic rebound after the economic crisis of 1974-5 had been only a modest one, and, although the unemployment rate fell, the rise in corporate and personal earnings had been less than that in the years 1970-73. Furthermore, there were successive rises in inflation in 1978, 1979 and 1980, although the government avoided the temptation of mandatory wage and price controls, preferring voluntary guidance. The oil crisis of 1979 contributed to a global economic downturn that helped the USA into recession in 1980.

The humiliation of the failure to rescue the American hostages held captive by Iranian radicals in the Tehran Embassy, particularly the unsuccessful rescue mission of April 1980, was scarcely a second Vietnam. Nevertheless it combined with other factors to associate Carter with repeated failure. Just as politics under Nixon had shrunk, or, at least, appeared to shrink to the Watergate case, so for Carter and the hostages. On the heels of Vietnam, the trauma arising from the hostage crisis and the failed attempt at rescue fuelled a sense of decline and desire for rejuvenation that Reagan understood and exploited.

THE REAGAN YEARS

Ronald Reagan was the beneficiary of this unpopularity. His sunny optimism provided encouragement, while his preference for homely dictums over sophisticated analysis helped him with most electors and was perfect for a television coverage that focused on 'sound-bites'. A millionaire with a smile, who managed to appear folksy, Reagan was an effective communicator. Personality, or at least appearance, was the crucial issue at stake in 1980, although policies also played a role. As Governor of California, Reagan, a former screen actor and a conservative trade unionist, had been associated with tax cutting and a rejection of the idea that government offered the solution to problems. The Republicans had rejected him as the Presidential candidate in 1968, seeing him as too extreme, but in 1980 he benefited from powerful grassroots backing. From the late 1970s there was greater unwillingness to pay taxes or sanction government borrowing for major projects to transform the infrastructure of human life. Proposition 13 in a California state referendum of June 1978 made huge cuts in local property taxes, setting off a taxpayers' revolt against big government that greatly affected American politics and public culture.

In opposition to the projected Medicare bill, Reagan in the 1960s had produced a record album, 'Ronald Reagan Speaks Out Against Socialized Medicine'. To Reagan, and his influential supporters, government was the problem, as he declared in his inaugural address in 1981. To them, 'big government' was associated with liberal lobbies and causes, and the redistributive nature of government expenditure entailed an economically and morally damaging, and socially enervating, movement of money, via taxation, into welfare. In part, electors understood this policy, and Reagan benefited from the popularity of tax cutting, which he presented as the way to push economic growth and thus raise tax revenues, enabling him to fund tax cuts and yet balance the budget and increase military expenditure. To critics this was voodoo economics, to supporters supply-side economics: growth through incentives.

He was also helped by the weakness of the Democratic coalition and by Republican success in making inroads into it. He won 50.8 per cent (43.9 million) of the popular vote, compared to 41 per cent (35.5 million) for Carter, the largest margin since Nixon's victory over McGovern in 1972. The Republicans also gained control of the Senate for the first time since 1952. There was a widespread reaction against what was seen as Carter's ineffectual nature and against McGovernism. At the same time, the notion of a landslide must be put in context. The votes in the Electoral College – 489 to 49 – were not proportional to the popular vote, the latter included 6.6 per cent (5.6 million) for John Anderson, an Illinois congressman whose policies, such as federal subsidies for mass transit, gun control and an Equal Rights Amendment, were scarcely those of Reagan, and a large percentage of the electorate did not vote. This percentage – 47 – was larger than those in elections earlier in the century. It revealed that Carter and the Democrats had lost touch with much of their traditional working-class support, hit hard by unemployment and inflation, but also indicated that it had not switched to Reagan. Instead, in the context of widespread disenchantment with the political process and, in particular, with the prospects of improvement through government action, much of the electorate had switched off national politics. It preferred to watch the television.

Reagan was to prove both popular and divisive. He was a successful head of state, helping to change the mood from 'can't do' to 'can do' and providing a strength of conviction that helped to overcome the sense of emergency in 1979–80, but yet a more questionable chief executive. Having done badly in the Congressional mid-terms of 1982, in part a comment on growth of negative 1.7 per cent that year, he was helped by substantial economic growth in 1983–4 and won re-election in 1984, defeating Walter Mondale by a very handsome majority: 58.8 per cent (54.3 million) to 40.5 per cent (37.5 million) of the popular vote. An ability to create 'Reagan Democrats', usually socially conservative, blue-collar workers, willing to break from their traditions and vote for Reagan, was important.

In foreign policy, Reagan benefited from a perception that Carter had not maintained national interests, and the new president was associated with a marked intensification of the Cold War. Military expenditure was greatly increased, and there was an active engagement against radicalism in Latin America and pro-Soviet states in Africa. More generally, Reagan revived the sagging American spirit. The 1970s had witnessed defeat in Vietnam and the stench of Watergate. Then in April 1980 the failed Iranian hostage mission seemed to put an exclamation mark on American military and diplomatic ineptitude. On Reagan's watch, this changed dramatically: American pride or swagger returned.

At home, in pursuit of his clear conservative vision, Reagan conspicuously broke with Democratic totems, both in policy terms and in his remarks. In 1981 air traffic controllers striking in defiance of a legal ban were fired, arrested and detained in manacles. Tax cutting became a goal and means of government, the defence build-up being financed, instead, by unprecedented borrowing. The Economic Recovery Tax Act of 1981 saw a massive cut in taxes, including income (both personal and corporate), inheritance, capital gains, business and investment taxes. Income taxes fell 25 per cent over two years and 60 per cent of capital gains was freed from taxation. The consequences of tax cutting reached out across the country, affecting both rich and poor, and hitting both affluent and poor beneficiaries of earlier legislation. For example, to get the cuts in taxation through Congress, the wide use of tax shelters was eliminated. This caused great losses in the financial community that dealt with these shelters, while the real estate, oil and other markets lost much capital infusion. The Alternative Minimum Tax was added to prevent the wealthy who paid no tax from escaping liabilities.

Reagan and his supporters criticized the liberal attitudes of the 1960s and '70s, not least in the field of judicial activism. Instead, in 1988 the Attorney General's Office of Legal Policy's 'The Constitution in the Year 2000' offered the prospectus of laws and justice that reflected 'conceptions of public morality' and 'traditional family values'. At the same time, although conservative judges were appointed, there was no attempt to pass constitutional amendments on abortion and school prayer as religious conservatives wanted. Reagan had benefited greatly from their support, especially from that of the Moral Majority, a religious pressure group pledged to conservative policies.

Reagan seemed a particularly appropriate President for a country that was increasingly aware of the pull of its Pacific rim and the declining influence of Europe and the East Coast. Yet, California had a maverick character in American culture and politics, and Reagan's success was not that of a narrowly regional candidate. Instead, he benefited greatly from reaching out to wider constituencies. Reagan's policies proved particularly attractive in the expanding Sunbelt, but far less so in traditional industrial areas in the North-East and Mid-West, which suffered from international economic competition and rising unemployment, sharing disproportionately in a national unemployment rate that rose to 10 per cent in the early 1980s. Company pensions lessened the shock, as did migration to the Sunbelt, but cities such as Detroit and Flint bore testimony to the economic strains of these years, which were particularly acute in 1981–2. It is unclear that the situation would have been much better in the long term had the government sought to influence it by large-scale intervention or greater social welfare, but this did not alter the severe disruption and serious hardship that resulted. With his smiling Goldwaterism, Reagan liked to joke that the most frightening words in the language were 'I'm from the government and I'm here to help'. The failure of Nixon's economic policies had helped to discredit government economic controls, and the Federal Reserve's experiment with credit controls in March–July 1980 was not seen as a success. Under Reagan, the government considered privatizing many activities, including the post system, but did not do so, although in 1987 it sold its share in Conrail, a government corporation based on railways that had gone bankrupt.

Reagan also cut government programmes for the poor in part in order to finance his policy of tax cuts, and this helped to accentuate indices of poverty, although tax cuts also fostered economic growth. One clear manifestation of poverty was a rise in homelessness, and this probably contributed to rising crime rates. To critics, the assault on government represented not simply the abandonment of the poor, but also a recourse to a Darwinian system of survival of the fittest in which individuals had to rely on themselves. The resulting isolation was presented in David Mamet's play *Edmond* (1982), with the title-character declaring: 'There is no law ... there is no history ... there is just now ... and if there is a god he may love the weak, Glenna, but he respects the strong. And if you are a man you should be feared.'

Nevertheless, the USA adjusted to the economic challenges of the 1970s and '80s with far less difficulty than the Communist states, and shaped the opportunities of the period far more successfully. In the 1930s the crisis of the capitalist model had helped to produce a new authoritarianism in the shape of Nazi Germany and other states characterized by populism, corporatism and autarky. In contrast, widespread fiscal and economic problems in the West in the 1970s, early '80s and early '90s led either to the short-term panacea of welfare, or, in the USA, particularly under Reagan, and in Britain, especially under Margaret Thatcher, to democratic, conservative governments that sought to 'roll back the state' and that pursued liberal economic policies, opening their markets and freeing currency movements and credit from most restrictions. In the USA economic crises did not lead to authoritarianism, the governmental direction of national resources or the rise of extremist political parties. Furthermore, like Thatcher, in some respects Reagan built on the policies of his predecessors. Carter had deregulated the airline industry in 1978, followed by road freight and aspects of banking in 1980, and had also begun the process with the rail industry. He had also tried to cut capital gains taxes in 1978, only to be defeated by Congress. In 1980, however, Congress approved the Depository Institution Deregulation and Monetary Control Act, which provided for the removal of interest rate controls and ceilings on deposits at commercial banks and thrifts, and freed residential mortgages and agricultural and business loans from state usury ceilings. It left states the option of restoring these ceilings later, but few if any did. The Act also gave federally chartered Thrifts (Savings and Loans) the freedom to enter the market for consumer and business loans and to purchase corporate debt securities. Formerly, their main business was home mortgages. In effect, in a major deregularity move, banks were set free to compete for customer deposits by offering attractive interest rates, and thrifts to compete with banks in the business-loan market.

Looked at differently, under Reagan a group of extremists took over government and ran it blatantly for the interests they represented. Choices of administrators, such as James Watt, Interior Secretary from 1981 to 1983 and an opponent of environmentalism, were scarcely an advertisement for national stewardship under Reagan. Nor was Watt an isolated example. The head of the Food and Drug Administration was replaced, which, it was subsequently claimed, may have helped to ensure that the sweetener aspartame was granted a licence. This was, it was claimed, despite doubts about the carcinogenic character of the substance expressed by FDA scientists and concerns about the studies submitted by the manufacturer, G. D. Searle. Furthermore, Reagan's appointee as the head of the Environmental Protection Agency was not a conspicuous opponent of pollution, and in any case the government made clear its lack of confidence in the agency's value by cutting its budget. This was part of a bonfire of regulation that included cuts for the budgets of the Securities and Exchange Commission and the Occupational Health and Safety Administration. The recall of about 13 million radial tyres in 1978 by Firestone, after a long battle between the company and the National Highway Traffic Safety Administration, would have been less likely in the Reagan years.

Looser regulation fed into the speculative fascination of risk on Wall Street, in the linked form of mergers and junk bonds, and into the unwise speculations that drove part of the deregulated Savings and Loans (S and L) Industry into unsafe practices and in some cases fraud. One of the causes for the Savings and Loans failures, however, was national fiscal policy. Paul Volcker, the Chairman of the Federal Reserve, introduced a tight money policy in 1979 that eventually helped to bring inflation under control (from 11.3 per cent in 1979 to 1.9 in 1986) through a tight grip on monetary policy that led to very high short-term interest rates, home mortgage rates rising to 18 per cent in 1981, and 90-day Treasury bills to 16 per cent. This helped to drive the dollar up. As a result of high interest rates, the S and Ls had to pay high rates to attract capital at the same time that they were locked into long-term mortgages. In response, there was a turn to more speculative ventures, which put added risk on the S and Ls. Poorly managed, they were unable to manage the risks and failed to get the necessary returns. Between 1988 and 1991 about one third of S and Ls went bankrupt. The subsequent bail-out cost the government, that is, the public, about $200 billion.

At the same time, this lack of regulation helped in the free movement of capital, trade, people, and economic and technical information to the USA. This contributed greatly to economic growth both in the USA and in the global economy, and also helped in the Cold War confrontation with the Soviet Union. Political misdemeanour also played a role, since the 'Iran-Contra Affair', revealed in 1986, indicated that Reagan, like Nixon, was also prepared to circumvent the law and to run covert activities and even agencies. Reagan was fortunate that the domestic political situation was more favourable than the one that Nixon had encountered. There was also a sense that the prime victims of the somewhat complex scheme were foreign, unlike in the Watergate affair, although in practice the illicit financing of the Nicaraguan Contras was a direct defiance of Congressional authority. Tension over foreign policy was also revealed that year when the Senate overrode Reagan's veto of a bill imposing sanctions on the white racist government of South Africa, the first such blow for Reagan and one that reflected the extent to which his opposition to anti-apartheid legislation had isolated him.

In 1986 Reagan also chose William Rehnquist as Chief Justice. This was highly indicative, since Rehnquist had supported Presidential authority during the Nixon years. Assistant Attorney-General in the Office of Legal Counsel, Rehnquist propounded the administration's opinions on wire-tapping and police immunity. Nixon chose Rehnquist for the Supreme Court in 1971, and he subsequently offered a dissident voice in the legalization of abortion. This was Reagan's choice for Chief Justice, and the angrily contested confirmation hearings revealed that, in the 1950s, Rehnquist had opposed desegregation of schools and public housing in Arizona.

Another legacy of the Reagan years was the imprisonment of an unprecedented number of citizens. Punishment was pushed more aggressively in response to public concern about crime rates, which had risen markedly since the 1960s, and to the emphasis by conservatives on personal responsibility, rather than social problems, as the cause of criminality. In California, the 'three-strikes' law made imprisonment an automatic provision (and an attempt to revise it was defeated in a referendum in 2004). The clear rightward drift of the Supreme Court and the federal judiciary under Reagan contributed to this process, as did a marked rise in drug use, particularly a crack wave.

The process continued under Reagan's successors. Between 1993 and 2003 the number of prisoners rose significantly to reach 482 for every 100,000 people, compared to 91 in France. There had been a marked growth from 1993 to 1999, but thereafter the rate slowed. This was a response to the changing crime rate, which may have reflected the decline in the use of crack. Although surveys face major difficulties in presenting an account of events, the annual National Crime Victimization Survey indicated a marked decline in violent and property crime from 1993 to 2004: by 57 per cent and 50 per cent respectively, a decline that was particularly marked in the 1990s. In 2004 the rate for property crime was 161 for every 1,000 people, and there were 1.37 million violent crimes, 465.5 for every 100,000 people, the lowest rate since 1974. In 2004 there were 16,137 murders, 5.5 for every 100,000 people, the lowest rate since 1965, when the figure was 5.1.

In order to meet rising demand in what was, by Western standards, a country of incarceration, in the 1990s there was an expansion of private prisons, as an aspect of a more widespread privatization of state activities. Private prisons were able to undercut the costs of public-sector prisons, in part because they are far less unionized. As another instance of geographical contrasts, private prisons are weak in the liberal North-East, but strong in the South and the West, bar California, where the ten-year plan unveiled by the Governor in January 2006 included two new prisons. Socially, the impact of the retributive power of government was accentuated by the prevalence of probation and parole. Social, racial and geographical considerations all played a role in patterns of crime and punishment, although film audiences preferred to treat policing as a comedy, as in the *Police Academy* series, or *Beverly Hills Cop*, the biggest hit of 1984, or as an adventure. Those imprisoned were disproportionately poor, black and urban. The war on drugs hit hard at the economy of many young urban blacks, while not having the same impact on their clients, a reprise of the earlier position on prostitution.

Reagan was succeeded by his Vice President, George H. W. Bush, in 1988. Bush went into the campaign well behind his Democratic challenger, Michael Dukakis, but the East Coast liberalism of the Democratic Party proved of limited lasting popular appeal, not least after the Republicans had depicted it as soft on crime, exploiting the Willy Horton case in particular. Like Mondale in 1984, Dukasis had tracked to the left to help win the nomination, but then found it difficult to regain the centre. Although, by background, a member of the East Coast elite, Bush had been careful to present himself as Texan by adoption. This was a matter not only of his oil interests, but also of his representation of a Texan congressional seat. This re-identification was crucial to Bush's success, both in the Republican Party and in the country. Bush took 54 per cent (48.9 million votes) of the popular vote.

An experienced office-holder, Bush, however, lacked Reagan's charisma and popularity. Furthermore, although there had been a rapid recovery from the major stock-market crash in late 1987, he was also hit by the overhang of the vast Reagan deficit, the need to bale out the Savings and Loans institutions, for which the federal government was the guarantor, and an economic downturn. This led him, in the face of falling government revenues, to raise taxes in 1990, despite having promised in his Presidential campaign not to do so. The Savings and Loans bale-out was also responsible for the tax increase. Serious economic problems in the early 1990s, with a recession that reached a trough in March 1991 (General Motors nearly went bankrupt the following year), indicated the reliance of the economic and financial systems on a sense of boom, and led to concern about American competitiveness. This focused on anxiety about Japan, which was seen in the book *The Coming War* (1991).

THE CLINTON YEARS

Nevertheless, sweeping victory over Iraq in the First Gulf War in 1991 led many commentators to conclude that Bush would win re-election the following year. As a result, the Democratic field was weak. This provided an opportunity for Bill Clinton, the young Governor of Arkansas, a brash and bold populist who sought to recreate the Democratic coalition. Although personally agreeable to East Coast liberals, who provided much of his campaign finance, Clinton sought to move the Democrats from the liberal causes that he argued had helped to ensure defeat in 1984 and 1988. Instead, in line with the New Democrats, who had called for change in 1990, he favoured searching for the middle ground, and defining Democratic aspirations for Middle America. This was a matter of social image as much as policy. Bush was made to seem like a 'Country Club' Republican and Clinton as a neighbour at the barbecue. Born in 1946, Clinton also benefited from his youth. Bush's failure to respond effectively, not only to economic problems but also to riots in Los Angeles and to Hurricane Andrew in Florida, made him appear ineffective, while he had been damaged by the challenge from the more doctrinaire Pat Buchanan in the Republican primaries. Bush's willingness to raise taxes was a major issue in sapping Republican support for his candidacy.

A fair amount of packaging was involved in Clinton's presentation, but it worked, and did so again when he beat Robert Dole, an experienced senator, in 1996. In 1992 Clinton won 43 per cent (44.9 million) of the popular vote, compared to 38 per cent (39.1 million) for Bush, and 19 per cent (19.7 million) for the anti-government, multi-millionaire, third-party candidate Ross Perot. The strength of anti-government feeling was shown in Colorado, where voters passed the Taxpayer's Bill of Rights. It linked government spending to growth in population and consumer prices, and ensured that surplus revenue was returned to voters.

The Clinton years were a period of economic growth, a marked increase in the number of jobs and a major fall in poverty, in which the USA also benefited from the collapse of the Soviet Union. Sound economic fundamentals and skilful economic management, particularly by Alan Greenspan, Chairman of the Federal Reserve Bank from 1987 to 2006, ensured sustained growth without inflationary pressures. Greenspan put the maintenance of economic growth as a central goal. He avoided an inflation target, as well as measures to further full employment, preferring a flexible and fluid approach to management. Soviet collapse, however, led to complacency about America's international position, while the stock-market bubble of the late 1990s ended in a bust. Greenspan indeed warned in December 1996 about 'irrational exuberance' and 'unduly escalated asset values' in the stock market. The Dow Jones Industrial Average, which had risen past 1,000 in late 1982 and 2,000 in early 1987 before falling in late 1987, rose to an average of over 5,000 in November 1995, 6,000 in October 1996, 7,000 in April 1997, 8,200 in July 1997 and 11,400 in December 1999. NASDAQ rose from a daily average of 755 for January 1995 to 4,000 in December 1999.

The emphasis on the stock market led to a focus on the short term: the financing of company activities was increasingly by the stock market rather than, as before, by banks. Important business and financial interests were perceived in a context of optimism, hot money and hostility to regulation, and regulators found it difficult to resist pressures towards both financial speculation and commercial consolidation. Banks proved willing to lend at very optimistic valuations, while big companies, such as Wal-Mart (which spread into California in 1990 and New England in 1991), proved successful in hitting local competition, strengthening the growing homogeneity of the retail world. Congress did, however, continue its long-term resistance to monopolies. In 1999 the Gramm-Leach-Bliley Act underlined the separation of retail from financial services.

The Clinton presidency struck many as wasted years, although, at least compared to those of his successor, they were a model of fiscal probity. In particular, the budget was balanced and progress was made in reducing the debt. Clinton, a charming but also lazy and self-indulgent figure, however, did not win the support of Congress in pushing through reforms. Instead, he allowed the Republicans to make his personal life into a key issue, particularly in 1998–9 with the Monica Lewinsky case, thus taking culture wars into Presidential sexual habits. Clinton was also accused of corruption, particularly in the shape of questionable land deals. Claims about impropriety extended to concern about Chinese attempts to fund the Democrats. Given the domestic and, even more, international problems that were to emerge on his successor's watch, the impression was one of wasted opportunities. The failure in 1994 to provide the universal health insurance for which Clinton had pressed hard revealed the President's inability to manage the legislative process to achieve change comparable to that coaxed through by Johnson.

This failure also indicated the strong conservatism of the political system, the role of vested interests and the unwillingness to accept fiscal changes that might benefit others. Clinton was accused of trying to socialize American medicine. The poor, who were the uninsured, were widely regarded as lacking merit and self-reliance, and their dependence on governmental action (a target of conservative populism) was seen as demonstrating this. The fact that they were disproportionately black added to the unpopularity of Clinton's attempt to engage with poverty, and this prepared the way for the Congressional elections of 1994. The verdict of those who voted was delivered clearly when the Republicans under Newt Gingrich gained control of the House of Representatives for the first time in 40 years: they won 52 seats there, as well as 9 in the Senate. Gingrich attacked what he termed the 'liberal welfare state' and pressed for welfare reform and a balanced budget. The Contract for America proposed by the Republicans promised small government and an assault on cronyism, an instructive contrast with what was to happen in the mid-2000s.

The mid-terms in 1994 were a nadir for Clinton, and a testimony to Republican skill in exploiting their presentation of him as left-wing, not least as a result of his healthcare reforms, his support for homosexuals in the military and his interest in gun control. The Democrats were also affected by Congressional scandals involving powerful figures, Jim Wright and Dan Rostenkowski. The Republicans, however, were then wrong-footed, being perceived as extreme, not least for pushing un-fundable tax cuts and for intolerant moralizing, while Clinton recovered the centralist ground he had cultivated in 1992, coming down harder on law and order, restricting welfare and cutting the federal payroll. In short, he adopted a moderate Republican agenda, at a time when the Republicans had ceased to be moderate and could be presented as such. The Republicans were perceived as going further, challenging Social Security and Medicare, and they were under pressure from their right wing, pushed again by Pat Buchanan. Clinton was seen as more normal and moderate than the Republicans, and he also benefited from the apparent dullness of Dole, his Republican challenger in 1996. Dole also suffered from divisions within the opposition to Clinton, from the discrediting of the extreme critique of the President after the Oklahoma bombing of 1995 by right-wing extremists, and from Clinton's ability to package himself, particularly to women, as well as to focus on the issues of crime and education. In 1996 the percentages were 50 (47.4 million) for Clinton, 41 (39.2 million) for Dole and 9 (8.17 million) for Perot, who had behaved in a quixotic fashion during the election.

Having failed to defeat Clinton at the polls, the Republicans were then unsuccessful in removing him from office for lying over the Monica Lewinsky case. As the focus shifted to this issue, the Republican-dominated House failed to maintain its earlier pressure against spending. Whereas spending growth had fallen in 1995 and 1996 as a result of Republican pressure for a balanced budget, spending thereafter rose, as Clinton and the Republicans accepted each other's priorities for spending increases.

BUSH JUNIOR

Clinton's Vice President, Al Gore, won more votes (51 million) than his Republican opponent, George W. Bush (50.5 million), in 2000. The latter's policy proposals did not enjoy marked popularity, but Bush benefited from a presentation of Gore as dull. After a contest over the Florida return, finally settled on partisan lines in the Supreme Court, Bush won more seats in the Electoral College. To outsiders, the Presidential election of 2000 seemed to indicate a corrupt system, with voters' wishes deliberately ignored and the Supreme Court settling the matter on partisan grounds, stopping the Florida recounts. Both those factors were indeed present, but so were many others. Despite the popularity of local propositions for fiscal measures and policy-making, American politics at the federal level is not politics by referendum, and, although the practice appeared to violate democratic principles, it was entirely compatible with the Constitution for the candidate with the fewer votes to emerge victorious. Indeed, this could have benefited John Kerry in 2004, while in Britain, in 1951 and in February 1974, a party with more votes had fewer seats than its principal opponent. American elections also respond to other factors, not least a relationship between federal and state levels and agencies, which led to a practice of difference seen in particular in the ways of recording votes. At the state level, the number of votes in the Electoral College and the House of Representatives changes in order to reflect demographic shifts, but there is no such change in the Senate. To foreigners, this presents the absurd spectacle of Wyoming having as many senators as California, but this is an aspect of a federalism deliberately designed to prevent the most populous states from so dominating the political process that the remainder do not need to be considered, whether at election times or between them.

The role of the courts, both state and federal, in the election was also typical of a country that contests issues in judicial forums. Again, the proactive nature of European jurists leaves scant basis for criticism of their American counterparts. Furthermore, in the USA the courts offer a way to reconcile change with continuity, to introduce a measure of consistency into policy-making and to deal with political logjams. The large number of lawyers in politics also helps to ensure a normative role for judicial action.

The choice of Presidential candidates in 2000 was symptomatic of a trend in American politics. It was between two blue-blooded Americans, both male and each the son of prominent politicians: Gore's father had been a senator. Each had been educated at an Ivy League university. This tendency was to recur in 2004 with the choice between Bush and Kerry, while a family dimension in politics was suggested by the prominence of Hillary Clinton. The absence of class-based politics at the national level made it possible for both political parties to be comfortable with leaders who came from similar backgrounds. In part, this can be seen as willingness across the spectrum to recognize success, but, in some cases, success was more a matter of which beds politicians had been born in than subsequent achievement outside the field of politics. A similar trend can be seen in other aspects of society. By the early 2000s, when the median family income of Harvard students was $150,000, the 'legacy preferences', by which the children of alumni were given preferential access to Ivy League universities, were responsible for an important tranche of applicants, which helped to contribute to the affluent mediocrity that is one of their characteristics. The institutions and social practices of the old elite sat in the *curriculum vitae* of many of the prominent, with an inheritance of family names and old money, followed by private schools, Ivy League universities, marriages within a certain set and homes in particular areas.

If this indicated an oligarchic character to politics, it was also an oligarchy open to new members, talent and money. Money, indeed, was a principal characteristic of the system, with a large number of senators and governors, as well as of candidates for these posts, being millionaires or multi-millionaires. Nevertheless, alongside many indications of declining social mobility, the elite's composition changed. The role of WASP (White Anglo-Saxon Protestant) men in politics and society, while still important, is smaller than had been the case in the 1950s. George W. Bush's two successive Secretaries of State were blacks, the latter also a woman, while in 2004 the Democratic Presidential candidate was a Catholic who had remarried after a divorce, and in 2000 the Democratic Vice Presidential candidate, Joe Lieberman, was an Orthodox Jew. At the time of writing, one of the frontrunners for the Democratic nomination for President is Hillary Clinton.

At the local level, despite the over-representation of lawyers, the diversity of politics, in terms of the background of politicians, and indeed of individual politicians, was more apparent across the nation as a whole. The Democratic Mayor of Providence in 2005, David Cicilline, is openly homosexual, and is Jewish on his mother's side. His father was known in the 1970s as a mob lawyer.

In 2004, in contrast to the 2000 result, Bush was not only to win, but also to win 3.5 million more votes than his opponent. He therefore secured a more convincing election, after a very divisive campaign that saw a marked rise in the numbers voting for both sides, with the total number voting rising from 105.4 million in 2000 to 119.8 million, 59.5 per cent of the electorate. Despite benefiting from a powerful anti-Bush vote, and from considerable disquiet over the economy and the

Iraq War, John Kerry, the Democratic challenger, found it impossible to win the affection of the electorate or to overcome the widespread antipathy to liberalism, or, rather, how liberalism was presented. He reminded many of the defeatism of the Democrats of 1972. Kerry followed the strategy of bringing out the Democratic base, but the Republicans matched this, while the leftward move of the Democrats led the centre to gravitate to Bush. The geographical contrast was marked, with Kerry winning Hawaii, the three West Coast states, the Upper Mid-West (Minnesota, Wisconsin, Michigan and Illinois), and the North-East of the country down to, and including, Pennsylvania, Maryland and Washington, DC. Bush won everywhere else, sweeping the South and the hinterland West. Thanks to the energizing of his conservative base, Bush won 51 per cent of the vote and Kerry 48 per cent. Nevertheless, the Presidential decision hinged on the Ohio result, where Bush's margin of victory was only 135,000. In the campaign there he had benefited from the Democrats' focus on canvassing in their core areas rather than in the expanding suburbia round Columbus. The Republicans also won seats in the Congressional elections, the first time a re-elected President had done so since Roosevelt. Again, there was a clear geographical shift. The Democrats won Senate seats from the Republicans in Colorado and Illinois, but the Republicans won five Southern senatorial seats from the Democrats (Florida, Georgia, Louisiana, North Carolina and South Carolina), as well as South Dakota, where the Democrat Senate leader, Tom Daschle, lost in a victory for social conservatives. The Republicans elected to Congress were more conservative than their predecessors and, in particular, more hawkish on moral issues, such as abortion.

Bush is not the idiot widely depicted, and clearly has a considerable measure of political shrewdness, not least in following Reagan and Clinton in melding with the common man, at least in presentational terms. He also used his Presidential position with reasonable success in his first term to control the tempo of politics and to reward his supporters, although his skill and luck deserted him in 2005. But it cannot be said that Bush has proved a wise or enlightened leader, and in some fields, particularly environmental stewardship and fiscal policy, he has proved badly remiss. The tax cuts did not have the large-scale trickle-down effects their supporters predicted. The cuts in capital gains, dividend and income tax rates in 2003 led to a marked increase in household wealth, although this was as part of a socially skewed situation that saw no increase in the federal minimum wage throughout the Bush years, while median household income also fell in the early 2000s. Combined with low interest rates, tax cuts helped consumer demand, and thus economic activity and employment, although the cuts increased the deficit, which rose to about 3.6 per cent of GDP for the fiscal year ending in September 2004, with scant sign that this would do anything other than accumulate. In 2003 the budget reconciliation called for $1.3 trillion in tax cuts and $265 billion in mandatory spending reductions over the following decade. By 2005 there was a $319 billion government deficit.

Low interest rates discouraged restraint in government expenditure, which rose greatly, particularly on defence, homeland security, transport and Medicare, the likely cost of which was greatly expanded by the major extension of the programme agreed in late 2003. The Medicare prescription-drug Act of 2003, which came into effect on 1 January 2006, represents a massive expansion in entitlement that is predicted to cost more than $700 billion in its first decade. In accordance with Republican preferences, the benefit will be administered through competing health plans managed by insurance companies. This was the largest extension of entitlement to state benefits since Johnson's 'Great Society', although it was accompanied by the cutting of progressive social welfare schemes such as the Youth Opportunity Grant programme. From 1994 to 2005 domestic discretionary non-defence spending rose 70 per cent, with federal spending as a whole growing 30 per cent in Bush's first term. This led to increasing concern in late 2004 as the value of the dollar slid. Despite their anti-government rhetoric, Bush and the Republican-dominated Congress were responsible for a major extension of the cost, personnel and role of government, for example spending far more on the Department of Education; and this process was greatly accentuated by events in the shape of the large new Department of Homeland Security, as well as Hurricane Katrina. The crisis caused by the attacks on 11 September 2001 was a major and novel challenge. Reagan had vetoed the transport bill in 1987, but Bush did not veto a single spending bill, although many envisaged a much greater expenditure than he had requested. Furthermore, by September 2005, he had not used his power to propose not spending funds authorized by Congress. Reagan had done so to great effect, saving $43.4 billion during his eight years. Clinton saved $6.6 billion, whereas Bush has saved nothing. In February 2006 he presented a $2.8 trillion federal budget. There was also unprecedented expenditure and borrowing at the state level. The ten-year plan for California unveiled by the Governor in January 2006 has a projected cost of $223 billion and proposes covering this in part by $68 billion in taxpayers' bonds. Despite these problems, tax receipts have risen as a consequence of economic growth that would be the envy of the rest of the world: the percentage rise is lower than in, say, India, but the aggregate rise in the USA is greater.

Government under Bush also served as a way to reward supporters, scarcely new in American politics, but not a way to achieve effectiveness. Democratic administrations had also used office-holding as a way to reward supporters, and indeed relatives. Kennedy made his brother Robert Attorney-General in 1961, while in 1993 Hillary Clinton became head of the Presidential review of healthcare policy. Cronyism not only fosters support, but also tries to ensure the presence of those who are trusted. This often has a strong regional, as well as an ideological, flavour, as seen with the Georgians who followed Carter to the White House, the Californians who followed Reagan and, far more dubiously, those from Arkansas who followed Clinton. His last pardons caused particular outrage. Republicans might be regarded as especially prone to cronyism on account of their anti-government ethos and its associated critique of bureaucratic professionalism, much of which they saw as instinctually liberal. Democrats lacked that response, but their smaller role than Republicans in business ensured that public service became a crucial means for upward mobility for the many and enrichment for the few.

Bush continued the tradition of putting Party supporters into crucial embassies, leaving, for example, a singularly ineffective ambassador in London during the run up to the Gulf War. Favouritism encouraged the questionable lobbying associated with figures such as Jack Abramoff. Hurricane Katrina exposed the problems created by jobbery, with the ineffective Michael Brown, the head of the Federal Emergency Management Agency, apparently owing his post to friendship with a friend of Bush. Bush's preference for rewarding friends, indeed his clientage and fealty approach to politics, was further shown in 2005 when he nominated Harriet Miers, his former personal lawyer, for the Supreme Court, a move that attracted massive criticism, which led her to withdraw her name from consideration. Although she was clearly a very talented lawyer, and in 1992 the first woman elected President of the Texas State Bar, Miers's career indicated the value of political connections. As Governor, Bush appointed her Chairwoman of the Texas Lottery Commission, and as President, successively, White House Staff Secretary, Deputy Chief of Staff for Policy and White House Counsel. It is interesting to compare Bush's policy with that of lower-rank politicians charged with offences under, for example, the Shakman Act of 1972, which banned the allocation of city jobs (other than senior policy posts) on the basis of political affiliations, leading, in 2005, to the charging of senior officials in Chicago. The same year, George Ryan, the former Governor of Illinois, went on trial for corruption. Disputes over alleged corruption at the national level recall the tensions of the early 1970s, as do scandals concerning domestic individual rights, specifically wiretapping without a warrant and the acceptability of torture. Bush argued that his authority as Commander-in-Chief during the 'War on Terror' entitled him to extend executive power, but there was resistance in both Congress and the courts.

Although his supporters would very much contest the charge, Bush has also proved a maladroit war President, finding it difficult to understand issues and assess options other than through the prism of his own convictions and those of his close supporters. Furthermore, while promising compassionate conservatism and, after his elections, to be a unifier, he has proved a clearly partisan figure, and has been perceived as such, with the contrast between Republican and Democratic approval greater than for previous Presidents. In large part, this partisanship reflects the convictions of rectitude that stem from his religious beliefs and his sense of politics as a battlefield where victory is the sole option. Bush is determined to push America in a more conservative direction, and is certainly doing so. At the same time, conservatism is not a one-fit philosophy or policy, and, although a conviction politician proud of his integrity, Bush is tolerant in some directions. This is seen particularly in his greater willingness than most of the Republican Party to accept immigration and to embrace its consequences. In part, this is a matter of cheap labour, but Bush's vision of America as a set of values was also one that he was happy to expound for all Americans and, indeed, for all non-Americans.

STABILITY AND VIOLENCE

A focus on Presidents and elections, albeit with reference to Civil Rights activism and the Kennedy assassination, provides a narrative that makes sense of politics in a country where changes of power take place peaceably. Despite the hugely controversial nature of the 2000 Presidential election, there was no civil violence at any level. Failure in Vietnam did not lead to the overthrow of the political system, in contrast to France, where failure in Algeria led to the fall of the Fourth Republic. The military, heavily Republican in sympathy, was willing to put up with Clinton, a President for which the generals had limited time. When a former senior army general, Wesley Clark, stood for the Democratic nomination in 2004, voters and politicians, with good reason, gave no thought to the idea that Clark might try to marshal military support in a bid to run roughshod over an election process that he could not manage in his favour.

Furthermore, unlike other populous democracies, such as India, Indonesia, Britain, Spain and France, the USA does not face a separatist movement. Its political parties are national. Nevertheless, there is a regional dynamic to politics, and this is one that has changed greatly during the period. In part, as indicated by the impact on the South of Civil Rights, this is a matter of the effects of policy, but demographics and economic shifts also play a role. Thus, the movement of retired people to the warmer South helped to make it more conservative (albeit New Yorkers in Florida could be liberal), while the search for economic opportunity in the Sunbelt also had the same effect, since those who moved as a result tended to put an emphasis on self-improvement rather than a culture of collective populism. In part, internal migration has lessened regional contrasts in politics, as has national television news. They are certainly less stark than in the 1960s, but they are still insistent.

The large-scale private ownership of guns, including automatic weapons, rests on a widespread belief in rugged individualism. It is protected by the combination of claims to principle and assertive lobbying that is so typical of American politics. Attempts to use the law to limit the consequences have therefore been resisted. In 2005 an Act protecting the firearms industry from lawsuits brought by victims of crime was designed to end litigation to this end. The widespread availability of guns does not lead to the routine use of organized violence in politics, although it does encourage the police to arm themselves heavily. In David Mamet's play *American Buffalo* (1975), the thug Teach declares of the police: 'They have the right idea. Armed to the hilt. Sticks, Mace, knives . . . who knows what the fuck they got. They have the right idea. Social customs break down, next thing everybody's lying in the gutter.' In practice, policing reflected social structures and the use of heavy armament by the police, such as the aerial attack capability employed in Philadelphia, was limited outside inner-city areas. The development of Taser stun guns, able to deliver a 50,000-volt shock, was an instance of technology employed to provide a non-fatal alternative to conventional guns.

Yet such remarks can seem overly congratulatory. There is also a potent strand of violent contention. This can be variously defined, charted and explained, but it is nevertheless insistent. Episodes included the rising at Attica prison in 1971, the Waco storming in 1993 and the Oklahoma bombing in 1995. This strand was very diverse, and indeed divided, not least between black power and religious extremist tendencies. In contrast to most other large states, regional separatism was not much of an issue. The Boricua People's Army formed in 1976 used violence in an unsuccessful attempt to pursue its goal of independence for Puerto Rico. Apart from attacks on federal facilities in Puerto Rico, the movement was responsible for a major attack on a Wells Fargo depot in Hartford, Connecticut, in 1983. However, there was little support for the movement in Puerto Rico.

Other tendencies towards direct action included environmental activism such as freeing animals from laboratories or resisting the cutting down of trees. In 1978 the 'Bolt Weevils' attacked power lines in Minnesota. The strand was as one in its defiance of the prerogatives of government and its willingness to use force to defy legal authority. Far more violently, the Los Angeles riots of 1992 touched off by police brutality and racism, led to 53 deaths and also awoke memories of 1960s riots. More than 2,000 people were wounded in Los Angeles and more than $1 billion of damage caused in the riots. As another instance, the violence associated with rap artists, such as Tupac Shakur, shot dead in 1996, was a vivid demonstration of the counter-cultural potential of such popular culture. The relationship between the strand of violent contention and conventional politics is not one that is generally probed, other than by conspiracy theorists, but it exists. Furthermore, the relationship also flows both ways. For example, the unpopularity of the Vietnam War, and the prevalence of the illegal drug culture, led to clashes between radicals and the police in the late 1960s. This fed into a widespread violence that was linked to black opposition to the integrationist model, opposition expressed in riots and also in crime, although many of the victims were also black.

Although each of these types of direct action has its own dynamic, violent contention that might be typecast as irrational or violent is significant and engages with many Americans. Furthermore, although the mainstream may rely on democratic mandates, and be perceived as normal, rational or peaceful, no system of government is a guarantee of these qualities. Nor is violence, or the threat of violence, far from the experience or fears of many. This is a point imaginatively strengthened by Hollywood's focus on the psychotic and threatening, as in *A History of Violence* (2005). In practice, the threat at the individual level is more likely to come from dangerous drivers, and the USA is safer as far as violent crime is concerned than it has been since the early 1970s. In large part, this is caused by economic growth and low unemployment, although some argue that the impact of abortion in lessening the number of unwanted children is important, as is policing in the shape of New York's policy of zero-tolerance. Some areas, however, for example, black neighbourhoods in Philadelphia, remain or have become very violent, in part because of a combination of drug culture and a breakdown of restraints among a cohort of young men.

A focus on the Bush years in terms of national politics in part misses their significance, for the contours of these politics reflected the strength of both longer-term and local configurations, although the latter were, in turn, affected by national policy, as in the appointment of many conservative judges to lower courts. Nevertheless, local political configurations became more powerful as the incumbency factor became stronger: by the early 2000s 98 per cent of congressmen competing for re-election were successful. In part, this was a consequence of the rampant gerrymandering of electoral districts, as in Texas by the Republicans in 2003, in order to ensure predictable, as well as favourable, results: affirmative action for politicians. This predictability encouraged candidates to woo activists rather than electors, who can be taken for granted, and also accentuated the investment in politics seen with lobbying and related practices. K Street, the lobbyists' base in Washington, DC, in the 2000s, became a major centre of politics, and one that was particularly close to the Republicans in Congress, leading to the fall-out from the Abramoff scandal in 2005-6. More generally, given that posts are filled thanks to a combination of investment and favouritism, it is not surprising that politicians openly represent special interests, nor that policy-making involves trade-offs. The Securities and Exchange Commission demonstrates the practice of controlled allocation. Of the five commissioners, three traditionally come from the President's party; the other two are nominated by the Senate leadership of the rival party. Companies push lobbying hard to the benefit of politicians. For example, the expertise of Billy Tauzin Jr as Chairman of the House of Energy and Commerce Committee, did not hinder his son from becoming a lobbyist for BellSouth before standing for his father's Louisiana seat when the latter retired.

The oligarchic tendency in American politics was a matter not only of the politics of lobbying, but also of the willingness of the wealthy to enter politics and to spend their own money in the pursuit of victory. This was seen in November 2005 with the mayoral election in New York and also in the victory of the Democratic candidate for the governorship of New Jersey.

Yet alongside this is the democratic practice in which large numbers of posts, including non-federal judgeships (nine out of ten judgeships) and sheriffs, are filled by election. This process became more partisan in the 2000s, since rules in some states restricting this have been relaxed under pressure from populist partisanship. As a result of this electioneering, there is a marked contrast to the European pattern, since in the USA the bureaucratic politics of Europe is tempered by at least a semblance of populism. This, however, is not always conducive to professionalism, while populism is itself constrained by political manipulation; not that the two are necessarily separate processes. In 2003 Clarence Norman, the head of Brooklyn's powerful Democratic Party, was charged with selling judgeships; this practice was possible because of the role of majority-party nomination in New York.

Democracy also means the representation of special interests, as seen, for example, in the determination to achieve the most beneficial tax/benefit combination. This is true of election campaigns and of lobbying between elections, and encouraged the bribing of the electorate with their own, or another part of the electorate's, or the future electorate's, money. This, of course, is a habitual aspect of politics, democratic or otherwise. In the USA, the popularity of bribing the electorate by borrowing against the future has helped to weaken fiscal restraint and undermine good government. The promise not to raise taxes became a crucial *leitmotif* of one strand of populism, and indeed helped Schwarzenegger to victory in California in 2003. Hostility to immigration was another aspect of populism, and in 1994 it helped the Republicans to win support in California. The allocation of government funds, for example road finance or disaster relief, by both parties also displays the role of special interests. The ready availability of relief in Florida after hurricanes during George W. Bush's first term helped him there in the 2004 Presidential election. Combined with the nature of political representation, the role of money and gerrymandering in electioneering, and the distribution of power between national and state authorities, this role suggests that the USA is truer to its eighteenth-century roots than might be anticipated. The ability to sustain oligarchy in democracy is far from unique, but its American character is distinctive.

Chapter 7

Imperial State

THE CULT OF AMERICA

On 15 May 1950 the cover of the leading news magazine *Time* showed a globe with facial features eagerly drinking from a bottle of Coca-Cola, with the caption 'World and Friend. Love that piaster, that lira, that tickey, and that American way of life'. Post-1945, American culture, indeed, offered a seductive worldwide model. It seemed fresh, vital, optimistic and democratic, certainly compared to the war-scarred and exhausted societies of Europe. This appeal was an important part of American 'soft' power, compared to the 'hard' power of the military. With the political cultures of Western Europe weakened, or discredited, by defeat, collaboration or exhaustion, their societies, especially that of West Germany (part of which was occupied by American forces), were reshaped in response to American influences and consumerism, which were associated with prosperity, youth, fashion, glamour and sex appeal. American culture also replaced European models elsewhere, particularly in Canada, Australia and Latin America, and was influential in Japan, which the Americans occupied. This culture thrived on the new consumerism, and was particularly attuned to the worlds of television, the car and suburbia, which were increasingly influential from the 1950s. Encouraged by the role of American films, television programmes and popular music, and of American-derived products in consumer society, the mystique of America as a land of wealth and excitement grew greatly in the 1950s.

More than consumerism was involved. There was also a cultural content that was more democratic, accessible and populist than that elsewhere. For example, composers such as Barber, Bernstein, Copeland, Gershwin and Ives created a musical language that successfully and vibrantly spanned classical and popular idioms, and drew heavily on the latter. Rock ensured that the USA made a powerful impact on popular music in the 1950s. Hollywood helped to redefine norms and values in the Western world, and was increasingly powerful as norms were set by visual means and the latter was dominated by film. This was to be a lasting impact. The Disney theme parks in Anaheim (1955) and Orlando (1971) were followed by others abroad: in Tokyo (1983), Paris (1992) and Hong Kong (2005). All were very popular and received more visits than famous 'high cultural' tourist sites. Orlando became the most popular destination for British tourists to the USA.

As the world consumed images of American culture, so in America there were attempts to draw on the cultural inheritance of the world. This included the recruitment of leading practitioners, such as conductors, ballet dancers and even academics, and the commissioning and purchasing of works by living artists, as well as the acquisition of works by dead ones. The number and combined wealth of private collectors was greater than that of any other country. A desire to demonstrate cultural leadership combined with a very favourable tax regime to encourage the display of these holdings in museums open to the public. The most dramatic was the Getty Museum, founded in 1953 by John Paul Getty, an oil billionaire. This rapidly growing collection was successively rehoused in the Getty Villa, opened in 1974, which was modelled on that of Julius Caesar's father-in-law, Lucius Calpurnius Piso, and in 1997 in the Getty Center in the Santa Monica mountains near Los Angeles. There were no equivalents on this scale in Europe. The process by which acquisitions were acquired, however, was not free from controversy: the Getty Museum was accused by the Italian government of receiving stolen antiquities, and in 2005 it returned three disputed treasures.

At the same time, there was also much support for American culture, with major collectors spending large sums to purchase paintings and to fund museums. In the early 2000s these included the Westervelt-Warner Museum of American Art in Tuscaloosa and the

Booth Western Art Museum in Cartersville, Georgia, both opened in 2003. The wealth of the Walton family, based on the Wal-Mart chain, is behind the Crystal Bridges museum, scheduled to open in Bentonville, Arkansas, in 2009. It will focus on American art and vast sums are being spent on acquisitions. All three museums are in the South and represent a move away from the previous focus on East Coast institutions with their emphasis on European art. The market for American art was such that, when in November 2005 Sotheby's in New York sold *Cubi XXVIII*, a large-scale stainless-steel sculpture by David Smith (1906–1965), for $23 million, it became the most expensive work of contemporary art sold at auction.

The cultural appeal of post-war America interacted with its role as the leader and defender of the free world, and both drew heavily on the country's economic and financial strength. This was compromised, however, in the late 1960s, when the Vietnam War led to serious domestic and international loss of confidence in the purpose of American power. Anti-war sentiment contributed to a widespread critique of American society.

TRAVEL

The emphasis in discussing America's global role generally focuses on its activities as a state, and specifically on a series of conflicts, particularly the Vietnam War. These will indeed be discussed, but it is important to note that America's role in the world was far more varied, and that this is even more the case if the emphasis is on Americans rather than on the state. It is necessary to underline the crucial role of America as a global economic power, and also its place in a variety of interactions, including culture, religion and travel. On the simplest level, more Americans travelled abroad than ever before (although most travelled within the USA), and more foreigners visited the country. This increase in travel was in part a consequence of American technology, but it also owed much to entrepreneurship and to a broad increase in individual wealth. The possibilities of long-distance travel were enhanced with the building of the first jet-propelled airliner: the British Comet, which had its maiden flight in 1949 and went into commercial service in 1952. But it was to be the Boeing 707 that dominated jet transport, becoming the fleet aircraft not only in the USA but also for many carriers throughout the non-Communist world. Jet transport brought much prosperity to Washington State, the centre of Boeing's activities, and promoted domestic and international flights. Air travel took over from long-distance liner services, so that the harbours of New York and San Francisco no longer defined the first view of the USA. Aircraft specifications progressively improved, with the 1960s bringing both more powerful engines and the wide-body design seen most successfully with the Boeing 747, the original Jumbo Jet, and a significant symbol of American entrepreneurial prowess. The arts followed, most graphically with the disaster film *Airport* (1975) and sequels, resulting in the spoof *Airplane!* (1980).

Demand for travel rose in the long economic boom of the years 1945–73, and travelling by air for leisure became normative. The development of long-distance tourism transformed the holiday parameters and experiences of large numbers. Many Americans flew to the West Indies and to the Yucatan peninsula in Mexico. What had been an elite activity, largely open only to the wealthy, was democratized, which helped to explain the success of wide-body jets. Long-distance travel was of great economic importance, literally transferring wealth, but it also had a major social impact. Although many tourists went to purpose-built resorts that reproduced much of what they were used to at home, others were affected by the experience of visiting different countries. The impact of tourism on the areas that were visited was considerable, not least the challenging of established patterns of activity.

Nevertheless, foreign travel remained a minority activity for Americans, certainly compared to Australians, let alone the inhabitants of Europe's far smaller countries. In the USA, there was a marked preference for taking holidays at home, not least because of cost, accessibility and familiarity. There was major development in leisure facilities in the USA, in part as a result of the growth in domestic air travel. This created new patterns of linkage, in which the hub system was particularly important, that were different to those of the rail and road eras. Delta's dominance in the South-East led to the remarks 'When you die and go to heaven, you have to connect in Atlanta' and 'If Jesus Christ comes back to Earth he'd have to go via Atlanta'. The changing relative position of airports reflected company success as well as economic development. By 2005 New York's Kennedy airport, for decades America's leading international air hub, had less jumbo-jet traffic than Los Angeles, although Newark grew as a major airport for the New York area.

Tourism to the sun increased in the late twentieth century, particularly to Florida and Hawaii, as did gambling-related holidaying, for example to Las Vegas. The entire resort is a testimony to the way that domestic tourism can transform the local economy: one of the monuments of the period is the MGM Grand at Las Vegas, with its 5,034 rooms. In 2004 only 34 per cent of Americans over the age of eighteen had a passport. This did not prevent foreign travel, since passports were unnecessary for travel to Canada, Mexico and the West Indies, but this exemption is for the chop, and anyway foreign travel has become less common for Americans in recent years, in part caused by uncertainties about the world outside the USA. Air travel declined after the terrorist attacks of 11 September 2001, which hit the profits of US airlines. Instead, there is a determination to take the USA abroad, seen in particular in the greater popularity of cruise holidays, especially in the Caribbean and to Alaska. Indeed, Carnival Cruises became the world's largest cruise business.

RELIGION AND THE WIDER WORLD

Religion also encouraged Americans to look abroad. Missionary activity was particularly important for Christians. Protestant Evangelicals were especially active in Latin America, which led to a major upsurge in Protestantism there, but Protestant missionary activity also took place across the Christian world. In addition, Catholics were well aware of being part of a worldwide communion. Furthermore, Mormons went on mission, while many Jews made personal commitments to Israel, either settling there or providing financial assistance. Accounts of American history tend to neglect this multiple activity. First, it does not meet with secularist perceptions of importance; secondly, it appears to have only limited significance; and, thirdly, it does not accord with the widespread belief that Americans are particularly insular. The sense of being a chosen people, and the willingness to reject the conventions, compromises and constraints of being just a part of international bodies, certainly suggests that religion cannot be used as evidence of cosmopolitanism without serious limits. The last was seen, for example, in the willingness of Episcopalians to ignore the views of fellow Anglicans in consecrating a gay bishop, and thus risking breaking with the worldwide Anglican communion, and in the Southern Baptists' willingness to depart from the international Baptist communion. Yet, the work of missionaries and the ample charity that Americans as individuals devote to foreign causes indicate the need to qualify automatic assumptions about insularity, while, in the Episcopal Church, traditionalist parishes responded to gay ordination by looking to Ugandan bishops.

THE COLD WAR

The commitment of Americans to the outside world was varied and extensive, but this world tended primarily to see America as a great power. This might be expected to begin a diatribe against the use, or rather misuse, of this power, but it is also important to note the extent to which the support of American power was ardently sought, keenly wished for, or at least reluctantly embraced, around much of the world throughout the period. America was correctly seen as crucial to the survival, as independent states, of Israel, Kuwait, South Korea and Taiwan, and to the security of Western Europe and Japan. How best to enlist American support was a central goal for many politicians, particularly in the establishment, maintenance and expansion of NATO. The peoples of Eastern Europe also sought this support eagerly as the Soviet yoke was thrown off.

This paralleled the widespread role of American society as a source of inspiration, as well as envy. Indeed, part of the reason for concern, even anger, over American policy in particular junctures stemmed not only from disagreements over choices between competing priorities for America (and her allies), but also from a strong sense of disappointment about tasks mishandled or not attempted. Hopes focused on the USA proved deceptive. In part, the failings were those of American policymakers and national priorities, but they arose even more from a failure, both in the USA and abroad, to accept that only so much could be achieved.

A polemicist might retort 'but what an achievement!', and that is certainly true, not least in contrast to the disillusionment of hopes focused on Communism and the Soviet Union and China, or the failures and weaknesses of the Non-Aligned Movement, the United Nations and the European Union. Nevertheless, it is ironic that a country that prided itself on being practical so often proved unable to fulfil expectations that it had engendered or encouraged. If this was true in both the domestic and the international sphere, it was most apparent in the latter. Indeed, it was as a beacon of hope and freedom that America's light dimmed in the 1960s.

This is associated primarily with Vietnam, but the 1960s also saw a continuation of the stabilization of Cold War boundaries that left the Communists in control over much of Eurasia. West Berlin was kept out of the Soviet bloc, with Kennedy making a conspicuous pledge of support for its freedom, but there was no 'roll back' of Soviet power in Eastern Europe, and the USA was unable to prevent the Soviets from suppressing the 'Prague Spring', an attempt to create a liberal Communist regime, in 1968, just as it had failed to act over Hungary in 1956.

For the American public, the most serious challenge was that of Communism in the Western Hemisphere. In the 1950s this concern had focused on domestic subversion, and in the 1960s there were to be many on the right who claimed that such subversion lay behind Civil Rights, anti-Vietnam activity, and other liberal causes. Despite such paranoia, the front line in the Cold War in the early 1960s ran not through the campuses and ghettoes of America but through the Caribbean, which was both nearer home than Eastern Europe and a traditional sphere of American control.

Kennedy had fought the Presidential election of 1960 in part on the platform that the Republican administration under Eisenhower (and Kennedy's opponent and Eisenhower's deputy, Nixon) had failed to maintain America's defences. Instead, he aimed for a strategic superiority over the Soviets and, once in power, increased defence spending to that end, beginning a process that helped to mould American strategic culture and force-profile. The prospect of massive US nuclear retaliation did lessen the Soviet threat in Europe, although American preparations also encouraged the KGB to report, inaccurately, that the USA was planning a nuclear first strike. In 1965 Robert McNamara, the Secretary of Defense, felt able to state that the USA could rely on the threat of 'assured destruction' to deter a Soviet attack. Major investment continued, for the logic of deterrence required matching any advance in the techniques of nuclear weaponry. The effort and cost were considerable. For example, having decided, in 1967, to proceed with the development of multiple-independently targeted re-entry vehicles (MIRVS), first tested in 1968, in 1970 the US deployed Minuteman III missiles equipped with MIRVS, thus ensuring that the strike capacity of an individual rocket was greatly enhanced. As a consequence warhead numbers, and therefore the potential destructiveness of a nuclear exchange, rose greatly. The technological development applied to the space programme was also devoted to nuclear deterrence. For example, the USA cut the response time of their land-based intercontinental missiles by developing the Titan II missile, which had storable liquid propellants, enabling in-silo launches, which reduced the launch time.

During the Kennedy administration the Soviet Union had deployed first bombers capable of carrying nuclear bombs and then missiles in Cuba. Under Fidel Castro, this was a newly Communist state that was threatened by American support for the opponents of its government, support that had led to an unsuccessful CIA-backed invasion by Cuban émigrés in 1961, the Bay of Pigs episode. The USA was in easy range of these missiles, and their deployment brought the world close to nuclear war in 1962, although, in practice, that very prospect may have helped to prevent conventional military operations, which would have begun with an air attack on the Soviet bases on Cuba. In the event, an air and naval quarantine was imposed in order to prevent the shipping of further Soviet supplies. The USA also considered an attack on Cuba and threatened a full retaliatory nuclear strike. In the event, Cuba was successfully isolated, the Americans deploying a total of 183 warships; the Soviet Union agreed to remove the missiles, which was presented as a major victory for Kennedy, in return for the USA withdrawing their outdated Jupiter missiles (which carried nuclear warheads) from Turkey, and agreeing not to invade Cuba. The crisis was readily limited, helping Kennedy to see off Republican claims that he was soft on Communism. Nevertheless, its aftermath continues to the present day to affect relations with Cuba. Fidel Castro remains in power and the USA continues to mount an ineffective blockade (enhanced under George W. Bush), which enables Castro to justify his authoritarian regime and to excuse its economic failures.

THE VIETNAM WAR

Success in brinkmanship in the Cuba crisis in 1962 encouraged a firm American response in other circumstances. It also accentuated a sense of the USA confronting an advancing Communism around the world. This was to focus on South Vietnam, a country that most Americans, and many politicians, could not have found on a map in 1960. The US government was concerned that a failure to support the government of Ngo Dinh Diem in South Vietnam against active Communist subversion would lead to the further spread of Communism in South-East Asia, a view described as the domino theory. Diem was an autocrat but his anti-Communism made him acceptable, while a generally racist American attitude to the South Vietnamese made a lack of democracy there seem reasonable. The commitment of American 'advisers' to South Vietnam, including the foundation in February 1962 of Military Assistance Command, Vietnam, in turn encouraged pressure for increased support, and by 1963 there were 16,000 military advisers there. American intervention did help to limit Viet Cong advances in South Vietnam in 1962, but the combination of the lack of fighting quality of much of the South Vietnamese army and flawed advice from the Americans, in particular an emphasis on fire-power, failed to win victory. Diem was assassinated in 1963 in a military coup in which the American government was complicit. Thereafter, the Americans supported the military rulers of South Vietnam.

An attack on American warships (however much provoked by American support for South Vietnamese commando raids) by the

North Vietnamese in the Gulf of Tonkin off Vietnam in August 1964 led Congress to pass a resolution permitting President Johnson 'to take all necessary measures to repel any armed attack against the forces of the United States and to prevent further aggression', in short to wage war without proclaiming it. This was the preferred option because Johnson wanted to avoid an explicit choice between war and disengagement. In a general sense, the credibility of US power seemed at issue, and there was a belief in Washington that the line against further Communist expansion had to be drawn somewhere, and that this was it. By acting in South Vietnam, the USA could affect the general struggle against Communism. The power of the anti-Communist 'China Lobby', the supporters of Taiwan, was also significant in encouraging action.

The American response was initially limited by Johnson's wish to avoid anything that might compromise his chance of re-election in 1964, but thereafter the dispatch of troops increased, numbers peaking at 541,000 in January 1969. The war, however, proved intractable, with American strategy wrongly based on the assumption that unacceptable losses could be inflicted on the North Vietnamese in the way that they could on the Americans. Disillusionment at continued signs of North Vietnamese vitality, combined with domestic economic problems, as well as political opposition, to lead Johnson, in March 1968, to reject the request from his commander in Vietnam for an additional 206,000 troops there. Military difficulties combined with political pressures within the USA, encouraging a shifting of the burden onto South Vietnam. Their leadership divided on policy, the Americans had lost the strategic initiative, but there was already a lack of deep commitment. Dean Rusk, the Secretary of State, later commented:

> we never made any effort to create a war psychology in the United States during the Vietnam affair. We didn't have military parades through cities. We didn't have beautiful movie stars out selling war bonds in factories and things like that as we did during World War II. We felt that in a nuclear world it is just too dangerous for an entire people to get too angry and we deliberately played this down. We tried to do in cold war perhaps what can only be done in hot blood.

By denying the USA victory in the field and continuing to inflict casualties, the North Vietnamese and the Viet Cong helped to create political pressures within America and to sap the will to fight, although their objectives were focused on success in South Vietnam: affecting American public opinion was only a side issue. In the USA the absence of victory led many to see the continuing casualties as futile. The conscription necessary to sustain a large-scale American presence in an increasingly unpopular war played a major role in the growth of disenchantment both in the USA and across the world. Most Americans who went to Vietnam were volunteers, not draftees, but in the years 1965–73 about two million Americans were drafted, while draftees accounted for a third of American deaths in Vietnam by 1969. The draft led to a massive increase in anti-war sentiment. Opposition was widely voiced and 'draft dodging' common, many Americans taking refuge in Canada. The war was fought with soldiers who were, on average, younger and less educated than those who had fought in World War Two. The education exemption and family 9 (fatherhood) exempted many citizens. The army disproportionately was made up of the poor, a crucial aspect of the social politics of the war that looks towards the current situation.

Johnson abandoned his re-election bid in March 1968 because he had failed to end the war. Once elected, his successor, Nixon, who had promised peace with honour, at least eventually brought the men home. Although seen as realists, beginning negotiations with the North Vietnamese in January 1969, Nixon and his Secretary of State, Henry Kissinger, initially stuck with the Vietnam War. Indeed in 1970 they widened its scope, invading neighbouring Cambodia in order to destroy Communist bases there. Successful on the ground in the short term, the 'incursion', which was of dubious legality, further lessened support for the war in the USA and helped to create a feeling of a government not willing to limit its goals. Withdrawals of troops ensured that, by the end of 1971, there were only 156,000 American troops in South Vietnam, but a feeling that the continuing conflict was pointless hit morale and discipline among them, while the South Vietnamese army was unable to achieve victory.

Away from the battlefield, Nixon strengthened America's diplomatic position, exploiting poor relations between China and the Soviet Union and overtures from the Chinese leader Mao Zedong, in order to negotiate a *rapprochement* with China in 1972, an arresting step for such a noted anti-Communist, and one he would have bitterly decried had there been a Democratic President. This opening made it less serious to abandon South Vietnam, just as in Indonesia the CIA-backed defeat of Communism and overthrow of the Sukarno government by the Indonesian military in 1965–6 had made the fate of Vietnam less significant geopolitically. In 1973, after negotiating a peace settlement, American forces withdrew from South Vietnam, but the conflict continued until, in 1975, South Vietnam was finally overrun. Communists also prevailed that year in Cambodia and Laos.

It is possible to argue that, had the USA continued to provide the aid they had promised, but that Congress cut off, then the South Vietnamese forces would have gone on fighting successfully. However, South Vietnam was weak and exposed. The stress to this day on how continued US intervention might have altered the situation is part of a longstanding tendency among Americans to see the conflict in their own terms, to underrate the extent to which the Vietnam War was an Asian civil war, and to find failure difficult to accept.

The Vietnam War demonstrated that being the foremost world power did not necessarily mean that less powerful states could be defeated, both because power existed in particular spheres and because its use was conditioned by wider political circumstances. Apart from the 58,000 fatalities (there were, of course, far more Vietnamese military and civilian casualties), large numbers of American troops were wounded physically or mentally, the last leading to a considerable number of suicides. Collectively, the personal traumas were a major social issue, although far, far less than the casualties and damage that the Vietnamese suffered. More generally, a sense of defeat and division had a major impact on American society and politics, both in the 1970s and thereafter. This sense also left a legacy in the arts, as in David Rabe's plays, including *The Basic Training of Pavlo Hummel* (1971), and films such as *The Deer Hunter* (1978), *Apocalypse Now* (1979) and *Platoon* (1986), which won the Oscar for Best Picture in 1987. Oliver Stone followed *Platoon* with another Vietnam film, *Born on the Fourth of July* (1990).

The war also led to a significant rethinking of the political context of force projection. The War Powers resolution passed in November 1973, by a Democrat-dominated Congress over Nixon's veto, stipulated consultation with Congress before American forces were sent into conflict, and a system of regular Presidential report and congressional authorization thereafter. This law was to be evaded by successive Presidents, and was not to be enforced by Congress, but it symbolized a post-Vietnam restraint that discouraged military interventionism in the 1970s, and helped to ensure that, in the 1980s, the more bellicose anti-Communist Reagan administration still did not commit ground forces in El Salvador or Nicaragua, let alone Angola. In 1991, after defeating Iraq, George H. W. Bush stated: 'By God, we've kicked the Vietnam syndrome once and for all', but the legacy of the conflict continued to influence not only civilian attitudes, but also views among military leaders, leading, in particular, to a reluctance to get involved in counter-insurgency operations. At the same time, what was seen as an anti-Americanism on the Left helped to lead to a revival of conservative thought, not least among some former liberals, such as Norman Podhoretz, the editor of *Commentary*, who moved to become crucial voices of a developing neo-conservatism.

AFTER VIETNAM

Failure in Vietnam was not the sole source of apparent crisis for American policy-making in the 1970s. The economic strength of the West seemed compromised by the strains following the oil price hike after the Arab–Israel war of 1973. Poor leadership also appeared a major issue. Nixon's resignation in 1974 was followed by the worthy, but uninspiring, leadership of Ford (1974–7) and Carter (1977–81), neither of whom gave the impression that they could dominate events at home or abroad. The USA in fact took an active role in several regional crises, not least supplying anti-Communist forces in the civil war in Angola. Nevertheless, the mid-1970s saw a number of treaties, especially the Helsinki Treaty of 1975, that recognized the position and interests of the Eastern bloc, which appeared to consolidate its position and stabilize the Cold War. It did not do so by marking any victory of the West. Instead, it seemed that both East and West still had all to play for in a world adapting to the end of the Western European colonial empires. There was a particular focus on the Middle East, with its concentration of oil production and reserves, and here the USA tried to ease regional pressures. The Carter administration helped to arrange a peace settlement between Egypt and Israel, with the Camp David Accords of 1978 followed by the Egypt–Israel treaty of 1979. However, the overthrow of the Shah of Iran, America's leading ally in South Asia, in January 1979 and his replacement by a hostile theocratic state, combined with the Soviet invasion of Afghanistan at the end of 1979 to suggest that the USA might lose the struggle for regional hegemony.

THE REAGAN YEARS

The 1980s, in contrast, were to reveal a more robust American stance and a resurgence of overseas activism. This was a matter of political resolution and economic strength. The resilience of the economy and the ability of the government to use its capacity to raise money in the bond markets permitted a mobilization of resources for a military build-up that the Soviets could not match. They lacked the money, and could not raise the credit. Even before the bellicose (or, at least, pro-defence) Reagan presidency, the Carter administration had taken a more assertive stance, as well as enhancing American military and intelligence preparedness. The overthrow of the Shah led, in early 1980, to the Carter Doctrine and to the establishment of the Rapid Deployment Task Force, which was to become the basis of Central Command, the Tampa-based Area Command, later responsible for the Gulf Wars, which was co-equal with other American regional commands. This Task Force was presented as a body able to provide a rapid response across the world. Since it contained both army and marine units, this was also an important initiative in joint military structures.

The subsequent marked build-up in the military focused on the deployment of tactical nuclear weapons, carried on Cruise and Patriot intermediate-range missiles, but also included expansion in all the services. The military had advanced the doctrine of AirLand Battle as it reformulated its thinking and practice after the Vietnam War. Military preparations placed a renewed emphasis on protecting Western Europe, rather than planning for counter-insurgency operations elsewhere, an emphasis that responded to Soviet capability, but this was also doctrinally convenient for both the army and the air force, each of which had found the Vietnam War challenging. AirLand Battle led to a stress on the integration of firepower with mobility, maximizing the potential of American forces in order to thwart the Soviet concept of Deep Battle. Tensions between the USA and what Reagan termed the 'evil empire' (a term that pressed the buttons of deep-rooted American sentiments) rose to a peak in 1983. That year, the Americans sited Cruise and Pershing missiles in Western Europe, while the Soviets shot down over their airspace a Korean airliner suspected of espionage. With the KGB providing inaccurate reports of American plans for a surprise nuclear first strike, the Soviets also deployed more weaponry.

American proficiency in weaponry reflected the vitality of applied technology. From the 1960s computers had transformed operational horizons and command and control options. The American Defense Advanced Research Projects Agency took major steps to enhance computing, contributing in the process to the eventual creation of the Internet, and also developing a Strategic Computing Initiative that was responsible for advances in technologies such as computer vision and recognition, and the parallel processing useful for code-breaking. In the 1980s weapons development and tactical planning drew on such advances as stealthy attack aircraft and 'smart' laser-guided weapons. Co-ordination was to be made possible by computer networking and a new generation of spy satellites capable of providing greater detail on the situation on the Earth, as well as AWACS (Airborne Warning and Control System) aircraft and the Global Positioning System. The launching of the Strategic Defense Initiative in 1984, designed to provide protection against missile attack, was seen by critics as an attempt to dominate space. At sea, there was a major bluewater reorientation in 1986 and an accompanying debate. Alongside the 'Maritime Strategy', there were calls for a 600-ship navy with fifteen carrier groups.

A vigorous American attitude was particularly marked in the Western Hemisphere. Under Reagan, there was a resumption of the earlier policy of supporting conservative regimes, as when Nixon encouraged the Chilean military's overthrow of the Marxist Allende government of Chile in 1973. Concerned about the risk of instability throughout Central America, and also about the spread of Cuban influence, Reagan applied economic, political and military pressure on the left-wing Sandinista government of Nicaragua. From 1981 funds were secretly provided to train and equip the Contras, a counter-revolutionary force based in neighbouring Honduras that helped to destabilize Nicaragua. Furthermore, in El Salvador, the Reagan administration provided advisers, arms, including helicopter gunships, and massive funds to help the right-wing junta resist the Farabundo Marti National Liberation Front. Ground troops were not committed, so the USA was able to define the struggle as low-intensity conflict, although it did not appear so to the people of El Salvador, since they were caught between guerrillas and brutal counter-insurgency action. In the Caribbean, the Americans did commit troops to seize the island of Grenada in 1983, in response to the possibility that a left-wing coup would lead to a Soviet military presence. In Panama, in 1989, overwhelming American force succeeded in rapidly overthrowing the government of General Noriega, which had played a prominent role in drug smuggling into the USA.

In contrast, a poorly conceived and managed intervention in Beirut in the years 1982–4 led to failure. In 1983 a lorry full of high explosives driven by a suicide bomber destroyed the American headquarters there. This, and the more lasting impact of the Vietnam War, encouraged the formulation of what became known as the Weinberger doctrine (after Casper Weinberger, Secretary of Defense). This doctrine pressed for commitments only in the event of predictable success and a clear exit strategy, and called for the use of overwhelming force. While prudent, it ensured that the protection of the military took precedence over diplomatic goals and, instead, became the strategic objective.

The international situation was transformed because the USA more than held the line, while the rise to power in the Soviet Union in 1985 of Mikhail Gorbachev, a leader committed to reform at home and good relations abroad, greatly defused tension, not least by leading to Soviet disengagement from Afghanistan and Angola, and by negotiating with the USA on arms control. The Intermediate Nuclear Forces Treaty in 1987 was followed, in 1991, by the START 1 agreement, which led to a major fall in the number of American and Soviet strategic warheads. Apart from reducing international tension, Gorbachev also ended the Cold War, thanks to the unintended consequences of his reform policies. Unintentionally, these unravelled the precarious domestic basis of government control, provoking political pressures that led to the fall of Communism, first in Eastern Europe in 1989 and then, in 1991, in the Soviet Union itself.

THE 1990S

As a result of Soviet collapse, the Western powers, led by the USA, were able to intervene decisively against states that earlier would have looked for Soviet support. In 1991, after a major deployment of American strength, Iraq was driven from Kuwait, which it had invaded the previous year. In the chaos of the former Yugoslavia, Western settlements were finally imposed in Bosnia in 1995 and in Kosovo in 1999, at the expense of the expansionism and ethnic aggression of a Serbian regime that unsuccessfully looked for Russian sponsorship. American air power played a crucial role in each crisis.

In Iraq, the USA organized a major coalition, providing more than half a million military personnel, and its victory helped to stabilize the Gulf region. The war showed the sophistication of American weaponry and the skilful professionalism of the military in its application. For example, the air offensive benefited from state-of-the-art weaponry: B-2 stealth bombers able to minimize radar detection bombed Baghdad – one of the most heavily defended cities in the world – and did so with impunity, while effective use was made of guided bombs. Thermal-imaging laser-designation systems were employed to guide the bombs to their target, and pilots launched bombs into the 'cone' of the laser beam in order to score a direct hit. The use of stealth and precision meant that it was possible to employ direct air assault aimed at overcoming the entire Iraqi air system, rather than mount an incremental roll-back campaign. This was a crucial prelude for the land assault, weakening and isolating Iraqi forces in the Kuwaiti theatre of operations. In the land campaign, the Iraqis were out-generalled and out-fought in a high-tempo offensive that benefited from better fighting quality, unit cohesion, leadership and planning. Superior technology enabled the Americans to provide precise bombardment: satellite surveillance, Cruise missiles and guided bombs were used in an integrated system. In the ground war, the Americans had 143 battle fatalities, the Iraqis more than 50,000.

The success of the Gulf War of 1991 led, in the early 1990s, to talk of a 'new world order' and the 'end of history'. These claims rested on the belief that the fall of the Soviet Union represented a triumph for American-led democratic capitalism, and that there would be no future clash of ideologies to destabilize the world. The anchoring of East Asia to the American economy and the major rise in US foreign trade from 1993 to 2000 seemed to vindicate this.

This confidence, however, was quickly tarnished after the Gulf War, since the upsurge of ethnic violence in Yugoslavia, the Caucasus and much of sub-Saharan Africa indicated the persistence of deep-seated tensions, while the unsuccessful UN intervention in Somalia in the years 1992–4, in which the Americans played a major role, proved a huge humiliation. Thereafter, no US troops were sent on peacekeeping missions to Africa, and in 2003, when pressure built up for UN intervention in the mounting crisis in Congo, the US administration made it clear that it would not send troops, while in Liberia the USA essentially provided only logistical support for Nigerian peacekeepers. In Haiti in 1994, however, the USA deployed 20,000 troops to restore a President deposed by a military coup, and as a way to stop the flight of Haitian refugees to the USA.

Global politics were widely reshaped in the 1990s. An imploding Soviet Union did not challenge American hegemony, and, unlike France in the years 1789–92, Russia did not swing from revolution to dangerous war-maker. Across much of the world, however, identity and conflict were shaped and expressed in terms of ethnicity, a practice that did not provide opportunities for American leadership. Furthermore, the internationalism that had greatest impact was that of religion, particularly Islam. In many countries, hostility to globalization meant opposition to modernism and modernization, and thus could draw on powerful interests and deep fears. The hostile focus was frequently on the alleged standard bearers of globalization, particularly the USA and multinational companies.

THE NEW MILLENNIUM

In September 2001 the ability of a virulently anti-American Islamic terrorist organization, Osama bin Laden's al-Qaeda movement, to strike with brutal impact on New York and Washington focused and accentuated American concerns about developments in the Islamic world and their own vulnerability. The optimism that had followed the fall of the Berlin Wall and the success in the Gulf War of 1991 was finally shattered. The newly revealed vulnerability led to a determination to try to use America's power in order to transform the situation and end the threat. The attacks helped to ensure that the administration took a more determined position in warfare in the early 2000s than had been the case in the Balkans in the 1990s. The replacement of Clinton by George W. Bush was also significant. In a 'War on Terror', the Bush administration attacked what were identified as terrorist bases and supporters, a crucial stage in the movement towards action that had followed the end of the Cold War. In 2001 the Taliban government in Afghanistan, which had refused to hand over al-Qaeda leaders, was overthrown, with American air and financial support for the Northern Alliance of Afghans playing a central role. American policy also had domestic consequences. The Patriot Act (2001, renewed in 2006) authorized the government to gather information in order to scrutinize the population and identify potential terrorists.

In 2003 the focus was on Iraq – a definite and defiant target with regular armed forces – rather than on the more intangible struggle with terrorism. The attack, in which American forces played an even greater proportionate role than in 1991, providing 125,000 troops, was presented as necessary to destroy Iraq's supposed capability in weapons of mass destruction, specifically chemical and bacteriological weapons, as well as to eliminate a regime allegedly supporting terror-ism. The first was proved wrong, although the Saddam regime would have acquired such weapons had it been able to do so. The second goal was successful in that it destroyed a cruel despotism, but not in terms of ending terrorism. The American attack indicated the technological proficiency of their military and its skill in regular warfare. Particular use was made of Joint Direct Attack Munitions, which used Global Positioning Systems to make conventional bombs act as satellite-guided weapons. Effective use was also made of unmanned aerial weapons.

A prime element of debate before the campaign related to the number of troops required for a successful invasion. The Secretary of Defense, Donald Rumsfeld, and other non-military commentators had been encouraged by the overthrow of the Taliban to argue that air power and special forces were the prime requirements, and that the large number of troops pressed for by the army leadership, both for the invasion and for subsequent occupation, was excessive. In the event, too few troops were dispatched, in large part because the difficulty of securing support within Iraq had been underrated, and there was totally inadequate preparation for post-war disorder.

As under Reagan, there was a major build-up in military expenditure under George W. Bush. In 2000 the USA spent $295 billion on its military budget, and Russia and China combined $100 billion. By 2001 US military spending, which had been $276 billion in 1998, had risen to $310 billion, more than the next nine largest national military budgets. For 2002 the sum was about 40 per cent of the world's total military spending, although expectations of, and costs for, items such as pay, food and social benefits varied greatly across the world. In February 2006 Rumsfeld proposed a defence budget of $439.3 billion. This expenditure was very important to local economies, as shown in contention over base and procurement issues. Thus naval shipbuilding was crucial on the Gulf of Mexico and also in Maine.

Expenditure was linked to strategic ambition. The National Security Strategy issued in September 2002 pressed the need for pre-emptive strikes in response to what were seen as the dual threats of terrorism and 'rogue states' possessing or developing weapons of mass destruc-tion, and sought to transform the global political order in order to lessen the chance of these threats developing. To that end, the first paragraph proposed a universalist message that linked the end of the Cold War to the new challenge and proposed the global extension of American values as the answer:

> The great struggles of the twentieth century between liberty and totalitarianism ended with a decisive victory for the forces of freedom . . . These values of freedom are right and true for every person, in every society – and the duty of protecting these values against their enemies is the common calling of freedom-loving people across the globe and across the ages . . . We will extend the peace by encouraging free and open societies on every continent.

To that end, Bush pressed for democracy in the Middle East and China. He also argued, in a speech given at Tiblisi in May 2005, that the peace settlement of 1945 had been flawed because it had left Eastern Europe under Communist control, an implicit criticism of the Democratic government of the period. The Bush doctrine, which was reiterated in the version of the National Security Strategy issued in March 2006, was the opposite of isolationism, and this was underlined in Bush's address to the United Nations in September 2005. He sought support in the struggle against Islamic terrorism. At the same time, this was multilateralism very much on American terms. Unsurprisingly so, given the grandiose self-interest of French policy under Chirac, but more generally, the notion, seen clearly with the Bush administration, that the mission defines the coalition and is determined by Washington destroys any semblance of policy-making among allies. Meanwhile, the widespread unpopularity of American policies, for example over climate change and the Middle East, weakened its 'soft power'. Around the world, anti-Americanism, at least in terms of the policies and supposed goals of its government, was much on display, for example at the Summit of the Americas in Argentina in November 2005. Under Bush, there was indeed a clear determination to defend American prerogatives. In 2005, for example, the USA successfully rejected a Chinese and European Union attempt to lessen its control of the computers that direct traffic on the Internet, which, indeed, was conceived as a Defense Department project. The US-based non-profit Internet Corporation for Assigned Names and Numbers controls domain names, and the USA is unwilling to see this brought under the control of an inter-governmental agency or possibly the United Nations.

Looking to the future, theorists often discuss China in terms of likely future confrontation with the USA, not least on the basis of a 'neo-realist' assumption that states naturally expand and compete when they can, and that China's ambitions will lead it to clash with the USA. Yet, alongside the view that clashing interests over Taiwan will lead to confrontation between China and the USA, it is possible that China's attempts to develop its strength and regional ambitions will involve India, Japan and Russia more closely than the USA. This is linked to America's attempt to strengthen relations with India and Japan.

Possibly, the USA will have a choice over how far to intervene. The international system involves a number of complex regional situations, with the USA taking the leading role, not because it is able to dominate the other powers (as might be implied by the word hegemony), but rather because, apart from its regional dominance of the Americas and the Pacific (the first of which is contested), it is the sole state able to play a part in these other regional situations. As a result, any return of the USA to isolationism would be a major problem for other states opposed to aggression, for example the European states and Canada, something that Western critics are prone to ignore. Isolationism itself is unlikely given America's commitments, not least in the shape of energy dependency. This ensures an interest not only in the Middle East, but also, for example, in Central Asia and West Africa, where Nigeria, Cameroons and Angola are already important producers, and in Venezuela, which, by 2005, provided a seventh of America's oil imports. Sensitivity over Venezuela contributed to the situation in which President Chávez blamed the USA for a coup against him in 2002. US involvement is unclear. If it was a factor, then the failure to remove Chávez was a serious one.

To leave an account of America as an imperial power with a brief noting of recent campaigns would do justice neither to the impact of this power on American society and politics, nor to the extent to which its imperial character is debated within the USA. The first can be powerfully glimpsed at elections. Candidates vie to draw attention to their personal commitment to the military, in contrast to their opponents. In the 1960 Presidential campaign, much was made of Kennedy's war service, while in the 1988 campaign Dukakis was made to seem ridiculous when he posed in a tank. This was a comment on images of leadership and, indeed, masculinity. In contrast, in 1988 George H. W. Bush was able to present himself as a war hero. As with Kennedy, the junior wartime position held by the candidate and the lack of success – Kennedy's boat was sunk, while Bush was shot down, both by the Japanese – were not the issues. Instead, there was an emphasis on resolution when in danger, on courage and on leadership skills. But Bush's use of his war record did not help against Clinton in 1992, no more than Dole's record of being wounded while fighting for his country helped in 1996. In 1964 being a General in the Air Force Reserve served largely only to confirm Goldwater's status as a hawk, and he was rejected.

In 1988 and 1992 the military service in the National Guard of Bush's running mate, Dan Quayle, threw another issue into prominence. It was claimed that he had deliberately chosen a soft option in order to avoid service in the Vietnam War, and this charge was to be repeated against Bill Clinton and George W. Bush. In fact, the election of 2004 saw a bitter Republican-linked attempt to divert attention from the issue by criticizing John Kerry's service and patriotism record, questioning his war service in Vietnam and challenging the patriotism of his subsequent criticism of the war. Kerry had made much of his service record in his bid for the presidency.

Similar strategies were followed in some Congressional races. They were deemed particularly important in states with a large number of veterans, and also in states where the emphasis was on military values, or at least masculinity defined in terms of outdoor pursuits including shooting. This was particularly, but not only, the case in the South. In contrast, such claims and values played a minor role in the politics of Australasia and Canada.

The significance of this subject for the issue of a divided society is considerable, for it exemplifies differing views of value and links them to supposed character types and to the emotive issue of service to the country. In part, this is a matter of the ideal type, but that is a potent one. At the same time, from within the military comes the complaint that civil society is less understanding of its needs and values, of the specific requirements of preparing soldiers for combat, and of the need to segregate them from the different values of civil society. This has been linked to the ending of conscription and the emphasis on a smaller, professional army. As a result, the percentage of the population that serves in the military, or has a partner or child who serves, has fallen. This is a cumulative process, and the percentage that has served is also declining. At the same time, there are generational issues. The cohorts that reached adulthood in the 1940s, '50s or early '60s tend to have a high participation ratio, as well as a positive view of the military. They often feel alienated from the Vietnam generation, whose response to military service was far more divided and frequently critical.

The divergence between the bulk of the population and the military takes a number of forms. The military are far more likely to vote Republican than the average voter, and a majority of the military is religious, many being Evangelical. Yet there are also powerful social and political pressures on the military and constraints within which it has to operate. The rise in individualism ensured that conscription was no longer an option. In 1993 there was a public dispute when the military resisted the Clinton administration's pressure to accept overt homosexuality in the forces. The population's growing obesity and lack of fitness are also issues, with many unfit to serve. The contrast between the high-tech military, the most sophisticated and expensive ever in the world, and both the difficulties it encounters in achieving its goals, and the more varied character of American society, is one more generally indicative for state and country.

This contrast may be partly responsible for the support shown in 2005 for military intervention in the event of emergencies. Hurricane Katrina created an impression of a clear contrast between military effectiveness and civilian failure. Polls reveal that trust in the military is greater than in federal officials. In part, this is a result of the US military's professionalism and commitment, but there is also a somewhat naïve response to the extent to which a military removed from some of the obligations of democratic politics and public government is able to appear more praiseworthy than the latter. In practice, internal politics, patronage, lobbying and 'pork' heavily affect the military, but these are largely kept from the public eye. Instead, there is more concern about political direction. In November 2005 this led the Senate to demand a clear plan for withdrawal from Iraq, one that was monitored by regular reports to Congress.

CONCLUSIONS

The potential challenge that social developments offered to national security could be matched in the economic sphere. Globalization and free trade acted to strengthen the USA, by spreading its values and interests, but the terms of both created serious problems, not least as a result of deficit financing at governmental and personal levels. A lack of competitiveness was also seen in important sectors of the American economy, including the iconic one of car manufacturing. In 1960 General Motors accounted for 60 per cent of the American market, and Ford and Chrysler for much of the rest, but by 2003 Japanese, South Korean and German models were responsible for half the cars sold, and by February 2006 General Motors' share was only 23.4 per cent. This was a testimony to the appeal of the American market to foreign companies and investors, and many of the foreign models were anyway manufactured in the USA, but the impact on the collective psyche was important. Although such developments did not lessen America's ability to act as an imperial power, business competition contributed to the sense of the country under pressure. In 2005 hostility to the idea of Chinese control blocked a bid by its state oil enterprise for Unocal, a California oil company, and in 2006 there was vociferous and successful opposition to the sale of ports to a Dubai-based company.

The sense of a country under pressure might seem ironic given the size of the American economy, but a concern, often paranoid, about the supposed threat from outside forces has long been a major theme in American public culture, as in many other countries, for example France. This concern is an important aspect of the xenophobia as nationalism that can be readily detected. Jobs have always been one of the touchstones of this sensitivity, but it is accentuated when the competition appears to come not only from abroad but also from within. In the 2000s concern was strengthened by large-scale immigration, both legal and illegal, and by the fall in the number of well-paid blue-collar jobs. Seen as a crucial American legacy, blue-collar jobs can also be regarded as high pay but low skill, and therefore as unsustainable in the competitive international order that the USA sought (on terms), and also found itself increasingly part of, while yet unable to dictate the terms.

This was very difficult to explain in terms of the populist ethos of public politics, and the problem contributed greatly to the sense of threat. So also did division within the USA, as concern about jobs, pay and status interacted with widespread concern about affirmative action, legal or simply political, on behalf of rival groups. Some whites perceived themselves as a minority in many localities, combining the widespread concept of victimhood with that of paranoia about the 'other'. The particular crisis stemming from the attacks of 11 September 2001 accentuated this tendency by lending institutional force and continuity to the notion of the enemy within and without. That there were indeed such enemies only served to anchor a much wider and more vaguely diffused sense of unease.

Such issues may seem far removed from the discussion of America as an imperial state, but, in fact, public attitudes were important in sustaining a sense of challenge that helped to make bellicosity possible. So far the critical political success has been to direct this bellicosity to foreign states, rather than to allow domestic tensions to spill over into more than episodic internal violence. Given the degree to which arms are readily available, the latter is a major achievement. Whether it will be a lasting one is less clear.

Chapter 8

Conclusions

Amidst the rush of change, there are striking continuities. Many are those of physical geography, from the mighty imperatives of terrain and climate to the detailed configurations that provide the weft of local life. It may be that the distribution of slope features and surface waters now ensures that particular fields sprout houses rather than crops, since farmers find developers offer the best prices, but there is still the pattern of influence. Other continuities arise from social patterns. Alongside the pressures for both change and homogeneity, it is easy to turn from the highroads and find byways where there is still a strong sense of place and one that is specific and distinctive in character. The causes and consequences vary, and is often a mix of race and religion, topography and livelihood, climate and distance, but these particularities are important and numerous. That is the most important conclusion, the traveller's conclusion. Look and listen, and America and Americans refract through the prism into kaleidoscopes of contrast. These can be compartmentalized and analysed – blue and red states, liberals and conservatives, metro and retro, 1960s and '50s values, and so on – but these are all too often attempts to categorize and classify varieties in order to make them simpler and more explicable than is the case.

Novelists keen to offer a realistic account of particular states of mind have ably captured these varieties, such as Larry McMurtry's accounts of Texas, particularly of rural and small-town Texas, as in

Moving On (1970) and *The Desert Rose* (1983). Crime writers offer the same sense of place, as in the distinctive Los Angeles setting of James Ellroy's works. At the same time, different writers capture the same setting in very varied ways.

Diversity, a diversity that after the election of 2004 led to foolish fantasies about secessionism by the blue (Democratic) states to join Canada, is the antithesis of much politics with its alternative emphasis on true identities, crucial values and natural pathways – which always seem to be those of the seer in question. Indeed, the organic theory of society rests on a denial both of popular diversity and of the inherently contradictory characters of free expression and democratic politics. The mid-2000s, however, saw much emphasis on diversity. In part, this was a matter of politics, more specifically the depths of division revealed in the 2004 election. Such divisiveness is not new, and it no more led to violence than the contested Florida returns in 2000 had done. However, the 2004 election led many commentators to focus on the extent to which political divisions reflected deep-seated cultural contrasts, contrasts that reflected not only distinctive identities but also powerful anxieties about fellow Americans. Furthermore, some politicians took up the theme of deep divisions, most prominently John Edwards, the Democratic Vice Presidential candidate, who referred to 'two Americas' as he considered the extent and impact of major contrasts in wealth and opportunity. In 2005 Edwards highlighted the contrast in average net wealth between whites and, on the other hand, blacks and Hispanics. That he, like John Kerry, was wealthy did not lessen the strength of this analysis.

In part, this contrast reflects the misleading use of average returns. Many blacks in practice have done reasonably well. Most are not close to the poverty line. In 2002 a majority of blacks earned more than $25,000 annually, and the percentage doing better has risen. Thanks to the marked expansion of the black middle class, a product of opportunities in both the public and private sectors, 27 per cent of blacks were earning more than $50,000 annually by 2002, whereas in 1980 the percentage was 16.8 per cent; for $100,000 the figures were 6.4 and 1.5 per cent respectively. Furthermore, far from being stuck in a multiple failure, the percentage of blacks owning their homes and graduating from high schools was rising: from 44 per cent in 1996 to 49 per cent in 2004, and from 70 per cent in 1993 to 80 per cent in 2003 respectively.

Yet, percentages and averages can also direct attention away from major problems, and Hurricane Katrina highlighted these. It led to a massive outing for anger, much of it, of course, from comfortably-off commentators, and it is understandable, in the wake of a crisis brought home vividly by the media, and even magnified with exaggerated tales of disorder and casualties, that the theme of victimhood and national division was pushed hard. For example, the black novelist Alice Walker saw racism at play in the treatment of the black and poor in New Orleans: 'It's exactly where America is. It has not sufficiently dealt with the race issue, and it certainly has not dealt with the issue of poverty. In a sense it was nothing new, but it was shocking for the world to see this side of America.'

Walker's novels, such as *The Third Life of Grange Copeland* (1971) and *The Color Purple* (1982), reflect her perception of the savage impact on black men of the legacy of segregation and slavery. Copeland, an anti-hero, refuses to rescue a pregnant white woman from drowning, and the impact of the abuse of blacks is a major theme in *The Color Purple*, which received a Pulitzer Prize, the first for a black woman, and was turned into a film by Steven Spielberg in 1985 and into a Broadway musical in 2005.

More mundanely, the figures cited above to indicate progress also highlight continued disparities, as is to be anticipated. If 80 per cent of blacks were high-school graduates in 2003, the percentage for whites was 89. If 49 per cent owned their own homes, the percentage for whites was 76. Furthermore, in 2002 median family income was $45,086 for whites compared to $29,036 for blacks, and in many parts of the country the gaps between these medians grew in the early 2000s. Figures for both whites and blacks are based on public expenditure and the economy, both of which are unnaturally sustained by massive capital inflows (75 per cent of the world's surplus saving in 2004), and it is interesting to consider how far any change in these inflows might lead to a shift in the fortunes of groups within American society – and to a rise in racial and social tension. By 2005 the external deficit had more than doubled since 1999, and America was annually spending over $700 billion more than the economy produced. This was a sum that was made less formidable by major economic growth, which owed much to a rise in productivity, but it was still more than 6 per cent of annual output, twice the rate at its peak in the late 1980s. In November 2004 Alan Greenspan, Chairman of the Federal Reserve, described the current-account deficit as 'increasingly less tenable'. Much of the expenditure was in property, threatening a repetition of the 1970s when a fall in property, combined with a rise in the price of oil, helped to cause (and reflect) economic and fiscal problems.

Katrina suggests that poor blacks would suffer disproportionately from any crisis, but in practice the level of indebtedness is such that the affluent and moderately off, whatever their colour, will suffer from any major economic downturn. The extent to which currency inflows are a matter of sustaining consumption – since 2000, foreigners, notably the Chinese central bank, have invested in bonds, particularly Treasury bonds, rather than in American companies as previously – is of particular concern, since this means a lack of underpinning for long-term economic growth. Furthermore, American corporate investment in future productivity is greater than in Europe, but less than in East Asia. This is a particular problem, since it is linked to a lack of comparative advantage, which, combined with the size of the domestic economy, means that there is a shortage of exports to help service the foreign debt. At the same time, much of the Chinese export growth rests on the activities of foreign (including American) companies, via subsidiaries or joint ventures, which offers a way for foreign profit from this growth.

The foreign debt is the product of the heavy borrowing that comes with a loose monetary policy, such that by the mid-2000s there were more than 1.3 billion credit cards in the USA (and the design of wallets, and therefore of jackets, had to respond to the large number of credit and charge cards carried by individuals). This looseness of monetary policy, and the willingness to borrow, led to a marked rise in home ownership, and therefore house values, which has benefited all ethnic groups. This rise, however, has further encouraged borrowing, pushing up personal debt. Although George W. Bush has tried to encourage thrift in society, he has made only episodic efforts to do so, and the example set by the government is scarcely encouraging. Indeed, personal and governmental indebtedness interact in a disturbing synergy, carried forward by the heady drug of low interest rates and the ability to borrow. In December 2005 Alan Greenspan pointed out that the ability hitherto to finance the current-account deficit suggested a flexibility in global capital markets that could be threatened by protectionism, but that, anyway, 'deficits that culminate to ever-increasing net external debt, with its attendant rise in servicing costs, cannot persist indefinitely'.

Social tensions will doubtless open up if the situation deteriorates, and this might well exacerbate contrasts between ethnic groups. It will also challenge the uneasy relationship between the generations that, similarly, relies on a shared unwillingness to accept fiscal discipline: children push the responsibility for looking after their elderly relatives onto a state only too willing to take on unsustainable commitments about healthcare. The strength of the American economy, and the nature of its age profile, makes this situation less serious than the economic prospectus for much of Europe, but a recurrence of the downturn of the 1970s is possible. The causes and contours will be different, but the sense of malaise may be just as dangerous.

The USA, however, is less likely than much of Europe to face such a downturn. Today, whereas the banking community is stronger than ever in the USA, and has both grown and become more efficient in the movement of capital, the Japanese banking community is protected from admitting its losses, and many European banks are overly subject to political interference, not least in France and Spain. Over-protected banks, such as those in Japan, hold on to their losers, as compared to the USA, which, driven by shareholder interests and the pressure for quick profits, forces the banks to admit their poor managerial moves. An American approach would be to argue that, like a forest fire that improves the forest as a whole, failure in business benefits the economy. In contrast, in continental Europe and Japan this approach is seen as 'Anglo-Saxon values' or 'harsh capitalism'. Although the American method entails social disruption, in a crisis the resulting skills are greater than those of more protected societies. American flexibility was seen in the response to the stock-market meltdown of October 1987, and in the skill of Alan Greenspan, Robert Reuben and Larry Summers during the

Clinton administration in helping to create and support a powerful and sustained surge in the stock market, as well as in the successful risk-management seen in the management of the Mexican financial crisis, the Russian debt non-payment in 1998 and the Asian liquidity crisis. At the level of individual banks, since 1992 upgrades in creditor-worthiness assessed by the rating agency Moody's have outnumbered downgrades. Furthermore, the American economy demonstrates the creative destruction of capital with a major turnover of large companies: large and famous firms, such as Pan Am, disappearing, and others, such as Apple, Google and Microsoft, being created and developed.

Although distant from the immediate concerns of the poor, such growth does create opportunities for them as well as for the affluent. The understanding of poverty, however, involves vexed issues, particularly that of race. Any black–white dichotomy, not least with the misleading use of the oft-reiterated motif of slavery (which certainly does not describe current relations), is complicated, if not invalidated, by the extent to which diversity and variety fail to correspond to such a stark divide. For example, the statistics of inequality need to make sufficient reference to the Hispanics, a rapidly growing section of the population. Recent immigration ensures that they are often poor, although many, particularly in subsequent generations, display considerable social mobility, while the development of 'Spanglish' is an important aspect of the engagement of all Hispanics with the dominant culture. Nevertheless, in 2003 only 57 per cent of Hispanics were high-school graduates, and in 2004 only 48 per cent owned their homes. The Hispanic narrative is not one of slavery or of oppression within America. In part, this is because, despite harsh conditions, for example for transient farm workers, Hispanics are better off in the USA than in the lands they left, and others continue to seek to immigrate into the USA. This contrast is not present for blacks, because their African experience is centuries old and eclipsed by that of slavery. As a consequence of this contrast, the theme of division seen in some black rhetoric, and in part of the black experience, cannot be so readily applied as a model for other non-white Americans.

This can be seen further if religious belief and practice are considered. There are separatist black religious traditions, and they have a variety of manifestations, although none threatens integration or social harmony to the extent that Islam does in Europe. One manifestation of American black religious separation is the creation of a distinctive celebratory ritual, as with Kwanzaa, an alternative to Christmas that emphasizes a sense of pride in black history and achievements. Kwanzaa is a seven-day celebration celebrating the Seven Principles of Life: Umoja (unity), Kujichagulia (self-determination), Ujima (collective work and responsibility), Ujamaa (cooperate economics), Nia (purpose), Kuumba (creativity), and Imani (faith). Each day, a candle is lit in the kinara to represent each of these principles. Symbols for Kwanzaa include the Black National Flag, the Unity Cup and the candles – one black, three red and three green.

To restrict attention to Christianity, there is a major sense of separation (but not segregation) in religion, with black churches frequently having largely, or exclusively, black congregations and particular types of religious practice. Yet any emphasis on dichotomy is complicated by the extent to which there is a common Christian creed, and that many churches have both black and white congregants. Furthermore, the extent to which Hispanics focus on the Catholic Church helps to restrict the theme of ethnic difference within American Christianity, although there are obvious differences in Catholic practice between churches in, say, Boston, where Catholics of Irish descent remain important, and southern Arizona, where Hispanics are more numerous.

If America then is so diverse, it is not easy to contrast it with other diverse societies. One important basis for comparison arises from the extent to which diversity is accepted in the USA. In part, this is a circumscribed diversity. It is clearly strong when grounded in constitutional rights, but less so when merely a matter of social preference. There are indeed powerful pressures against diversity and for conformity. This is not simply a matter of pressures in long-established communities, but also in the new frontiers of advancing suburbia where new communities are being established and moulded. In this context, indeed, there can seem to be scant support for diversity, not least if it is defined and stigmatized as liberalism.

Such stigmatism is understandable in terms of mainstream conservative values, because the latter are conformist rather than libertarian.

The extent to which the last have been pushed since the 1960s is part of the dialectical dynamic of American culture: libertarian individualism and conformist conservatism feed off each other, requiring their perception of the other in order to provide an apparent need for rhetoric and action. This is amply demonstrated in the literature produced by those who like to see themselves on one of the sides, but less so in individual and family lives in which the emphasis frequently (but far from invariably) is rather on compromise and, in place of consensus, on the shifting bases of acceptance.

As an example of libertarian individualism, one could turn not to the idealists of the 1960s but to the brat novelists of the 1980s, with their concern with cynicism and selfishness, and their sense of society as lacking in values and immersed in consumerism. Drugs also frequently played a role in the action. Examples of such novels include Jay McInerney's *Bright Lights, Big City* (1983), *Story of My Life* (1988) and *Brightness Falls* (1992), each set in New York during the Reagan years, Tama Janowitz's *Slaves of New York* (1986), *A Cannibal in Manhattan* (1987) and *The Male Cross-Dresser Support Group* (1992), each again set in New York, and Bret Easton Ellis's *Less than Zero* (1985), *The Rules of Attraction* (1987), *American Psycho* (1991) and *Lunar Park* (2005). *American Psycho* was a very contentious work because it depicted a successful Wall Street banker keen on the good things of life, and also on serial killing and mutilation. A brutal book, this was also a satire on success. In *Lunar Park*, the suburbs are a site of horror and a cause of dread, both focused on concerns about children. Given the role of success, suburbia and the family in the collective psyche (success leads to the suburbs, where families are created and sustained), attacks on either, or all, of them are particularly threatening.

At the same time, the situation naturally is more complicated than the critical construction in terms of conservative conformism and liberal, or libertarian, individualism. There is also a liberal conformism in some spheres, one, moreover, that can be stridently asserted, not least in the language of the politically correct, and this conformism can be the antithesis of libertarianism. In accordance with American political culture, conservative conformism largely acts by means of trying to shift constitutional parameters, rather than to overturn the

Constitution. As such, any drive for conformity has to address the strong, and legally well-grounded, sense of institutional distinction and autonomy seen in such spheres as the judicial system, universities, the military, and state and local government. This is why the issue of appointments in these spheres is so important.

Furthermore, liberalism and conservatism are monoliths only to uninformed outsiders. The strains that Presidential policies placed upon Republican loyalties during the presidencies of George Bush, father and son, amply demonstrated the diversity of the right, not least over the role of government, the extent of public borrowing, the place of social conformism and the desirability of an interventionist foreign policy. Far from lessening, these tensions have grown. The Republican party has certainly not become a homogenous force (some politicians, such as Mayor Bloomberg of New York, are known as RINOS – Republicans in Name Only), and this is linked to the growing crisis in policy and personnel that affected it in the mid-2000s. These tensions raise the possibility of a very different leadership after the Bush term. Very different constituencies include the business establishment and the religious right – fiscal versus social conservatives, as well as the neo-conservatives who focus on a proactive foreign party.

Although the Democrats saw their conservative strand decline in the loss of much (but not all, as Louisiana clearly shows) of the Southern white vote, Democratic primary campaigns show that the same can be true of the left. There is particular tension over the extent to which the party should move leftwards or, as Clinton and the Democratic Leadership Council in the 1990s urged, to the centre. Liberalism and conservatism are both, in part, shaped as monoliths by outsiders who offer a false coherence (matching that of polemicists within each tendency), which fails to address the gradations and divisions of these tendencies. This is but part of a more general false consciousness of agglomeration, seen, for example, in the treatment of the 1960s both by those who see it as inspiration and by those who are appalled by it. The same is also true of other periods of time and of individual presidencies, for example 'the Reagan years'. In addition, religion and religious pressures, not least the Christian variety, dissolve under scrutiny into a range of dissonant drives.

Awareness of these and other variations poses problems not only for discussion of the present but also for the presentation of the past. The latter is of growing importance given greater political interest from the 1990s in the depiction of American history. The meeting on 30 June 2005 of the Subcommittee on Education and Early Childhood Development of the Senate Committee on Health, Education, Labor and Pensions heard an undertaking that when the 'No Child Left Behind' legislation came up for reauthorization, history would be added as a core element in the initiative's teaching programme, while the Executive Director of the National Assessment Governing Board announced that, from 2006, the Board would ensure that its US history test would be conducted every four years. This would be the basis for intended legislation to authorize a pilot study that would provide state-by-state comparison of US history and civics' test data, the approach taken in the proposed American History Achievement Act.

This emphasis on the need for history detracts attention from the problems posed by the subject. Public history is apt to be history as answers, not history as questions. There is a marked contrast between the questioning ethos and methods that are central to the modern notion of scholarship, and, on the other hand, a public use of history in which the emphasis is rather on answers, with public myths providing ways to make sense of the past. It is indicative that the historian who testified to the Senate Subcommittee in June 2005 was the popular writer David McCullough, who claimed that history texts were often written in a style that was far too boring to interest students and that, instead, it was necessary to emphasize the 'literature of history' and for teachers to focus on narrative history to reach students. Engaging students is clearly a central issue, but an understanding of the process of history is offered only by narratives that are alive to contrasting interpretations and to the problems of using evidence. If the Senate chooses to ignore this, as it probably will, then there is likely to be a false coherence in the narratives it sanctions.

As an example of the absence of monoliths in American public life, there is no institutional body to provide discipline in the cause of coherence, as the Communist Party seeks to do in China. Indeed, although the Democrats and the Republicans are each less diverse and therefore with fewer coalitions than in the past, they still lack the disciplinary centralization of political parties across much of the Free World. This approach can be taken further by referring to business, capital and labour, each of which resists direction and unification. The labour movement proved particularly divided in the 2000s. Within the political parties, the lure of conformity to dominant themes, particularly the ideas held by activists, is matched by a search for moderate support. This can be seen not only from politicians widely regarded as moderate, but also from those who are seen by opponents as extreme. Thus, despite the general presentation of him, George W. Bush in 2005 avoided nominating known doctrinaire conservatives for the first Supreme Court vacancy, and initially for the second vacancy, and he also made major efforts to woo black support, while, as she positioned herself for a Presidential run, Hillary Clinton changed her position on abortion and on power projection abroad.

These political shifts and expedients reflected the extent to which the electorate was less doctrinaire than the divisiveness of culture wars might suggest. Polls indicate a strong support for tolerance, especially among the young, but also a widely diffused patriotism and religious faith that contrasts with the situation in Europe. The combination of pre-marital sexual licence with the popularity of marriage and parenthood indicate that the values of both the '60s and the '50s remain important.

To some critics, diversity has become excessive and a threat to social cohesion and political interest. These arguments are applied in particular against liberal individualism and large-scale Hispanic immigration. Each, indeed, challenges any attempt at direction. Liberal individualism leads many conservatives to a sense of cultural and social crisis. In practice, few of the fears expressed in the 1960s have materialized. Drug use remains a serious problem, but although it has helped to cause serious social difficulties in inner cities, with savage consequences for many, it has not led to the general breakdown that was feared. In suburban areas, drug use is a cause of individual and family problems, rather than general societal crisis, and the same is true of violence. Ironically, suburban anxieties are more easily expressed by transposing them onto the inner cities. The marked rise in pre-marital sex in the 1960s did not lead to the end of marriage but to its postponement, with many young people having relatively stable relationships in the meanwhile, and not the promiscuity depicted by critics. The major increase in divorces in the late 1960s and early '70s has not led to the breakdown of the family, as was feared, but, instead, to an unprecedented rate of remarriage. Furthermore, many of these 'problem indices' improved in the early 2000s, with abortion, crime, divorce and teenage pregnancy rates all falling. This does not mean the end of culture wars, but rather that the charge that liberalism and 1960s values led to social breakdown can be rejected. Instead, American society has reshaped, with a differing mix of conformism and individualism to that in the 1950s. Generational issues played a major role in the reshaping, as issues were reformulated or new ones framed. The power of the Baby Boomers reached out in many directions, creating new expectations. For example, new approaches to generational issues, such as the menopause, hair loss and weight gain, influenced medical practice and drug companies.

This reshaping interacted with that of changes in the world of work. The make-up of the work force changed dramatically after 1950. Today the percentages are 3 in agriculture, 16 in manufacturing and the balance service-oriented. This change from a manufacturing to a service society is as great as it was in the latter part of the nineteenth century, when the USA was transformed from a predominantly ruralist agrarian society to an increasingly urban manufacturing one, albeit with important regional variations.

As the country has changed greatly since 1960, most particularly with the rising relative importance of the South and the West, this reshaping of society also has a geographical aspect. If the North-East has changed, so also has the South and the West. Outsiders perceive the latter in terms of homogeneous communities, and sometimes starkly so. I was assured in 2005 by one resident of Alabama, who was not locally born, that the state's politics were run by 'Bapto-Fascists', but, in fact, the Southern Baptists themselves have diverse views on social and political topics, while Alabama, like other Southern states, contains a variety that, while it is in aggregate different in tone to Connecticut or Massachusetts, is also far from homogeneous in particulars. Indeed, alongside the emphasis on uniformity as a consequence of national consumerism and other factors there are important factors encouraging variety. The hegemony of the television networks has fractured as new technology and media have allowed more ways to communicate and thus define identity.

More profoundly, the very themes of conformism have been greatly attenuated. This is not so much a consequence of 1960s values, but, rather, a broader process of economic opportunity, social individualism and an assertiveness that is not only a matter of youth and women but of all social groups and of most individuals. Assertiveness can, of course, be an aspect of conformism; for example, rejecting one's looks through diet, exercise, plastic surgery or hair transplants in order to share in social suppositions about appeal. Nevertheless, however much influenced by advertising and other factors, the relationship between conformism and choice has shifted towards the latter.

This is an aspect of the restlessness that is part of the essence of the American experience. This restlessness helps to explain the energy of Americans, which clearly has such positive and negative manifestations. The sources of this restlessness are cultural and environmental, the former in part an aspect of the extent to which America is an immigrant society whose people, directly or (with the exception of the blacks) through their forebears, chose to come to the USA. Furthermore, the presence of so much physical and material abundance (magnified by popular accounts and images) stirred the imagination and presented Americans with the idea of improvement and upward social mobility. Unity within so much diversity is to be found in a rough allegiance to the idea of America as a place where liberty and freedom (variously conceived) prevail, and provide opportunity. Technology corresponded to this unity within diversity. The spread of information technology that has been so important to productivity growth since 1995 – and has been significant culturally in creating common experiences and new languages – contributes to similarities and yet also provides a way in which to express different views.

As far as immigration is concerned, integrationists have to hope that immigrants will identify with what are presented as American values; they cannot be coerced into doing so, and this has led pessimists to fear a re-shaping of the USA as a result of its porous frontiers, external and internal. Yet, the re-shaping of the country is scarcely new, and the very drive to settle in the USA reflects the potent attraction of its opportunities and the appeal of its sense of possibility. That offers a powerful antidote to the reality of a prominent sector of American society that is mired in crime and drugs. Talking to Americans, it is clear that many identify the latter with inner cities and blacks, but that scarcely describes the reality of a far more widespread drug-taking, or indeed of criminality that is as much about Whitewater, Enron, WorldCom. and Tyco, as of the Willy Hortons that haunt much of the collective psyche. Indeed, polls in the early 2000s indicated considerable distrust of the leadership of large companies. In addition, structural factors led to disquiet about the probity of important tranches of business and public life. The investigation into mutual-fund fraud launched by Eliot Spitzer, New York's Attorney-General in 2003, suggested serious conflicts of interest. Whether this, or the blatant and destructive Savings and Loans scandals of the 1980s, or the problems facing Refco in 2005, when the major broker was accused of concealing transactions in order to make it more attractive for investors, deserve to be compared to the gerrymandering of political constituencies is a matter of opinion, but also a question worth asking. Furthermore, just as the political history of this period can be discussed, at least in part, in terms of violence and of cultures of fear, so the economic history can be considered, in part, in terms of crime and fraud. As with violence, this is a matter both of top-down activities, such as fraudulent accounting, and also of independent action by the many, for example, the piracy and downloading of videos and DVDs.

Other countries have similar and sometimes worse problems. However bad American crime figures might be, they are good compared to those of Brazil or South Africa. Although there is a popular apocalyptic fiction predicting environmental crisis, such as Kim Robinson's *Forty Signs of Rain* (2004) and *Fifty Degrees Below* (2005), in which Washington, DC, faces the flooding consequences of melting icecaps, in fact pollution and environmental degradation are worse in China and India. American geographical sectionalism is less acute than that of Canada. Yet, to take this course is scarcely to find much positive support for the aspiration that is America, and there is no consolation, at least in so far as comparisons with other major states are concerned, when the exceptionalism in sight is that of per capita energy consumption or widespread obesity. Australia also offers can-do optimism and the sense of a young country, and without some of the less desirable features of American society, including high levels of personal violence and cultural combativeness. If in the USA the material standard of life is much higher than in 1960, and there is no longer the challenge of nuclear extinction in great power conflict, this is more generally true of the developed world. However, American politicians played the crucial role in bringing the Cold War to a successful conclusion for Western values (freedom, democracy, liberal economics), while the rise in the material standard of life has been particularly marked in the USA when compared to Western Europe.

An exciting story, an uplifting ambition and more of a friend to liberty around the world than other major states, America captures the exhilaration and disappointment of freedom once it is translated into a political system. But the world, and not just the Americans', has been very lucky that the USA, and not Nazi Germany, or the Soviet Union, was the leading power of the last six decades. That this book can be sold in the USA without censorship is a reminder of the truly liberal character of its political culture. Whether, for the future, the USA can provide its own citizens, or indeed others, with a sense of freedom that encompasses necessary and desirable degrees of economic growth and environmental protection, social justice and national security, is for you to consider.

Selected Further Reading

1987 Census of Agriculture, I: Agricultural Atlas of the United States (1990)

A. F. Alkhafaji, *Restructuring American Corporations: Causes, Effects, Implications* (New York, 1990)

L. Allen, *The Global Economic System since 1945* (London, 2005)

S. E. Ambrose, *Rise to Globalism: American Foreign Policy since 1938* (Harmondsworth, 1988)

R. R. Archibald, *The New Town Square: Museums and Communities in Transition* (Oxford, 2004)

K. Auletta, *Media Man: Ted Turner's Improbable Empire* (New York, 2004)

E. L. Ayers et al., *All Over the Map: Rethinking American Regions* (Baltimore, MD, 1996)

A. J. Bacevich, *American Empire: The Realities and Consequences of US Diplomacy* (Cambridge, MA, 2002)

S. J. Ball, *The Cold War: An International History* (London, 1998)

D. Barlett and J. Steele, *America: Who Really Pays the Taxes?* (New York, 1994)

M. Barone, *The Almanac of American Politics, 2006* (Washington, DC, 2005)

J. Battelle, *The Search: How Google and its Rivals Rewrote the Rules of Business and Transformed our Culture* (London, 2005)

T. Bender et al., *The Education of Historians for the Twenty-First Century* (Urbana, IL, 2004)

D. Benjamin, ed., *America and the World in the Age of Terror* (Washington, DC, 2005)

L. Berlin, *The Man behind the Microchip: Robert Noyce and the Invention of Silicon Valley* (Oxford, 2005)

E. Black and M. Black, *The Rise of Southern Republicans* (Cambridge, MA, 2002)

A. Blinder, *Economic Policy and the Great Stagflation* (New York, 1981)

J. M. Blum, *Years of Discord: American Politics and Society, 1960–1974* (New York, 1991)

J. Bodnar, *Remaking America: Public Memory, Commemoration and Patriotism in the Twentieth Century* (Princeton, NJ, 1992)

R. J. B. Bosworth, *Explaining Auschwitz and Hiroshima: History Writing and the Second World War, 1945–1990* (London, 1993)

D. Buisseret, ed., *From Sea Charts to Satellite Images: Interpreting North American History through Maps* (Chicago, 1990)

H. J. Bull-Berg, *American International Oil Policy: Causal Factors and Effects* (London, 1987)

R. Burgoyne, *Film Nation: Hollywood Looks at US History* (Minneapolis, MN, 1997)

L. Cannon, *President Reagan: The Role of a Lifetime* (New York, 1991)

—, *Governor Reagan: His Rise to Power* (New York, 2003)

D. T. Carter, *The Politics of Rage*, 2nd edn (Baton Rouge, LA, 2000)

G. Carter, *What We've Lost* (London, 2004)

J. Carter, *Keeping Faith: Memoirs of a President* (London, 1981)

W. H. Chafe, *Civilities and Civil Rights: Greensboro, North Carolina and the Black Struggle for Freedom* (Oxford, 1980)

—, *The Unfinished Journal: America since World War II* (Oxford, 2003)

J. Chang, *Can't Stop. Won't Stop: A History of the Hip-Hop Generation* (London, 2005)

R. Clarke, *Against All Enemies* (New York, 2004)

C. T. Clotfelter, *After 'Brown': The Rise and Retreat of School Desegregation* (Princeton, NJ, 2004)

L. Cohen, *A Consumers' Republic* (New York, 2003)

J. M. Coski, *The Confederate Battle Flag: America's Most Embattled Emblem* (Cambridge, MA, 2005)

G. Critser, *Generation Rx: How Prescription Drugs Are Altering American Minds, Lives and Bodies* (Boston, MA, 2005)

G. Cross, *The All-Consuming Century* (New York, 2000)

J. Cullen, *The Art of Democracy: A Concise History of Popular Culture in America* (New York, 1996)

I. H. Daalder and J. M. Lindsay, *America Unbound: The Bush Revolution in Foreign Policy* (Washington, DC, 2003)

M. Dallek, *The Right Moment: Ronald Reagan's First Victory and the Decisive Turning Point in American Politics* (Oxford, 2000)

R. Dallek, *Lone Star Rising: Lyndon Johnson, 1908–1960* (Oxford, 1991)

—, *Flawed Giant: Lyndon Johnson and his Times, 1961–1973* (Oxford, 1998)

J. DeParle, *American Dream: Three Women, Ten Kids and a Nation's Drive to End Welfare* (New York, 2004)

R. A. Divine, ed., *Exploring the Johnson Years* (Austin, TX, 1981)

R. J. Donovan and R. Scherer, *Unsilent Revolution: Television News and American Public Life, 1948–1991* (Cambridge, 1992)

M. Duberman, *Stonewall* (New York, 1993)

M. Eberstadt, *Home-Alone America: The Hidden Toll of Day Care, Wonder Drugs and Other Parent Substitutes* (New York, 2004)

L. E. Farrington, *Creating Their Own Image: The History of African-American Women Artists* (Oxford, 2004)

N. Ferguson, *Colossus: The Rise and Fall of the American Empire* (London, 2004)

G. R. Ford, *A Time to Heal: The Autobiography of Gerald R. Ford* (New York, 1979)

R. V. Francaviglia, *The Shape of Texas: Maps and Metaphors* (College Station, TX, 1995)

—, *Mapping and Imagination in the Great Basin: A Cartographic History* (Reno, NV, 2005)

T. Frank, *What's the Matter with America: The Resistible Rise of the American Right* (London, 2004)

M. Frankel, *High Noon in the Cold War: Kennedy, Khruschev and the Cuban Missile Crisis* (New York, 2004)

L. Freeh, *My FBI: Bringing Down the Mafia, Investigating Bill Clinton and Fighting War on Terror* (New York, 2005)

M. Friedman, *The Neoconservative Revolution: Jewish Intellectuals and the Shaping of Public Policy* (Cambridge, 2005)

—, ed., *'Commentary' in American Life* (Philadelphia, 2005)

F. Fukuyama, *After the Neocons: America at the Crossroads* (London, 2006)

J. L. Gaddis, *Surprise, Security and the American Experience* (Cambridge, MA, 2004)

—, *We Now Know: Rethinking Cold War History* (Oxford, 1997)

M. C. Garcia, *Havana USA: Cuban Exiles and Cuban Americans in South Florida, 1959–1994* (Berkeley, CA, 1996)

D. Garrow, *We Shall Overcome: The Civil Rights Movement in the United States in the 1950s and 1960s* (Brooklyn, NY, 1989)

J. N. Giglio, *The Presidency of John F. Kennedy* (Lawrence, KS, 1991)

M. J. Gilbert, ed., *Why the North Won the Vietnam War* (New York, 2002)

S. Gillon, *Boomer Nation: The Largest and Richest Generation Ever, and How It Changed America* (New York, 2004)

T. Gitlin, *The Sixties: Years of Hope, Days of Rage* (Toronto, 1987)

—, *The Twilight of Common Dreams: Why America Is Wracked by Culture Wars* (New York, 1995)

N. Glazer and I. Kristol, eds, *The American Commonwealth* (New York, 1976)

L. L. Gould, *Grand Old Party: A History of the Republicans* (New York, 2003)

O. D. Gutfreund, *Twentieth Century Sprawl: How Highways Transformed America* (Oxford, 2004)

D. Halberstam, *War in a Time of Peace* (New York, 2001)

H. R. Haldeman, *The Haldeman Diaries: Inside the Nixon White House* (New York, 1994)

J. F. Hart, ed., *Regions of the United States* (New York, 1972)

D. Hayden, *The Grand Domestic Revolution: A History of Feminist Designs for American Homes, Neighbourhoods and Cities* (Cambridge, MA, 1981)

D. R. Herspring, *The Pentagon and the Presidency: Civil–Military Relations from FDR to George W. Bush* (Lawrence, KS, 2005)

G. Hodgson, *More Equal Than Others: America from Nixon to the New Century* (Princeton, NJ, 2005)

R. Hofstadter, *The American Political Tradition* (New York, 1974)

R. Hogan, *The Stewardess Is Flying the Plane! American Films of the 1970s* (New York, 2005)

D. Horowitz, *Betty Friedan and the Making of 'The Feminine Mystique'* (Amherst, MA, 2000)

S. P. Huntington, *Who Are We? The Challenges to America's National Identity* (London, 2004)

W. Issel, *Social Change in the US, 1945–83* (Basingstoke, 1985)

K. Jackson, *Crabgrass Frontier: The Suburbanization of the United States* (Oxford, 1985)

S. Jacobs, *America's Miracle Man in Vietnam: Ngo Dinh Diem, Religion, Race and US Intervention in Southeast Asia* (Durham, NC, 2005)

J. A. Jakle and K. A. Sculle, *Lots of Parking: Land Use in a Car Culture* (Charlottesville, VA, 2004)

P. Jenkins, *A History of the United States*, 2nd edn (Basingstoke, 2003)

—, *Dream Catchers: How Mainstream America Discovered Native Spirituality* (Oxford, 2004)

—, *Decade of Nightmares: The End of the Sixties and the Making of Eighties America* (Oxford, 2006)

C. Johnson, *Blowback: The Costs and Consequences of American Empire* (New York, 2004)

D. D. Joyce, *Howard Zinn: A Radical American Vision* (Amherst, NY, 2003)

W. L. Kahrl, ed., *The California Water Atlas* (Sacramento, CA, 1978)

D. E. Kaiser, *American Tragedy: Kennedy, Johnson and the Origins of the Vietnam War* (Cambridge, MA, 2000)

B. I. Kaufman, *The Presidency of James Earl Carter* (Lawrence, KS, 1993)

B. W. Kimzey, *Reaganomics* (St Paul, MN, 1983)

G. Klerkx, *Lost in Space: The Fall of NASA and the Dream of a New Space Age* (London, 2004)

A. N. LeBlanc, *Random Family: Love, Drugs, Trouble and Coming of Age in the Bronx* (London, 2003)

M. A. Lee and B. Shlain, *Acid Dreams* (New York, 1992)

M. Lerner, ed., *Looking Back at LBJ: White House Politics in a New Light* (Lawrence, KS, 2005)

M. Lewis, *Moneyball: The Art of Winning an Unfair Game* (New York, 2003)

A. Lieven, *America Right or Wrong: An Anatomy of American Nationalism* (London, 2004)

P. Limerick, *The Legacy of Conquest: The Unbroken Past of the American West* (New York, 1987)

D. Lindaman and K. War, *History Lessons: How Textbooks from Around the World Portray US History* (New York, 2004)

G. C. Loury, *The Anatomy of Racial Inequality* (Cambridge, MA, 2002)

M. J. Lytle, *America's Uncivil Wars: The Sixties Era from Elvis to the Fall of*

Richard Nixon (Oxford, 2005)

P. MacAvoy and I. Millstein, *The Recurrent Crisis in Corporate Governance* (Basingstoke, 2003)

Malcolm X, *Malcolm X Speaks* (New York, 1965)

D. Maraniss, *They Marched into Sunlight: War and Peace, Vietnam and America, October 1967* (New York, 2003)

G. Marsden, *Fundamentalism in American Culture* (Oxford, 1982)

M. Maynard, *The End of Detroit: How the Big Three Lost Their Grip on the American Car Market* (New York, 2003)

E. McCoy, *The Emperor of Wine: The Rise of Robert M. Parker, Jr, and the Reign of American Taste* (New York, 2005)

W. A. McDougall, *The Heavens and the Earth: Political History of the Space Age* (New York, 1985)

K. McQuaid, *The Anxious Years: America in the Vietnam and Watergate Era* (New York, 1989)

A. Matusow, *The Unravelling of America: A History of Liberalism in the 1960s* (New York, 1984)

A. Meier and E. Rudwick, *Black History and the Historical Profession, 1915–1980* (Urbana, IL, 1986)

D. Mervin, *Ronald Reagan and the American Presidency* (Harlow, 1990)

J. Micklethwait and A. Wooldridge, *The Right Nation: Conservative Power in America* (London, 2004)

J. Miller, *Democracy is in the Streets* (New York, 1987)

R. D. Mitchell and P. A. Groves, eds, *North America: The Historical Geography of a Changing Continent* (Totowa, NJ, 1987)

S. Mnookin, *Hard News: The Scandals at 'The New York Times' and their Meaning for American Media* (New York, 2004)

A. Molho and G. S. Wood, eds, *Imagined Histories: American Historians Interpret their Past* (Princeton, NJ, 1998)

P. O. Muller, *Contemporary Suburban America* (Englewood Cliffs, NJ, 1981)

G. B. Nash, C. Grabtree and R. E. Dunn, *History on Trial: Culture Wars and Teaching of the Past* (New York, 1997)

F. N. Nesbitt, *Race for Sanctions: African Americans against Apartheid, 1946–1994* (Bloomington, IN, 2004)

R. P. Newman, *Enola Gay and the Court of History* (New York, 2004)

S. B. Oates, *Let the Trumpet Sound: The Life of Martin Luther King, Jr* (New

York, 1982)

S. D. O'Connor, *The Majesty of the Law: Reflections of a Supreme Court Justice* (New York, 2003)

H. Parmet, *Richard Nixon and his America* (Boston, MA, 1990)

H. S. Parmet, *J.F.K.: The Presidency of John F. Kennedy* (Harmondsworth, 1984)

J. T. Patterson, *Grand Expectations* (Oxford, 1996)

—, *Restless Giant: The United States from Watergate to Bush v. Gore* (Oxford, 2005)

R. Perlstein, *Before the Storm: Barry Goldwater and the Unmaking of the American Consensus* (New York, 2001)

K. Phillips, *The Emerging Republican Majority* (New Rochelle, NY, 1969)

—, *American Dynasty: Aristocracy, Fortune and the Politics of Deceit in the House of Bush* (London, 2004)

G. K. Piehler, *Remembering War the American Way* (Washington, DC, 1995)

J. Prados, *Presidents' Secret Wars: CIA and Pentagon Covert Operations from World War II through Iranscam* (New York, 1986)

C. Prestowitz, *Rogue Nation: American Unilateralism and the Failure of Good Intentions* (New York, 2003)

H. Prince, *Wetlands of the American Midwest: A Historical Geography of Changing Attitudes* (Chicago, 1997)

N. Prins, *Other People's Money: The Corporate Mugging of America* (London, 2004)

R. Reagan, *An American Life* (New York, 1990)

J. Record, *Making War, Thinking History: Munich, Vietnam and Presidential Uses of Force from Korea to Kosovo* (Annapolis, MD, 2002)

J. F. Rooney, W. Zelinsky and D. R. Louder, eds, *This Remarkable Continent: An Atlas of United States and Canadian Society and Cultures* (College Station, TX, 1982)

H. W. Rose, *The Black Ghetto: A Spatial Behavioral Perspective* (New York, 1971)

B. Rubin, *Paved with Good Intentions: The American Experience in Iran* (Harmondsworth, 1981)

R. E. Rubin and J. Weisberg, *In an Uncertain World: Tough Choices from Wall Street to Washington* (New York, 2004)

W. Saletan, *Bearing Right: How Conservatives Won the Abortion War*

(Berkeley, CA, 2003)

D. Savage, *Turning Right: The Making of the Rehnquist Supreme Court* (New York, 1992)

M. Schaller, *Reckoning with Reagan: America and its President in the 1980s* (Oxford, 1994)

A. M. Schlesinger, *The Imperial Presidency* (Boston, MA, 1989)

—, *The Disuniting of America* (New York, 1992)

—, *War and the American Presidency* (New York, 2004)

J. C. Scruggs and J. L. Swerdlow, *To Heal a Nation: The Vietnam Veterans Memorial* (New York, 1985)

R. Shilts, *And the Band Played On: Politics, People and the AIDS Epidemic* (New York, 1987)

C. H. Sommers and S. Satel, *One Nation under Therapy: How the Helping Culture Is Eroding Self-Reliance* (New York, 2005)

K. Starr, *Coast of Dreams: California on the Edge, 1990–2003* (New York, 2004)

I. Stavans, *Spanglish: The Making of a New American Language* (New York, 2003)

D. Steigerwald, *The Sixties and the End of Modern America* (New York, 1995)

D. A. Stockman, *The Triumph of Politics: The Inside Story of the Reagan Revolution* (London, 1986)

D. K. Stumpf, *Titan II: A History of a Cold War Missile Program* (Fayetteville, AR, 2000)

L. H. Suid, *Guts and Glory: The Making of the American Military Image in Film* (Lexington, KY, 2002)

S. J. Summerhill and J. A. Williams, *Sinking Columbus: Contested History, Cultural Politics, and Mythmaking during the Quincentenary* (Gainesville, FL, 2000)

C. Sunstein, *Radicals in Robes: Why Extreme Right-Wing Courts are Wrong for America* (New York, 2005)

C. M. Swain, *The New White Nationalism in America* (Cambridge, 2002)

T. Terriff, *The Nixon Administration and the Making of US Nuclear Strategy* (Ithaca, NY, 1995)

G. Troy, *Morning in America: How Ronald Reagan Invented the 1980s* (Princeton, NJ, 2005)

I. Tyrrell, *The Absent Marx: Class Analysis and Liberal History in Twentieth-*

Century America (New York, 1986)

—, Historians in Public: The Practice of American History, 1890–1970 (Chicago, 2005)

M. Urofsky, The Continuity of Change: The Supreme Court and Individual Liberties, 1953–1986 (Belmont, CA, 1991)

D. R. Wells, The Federal Reserve System: A History (Jefferson, NC, 2004)

J. E. Westheider, Fighting on Two Fronts: African Americans and the Vietnam War (New York, 1997)

M. J. White, The Cuban Missile Crisis (Basingstoke, 1995)

J. Wiener, Historians in Trouble: Plagiarism, Fraud and Politics in the Ivory Tower (New York, 2005)

G. Wills, Reagan's America (Garden City, NY, 1987)

W. J. Wilson, The Truly Disadvantaged: The Inner City, the Underclass and Public Policy (Chicago, 1987)

J. Witcover, Party of the People: A History of the Democrats (New York, 2003)

R. B. Woods, Quest for Identity: America since 1945 (Cambridge, 2005)

B. Woodward, Veil: The Secret Wars of the CIA, 1981–1987 (New York, 1987)

—, The Choice (New York, 1996)

—, Plan of Attack (New York, 2004)

W. B. Wriston, The Twilight of Sovereignty (New York, 1992)

W. Zelinsky, The Cultural Geography of the United States (Englewood Cliffs, NJ, 1973)

F. E. Zimring, The Contradictions of American Capital Punishment (Oxford, 2003)

H. Zinn, A People's History of the United States, 3rd edn (New York, 2003)

Index

abortion 60, 98–9, 108–9, 126,
123, 182, 197, 237
Adams, John 143
agriculture 22, 31, 33–6, 40, 58
AIDS 71–3
air conditioning 52
aircraft 202–4
Alabama 59, 67, 79, 125, 161, 164,
237
Alaska 22, 29–30, 32, 40–43, 54,
55, 61, 76, 99, 120, 204
aliens 26, 142
Allen, Woody 141
al-Qaeda 218
Alther, Lisa 58
Alvarez, Julia 62
Anderson, George 177
Arizona 22, 40, 63, 76, 182
Arkansas 167, 171, 193
Atlanta 22, 23, 40, 45, 58, 84, 110,
166, 204
atom bomb 17–18, 20, 207
Austin 59, 129

Baby Boomers 22, 237
Baltimore 21, 165
banking 160
Baton Rouge 34
Beat Generation 143
Beat movement 23
Beaumont 43
Birmingham 164
Black Power 166
blacks 16–17, 72, 85, 90–94, 126,
136, 144, 163, 170, 187, 197,
227–8, 231
Boston 21, 33, 50, 84
Braunbeck, Gary 141
Bretton Woods Agreement 18,
148, 169
bridges 51–2
Buchanan, Patrick 133, 185, 187
Bush, George H. W. 131, 184, 212,
222, 234
Bush, George W. 26, 38, 44–6,
52–5, 61, 72–3, 83, 87, 92, 112,
121, 123–4, 126–8, 130, 154–8

California 17, 22, 27, 33, 39, 44, 51,
    54, 58–9, 61, 69, 79, 86–7,
    97–8, 100–01, 127, 129, 131, 155,
    157, 160, 166–7, 176, 179, 183,
    186, 188–95, 193, 199, 208,
    218–20, 222, 229, 234, 236
Canada 36
capital movements 18–19, 148,
    152, 154, 169, 229
cars 9, 21, 29, 47–9, 51–79, 154,
    224
Carson, Rachel 28
Carter, Jimmy 55, 122–3, 171,
    174–5, 177, 180, 193, 212–13
Catholics 16, 120–21, 204, 232
Charleston 51–2
Chicago 21, 49, 50, 64, 68, 88,
    165, 170, 194
China 41–3, 53, 60, 151–4, 164,
    186, 219–21, 224, 229, 239
CIA 21, 171–3, 207
Cincinnati 59
Civil Rights 161, 164
Civil War 15–16, 136
Cleveland 165
climate change 37–9, 52, 54, 71
Clinton, Bill 91, 124, 133, 147, 156,
    163, 171, 185–8, 191, 193, 195,
    222, 234
coal 10, 42–3
Cold War 132, 135–6, 178, 182,
    205–8, 212–16
Colorado 22, 33, 58, 60, 67, 185,
    191
Colorado, river 39
Condon, Richard 96

Connecticut 22, 68, 237
consumerism 12, 102–5
Coolidge, Calvin 13
cotton 36
credit cards 116–17
crime 76, 182–3, 197, 237
Critser, Greg 65
Crowley, Mart 70, 110
Cuba 11, 61, 162, 207–8
Cuban missile crisis 132, 207

Dallas 22, 40, 161
Davis, Gray 44
Dayton 59
Democrats 15–16, 21, 121, 126 128,
    156, 161–2, 170, 177, 185–7,
    234–6
demographics 47, 57–63
Denver 58
Detroit 17, 59, 79, 92, 165, 179
diabetes 68
diet 67–8, 70, 112
Dinkins, David 92
Disney 201
divorce 100–01, 111, 237
Dole, Robert 133, 185, 188, 222
drugs, narcotic 56, 71, 103, 114,
    124, 129, 167, 183, 197, 233, 236
drugs, prescription 34, 65–6
Dukakis, Michael 222

Earth Days 28
Eastlake, William 143
Edwards, John 83, 227
Eisenhower, Dwight 20–21, 23,
    166, 206

electricity 12, 24
Ellis, Bret Easton 233
Ellroy, James 227
Energy Act (2005) 45
environmentalism 28–9
evolution 129–30

Falwell, Jerry 123
Farrakhan, Louis 92
fishing 36–7
Flint 179
Florida 22, 32–3, 39–40, 58, 61, 76,
    86, 93, 185, 188, 191, 195, 204,
    227
food 74
Foote, Horton 140
Ford 47, 54
Ford, Gerald 172, 174, 212
Fort Myers 76
Foster, Andrew 71
Fredericksburg 50
Friedan, Betty 108
Fuller, Buckminster 107

General Motors 16, 28, 47–8, 78,
    154, 184, 224
Georgia 58, 79, 128, 167, 171, 191,
    193
Gingrich, Newt 171, 187
Ginsberg, Allen 143
Giuliani, Rudolph 92
Goldwinter, Barry 162–3, 167, 179
Gore, Al 171, 188
'Great Society' 163, 165, 192
Greatest Generation 135
Greenspan, Alan 185–6, 229–30

Gulf War (1991) 216–18
Gulf War (2003) 218–19
guns 119, 177, 187, 196

Haiti 13, 62, 217
Harding, Warren 13
Harrington, Michael 82
Hawaii 22, 94–6, 120, 168, 191,
    204
health 63–75, 109
Hispanics 8, 61–3, 85, 89–94, 97,
    231
History Standards 131–3
Hollywood 19, 88, 96, 103, 139,
    144–5, 197
homosexuals 124, 127–8, 187, 190,
    223
Hoover, Herbert 13
Hoover, J. Edgar 171
housing 45–8
Houston 22, 40, 43, 45
Humphrey, Hubert 167–8, 170

Idaho 22, 76
Illinois 22, 101, 166, 191, 194
immigration 14, 61–3, 77
imprisonment 182–3
Indiana 29
Internet 42, 115, 158, 221
Iowa 35
Iran 43, 149, 175, 178, 213
Iraq 43, 218

Jackson, Michael 144
Janowitz, Tama 233
Japan 12, 17, 19, 22, 148, 151, 200,

205, 230
Johnson, Lyndon 148, 162–5, 167, 192, 209–10

Kansas 22, 130
Katrina, Hurricane 38–9, 42, 55, 59, 83, 90, 93, 154, 159, 165, 192–3, 228
Kennedy, Edward 129
Kennedy, John F. 119, 121, 156–7, 161, 166, 193, 195, 206–8, 222
Kennedy, Robert 119, 162, 167, 193
Kentucky 79, 89, 93, 128–9
Kerry, John 123, 128, 171, 189–91, 222, 227
King, Martin Luther 91, 162, 166
Kopit, Arthur 143
Korea, South 20, 60, 151, 205
Korean War 20
Kyoto Protocol 52–4

language 8, 62, 130–31, 231
Larson, Jonathan 73
Las Vegas 40, 58, 88, 204
lawyers 69, 79
Lee, Spike 143
Los Angeles 23, 39–40, 45, 61, 90, 119, 142, 153, 157, 165, 174, 185, 197, 204, 227
Louisiana 16, 33, 59, 67, 85, 90, 93, 120, 167, 191, 234

Millett, Kate 108
Maine 76
Mamet, David 29, 180, 196
Marsalis, Wynton 143

Maryland 22, 191
Massachusetts 22, 44, 67, 99, 127–8, 170, 171, 237
McCarthy, Joseph 21, 132
McDonalds 68
McGovern, George 170, 177
McInerney, Jay 233
McMurty, Larry 226–7
meat 30–31
Medicare 77–8, 83, 192
Memphis 48
Miami 84
Michigan 86, 101, 128, 168, 191
microchips 115
Miers, Harriet 126, 194
Milwaukee 21
Minnesota 35, 168, 191, 197
Mississippi 59, 67, 85, 93, 128, 167, 171
Mississippi, river 39
Mogadon 65
Mondale, Walter 177, 184
Montana 22, 66, 128
Montgomery 91
moon, the 25
Moral Majority 179
Mormons 120–22
Morrison, Toni 143
mortgages 46–7
museums 201–2
Muslims 122

Nader, Ralph 28
NAFTA 41, 63, 88
Naples 76
NASA 25

Native Americans 32, 61, 137–8,
    143–4, 160
NATO 19, 205
Nebraska 99, 105
Nevada 22, 30, 32, 40, 76, 100, 161
New Deal 14–15, 21, 163
New Democrats 185
New Hampshire 76, 85
New Jersey 22, 85, 160, 198
New Mexico 22, 73, 85, 160
New Orleans 83, 90, 93, 119, 145,
    159, 228
New South 22, 166
New York 12, 23, 33, 45, 48, 50, 59,
    74, 84, 99–100, 109–10, 119,
    165, 174, 197–9, 204, 218, 233
Newark 165
Nicaragua 13
Nixon, Richard 143, 148, 156–7,
    171–5, 179, 164, 166–74, 182,
    206, 210–12
North Carolina 58, 60, 191
North Dakota 22, 59, 128
Nosick, Robert 87
nuclear power 29, 41–2

Obama, Barack 83
obesity 67–8
Ohio 86, 101, 128, 141, 191
oil 42–4, 47, 148–9, 154, 212, 221,
    224, 229
Oklahoma 105, 128, 188, 196
Oregon 17, 54–5, 58, 66, 68,
    128–9
Orlando 201

Paretsky, Sara 88
Parks, Rosa 91, 93
Patriot Act 218
Pennsylvania 130, 191
Perot, Ross 88, 185, 188
pets 31–2
Philadelphia 40, 196
Phoenix 40, 50, 58
Picker, Tobias 145
Pittsburgh 59, 143, 165
plastic 12
Pollock, Jackson 142
pollution 28, 34–5, 40–41, 70–71
'pork' 40, 51, 224
poverty 32, 82–3, 87, 103, 187
Prohibition 13, 100
pornography 117
property rights 55
protectionism 14
Providence 93
Prozac 65
Puerto Rico 96, 196

Quayle, Dan 222

Rabe, David, 211
rail 50–51
Rawls, John 87
Reagan, Ronald 95, 111, 119, 122–3,
    127, 129, 133, 136, 149, 167, 171,
    176–84, 191, 193, 212, 215
Rehnquist, William 126, 182
religion 16, 21, 26, 29, 53, 119–27,
    145, 204–5, 231–2
Republicans 15–16, 61, 126, 128,
    167, 187–8, 234–6

retirement 58, 75–8, 103, 195
Rhode Island 22, 67, 93, 129
roads 23, 48–51
Robertson, Pat 123
robots 116
Rochester 59
rockets 20, 207–8, 214
Rogers, Adrian 122
Romero, George 80
Roosevelt, Franklin Delano 14, 17,
   162–3
Rossner, Judith 108

San Antonio 40
San Diego 38, 40, 59
San Francisco 23, 48, 59, 110,
   112–18, 127, 149
Sanders, Lawrence 80
Saudi Arabia 43, 152
Savings and Loans 181–2, 184,
   239
Schiavo, Terri 128
Schwarzenegger, Arnold 54, 98,
   100, 111, 155, 157, 199
Scopes, John 129
Seattle 22
Selma 165
Sierra Club 24, 28, 63
Simon Neil 100, 141
Simpsons, The 146
social security 15, 163
South 15–16, 21, 23, 29, 48, 102,
   105, 126, 136–7, 161, 164–5, 167,
   168, 171, 191, 195, 237
South Carolina 58, 91, 191
South Dakota 22, 59, 99, 138

Space Race 25
Spielberg, Steven 228
Spock, Benjamin 113
sport 69–70, 105
St Louis 21
Stallone, Sylvester 111
standardization 23, 35
Star Wars 26
steel 16
stem-cell research 127
Sternbach, Leo 65
Stewart, Martha 102
stock-market index 153
Stone, Oliver 211
suburbanization 22, 33, 45, 48,
   139
Supreme Court 91, 97, 99, 120,
   125, 128, 129, 160, 170, 182, 194
surgery 64
Susann, Jacqueline 65
Swaggart, Jimmy 123
swine-flu 74

Taiwan 20
Tartt, Donna 7, 9
taxation 15, 46, 178–80, 176, 185,
   187, 191–2
television 19, 23, 30, 118–19,
   156–8, 196, 200, 238
Tennessee 58, 59, 79, 129, 171
terrorism 44, 56
Texas 40, 58, 61, 76, 79, 89, 105,
   109, 128–9, 140, 157, 161–2,
   166, 168, 171, 198, 226
tourism 202–4
Tower, Joan 145

trade unions 29, 48, 62, 101–2, 153
Truman, Harry 17–18
Tyler, Anne 140

United Nations 19
Updike, John 98–9
Utah 22, 40, 76, 121, 122, 128

Valium 65
Vermont 67, 76
Vietnam War 132, 134, 135, 143,
    148, 162–3, 167, 197, 202,
    208–12, 222
Virginia 91, 124
Volcker, Paul 181

Waco 196
Walker, Alice 228
Wallace, George 119, 161–2,
    167–8, 171, 174
Wal-Mart 70, 87, 150, 153, 186,
    202
Warren, Earl 125
Washington, DC 50, 84, 134–5,
    137–8, 165, 170, 191, 198, 218,
    239
Washington state 17, 128, 168
Washington, Harold 92
water 27, 34–5, 39–40
Watergate affair 156, 172–5
weathermen 171
West Virginia 42, 86, 93, 168
Westerns 142
Willis, Bruce 111
Wilson, August 143
Wilson, Langford 73

Winfrey, Oprah 92, 141
Wisconsin 191
Wolfe, Tom 46, 107
women 17, 97–101, 108–9, 112
Wurtzell, Elizabeth 65
Wyoming 22, 39, 76, 110, 189

youth 86, 112–13